HOPEFUL PESSIMISM

Hopeful Pessimism

MARA VAN DER LUGT

PRINCETON UNIVERSITY PRESS

PRINCETON & OXFORD

Published by Princeton University Press
41 William Street, Princeton, New Jersey 08540
99 Banbury Road, Oxford OX2 6JX

press.princeton.edu

All Rights Reserved

ISBN 978-0-691-26560-5
ISBN (e-book) 978-0-691-26562-9

British Library Cataloging-in-Publication Data is available

Editorial: Ben Tate and Josh Drake
Production Editorial: Jenny Wolkowicki
Jacket design: Katie Osborne
Text design: Carmina Alvarez
Production: Danielle Amatucci
Publicity: Tyler Hubbert and Carmen Jimenez

Jacket image: *Hope*, George Frederic Watts and assistants, 1886, oil on canvas. Album / Alamy Stock Photo

This book has been composed in Arno Pro

Printed in the United States of America

10 9 8 7 6 5 4 3 2 1

For my mother
and my brothers

Impossible, you say;
let me retreat
and find my rest.
What rest, my friend,
in these fragmented times?

—Toyohiko Kagawa

CONTENTS

. . . Why, then, not a philosophy of hopeful pessimism to guide us into the future? . . .

FIGURE 1. G. F. Watts, *Hope*. First ('green') version, 1885–86; see plate 1.

Introduction

A FEMALE figure sits upon a globe. The scene is one of solitude and desolation, as if a terrible catastrophe has taken place, leaving only the bare globe and the figure upon it, blindfolded, bending her head to hear the sound made by the last string on the last harp. She sits upon the globe as on the ruins of the world.

The writer G. K. Chesterton suggested that if a person strayed into a gallery and saw this painting for the first time, they would think it was called *Despair*. But in fact, it is called *Hope*.

The painting, made by G. F. Watts in 1885, disturbed some of its earliest viewers: it seemed so far removed from the usual portrayals of hope, as an anchor, something that bolsters the spirit—not this fragile, broken scene. But despite its desolate character, it quickly became popular and grew to have an intellectual life of its own. Both Martin Luther King and Jeremiah Wright drew on *Hope* in their sermons, which in turn inspired a young Barack Obama. But it is not clear that the message often drawn from the painting (that human resilience conquers everything; that even with only one string hope remains) is what Watts himself intended. Questioned about the painting, he resisted associations with both optimism and pessimism. 'Hope need not mean expectancy,' he said instead. 'It suggests here rather the music which can come from the remaining chord.'[1]

This is interesting: for it is not how we usually think of hope. We tend to interpret hope precisely as an expectation about the future and juxtapose it with attitudes that we call unhopeful, such as pessimism, passivity, despair. But what if, following Watts's cue, we took a different view of hope? What would hope be like if it was *not* about expectancy and optimism? Could pessimism itself be hopeful?

Hopeful pessimism: this sounds like a contradiction in terms, since hope is usually associated or equated with optimism, and pessimism with its opposite, despair. These, in an age darkened by the gathering storm of climate catastrophe, are terms we encounter every day. *Are you optimistic or pessimistic about our chances? Don't you become hopeless? Is there reason for hope? How can we stave off despair?* These are the kinds of questions writers, scientists, and activists are asked on a daily basis. It is as if we are all asked to take a stance, not just on climate change and what to do about it but on what kind of attitudes we have about the future—a future, meanwhile, that is marked by nothing so much as uncertainty.

Now there is nothing wrong with these questions insofar as they come from a position of open-mindedness and curiosity. But sometimes the questions that are asked, and the manner in which they are answered, are intensely morally charged. Underlying the demand to choose between *hope/optimism* on the one hand and *despair/pessimism* on the other is the stubborn assumption that to opt for the former is to be on the right side of history, while to give in to the latter is to give up altogether. One who caves in to pessimism, the narrative goes, enters a world of fatalism, defeatism, and apathy, where change is rendered impossible by the inability to envision it.

The *optimism vs. pessimism* binary (which is often, but not always, equated with *hope vs. despair*) is thus coupled with other binaries, such as *courage vs. giving up, right vs. wrong,* and *strength vs. weakness.* To be a pessimist, on this view, is to give in to despair, to fail in courage, and ultimately to be *on the wrong side,* which is the side of the deniers and barbarians, those who look away and do nothing—those whom history will not forgive.

Sometimes such demands on our hopes are brought to us by dubious sources, from techno-optimists to greenwashing politicians, but they are just as likely to come from authors who speak from the deepest commitment to justice and change. Noam Chomsky, in the tellingly titled collection *Optimism over Despair,* puts the question of optimism and pessimism as a forking path:

> We have two choices. We can be pessimistic, give up, and help ensure that the worst will happen. Or we can be optimistic, grasp the opportunities that surely exist, and maybe help make the world a better place. Not much of a choice.[2]

So too Jane Goodall believes that it is because people are 'overwhelmed by the magnitude of our folly' that they 'sink into apathy and despair, lose hope, and so do nothing.'[3] In a more complicated stance, Rebecca Solnit pits hope against *both* optimism and pessimism: 'Optimists think it will all be fine without our involvement; pessimists take the opposite position; both excuse themselves from acting,' because 'whether you feel assured that everything is going to hell or will all turn out fine, you are not impelled to act.'[4] The entrenched assumption remains: taking a dark view of things will lead, necessarily, to giving up.

Such expressions, by authors who deserve our utmost attention, are all perfectly well-intended—and to the extent that they have provided many with inspiration and moral fervour, they are to be applauded. But there is also reason for concern. In fact there are two: a misunderstanding and a danger, which underlie all expressions that pit hope/optimism against pessimism/despair. Untangling these will be the task and message of this book. But here is a first sketch.

The Misunderstanding

Authors who warn against the danger of pessimism and despair (which, as will become clear, are certainly not the same thing, though they sometimes go hand in hand) are motivated by an understandable fear. If we take a closer look at their expressions, it quickly becomes clear that what they are really combatting is not so much pessimism (the view that the future looks bleak) or even despair (a natural response to such bleakness) but the spectre of fatalism, apathy, and defeatism: the view that *nothing can be done, and so we may as well give up.*

This spectre, as we will see, sometimes takes very real and tangible forms, and when it does the fear of fatalism is justified: we are right to be concerned about those who say we should *just give up.* But there are few who say this—and, what is crucial, most pessimists do not.

The great misunderstanding, in the climate debate and more generally, occurs when optimism is equated with activity and commitment, pessimism with passivity, defeatism, or resignation. But it is simply not the case that pessimism is tantamount to giving up. As others too have argued, and history amply demonstrates, pessimism and activism are perfectly compatible—indeed, in some cases they have proven to be an especially powerful combination. After all, if optimistic activism hinges on the proximity of success, it is vulnerable to setbacks and disappointments: quick to burn up, quick to burn out. By contrast pessimistic activism, if rightly developed, can manifest as a slow-burning fire—one that does not need to be fuelled by either the expectation or gratification of successes on the way.

We are so quick to equate pessimism with passivity or fatalism or despair, and to reject it on that basis—for of course we do not want a philosophy that tells us to give up. But is that really what pessimism is, what pessimism means? As Joshua Foa Dienstag has argued in his book on the topic, far from leading to passivity, pessimism can be closely linked to a tradition of moral and political activism, as in the case of the French novelist and philosopher Albert Camus (whom we will encounter at length in chapter 2).

Even the darkest pessimists never said that life would only get worse or can never be better: this is but a caricature of pessimism, sketched quickly to dismiss it. Even Schopenhauer, the bleakest of them all, did not subscribe to it. On the contrary, he suggested that it is precisely because we cannot control the course of things that we can never know what the future holds: life may become worse *or* better. 'The pessimist,' in Dienstag's words, 'expects nothing.'[5]

This is not to say such pessimism is 'unhopeful', at least not in the sense that it believes there is no hope of change. If the future is radically open, this uncertainty is a danger as well as a possibility. There is always hope for the pessimist, because there is always uncertainty. This is hope without expectancy—and it may well be what Watts seemed to be getting at by calling his desolate painting *Hope*.

But if pessimism can be compatible with activism, what about despair? Surely despair at least is akin to giving up?

I'm not so certain. Yes, some versions of despair are to be resisted at all costs—the kinds that cause us to collapse into inaction, to admit defeat. But there are other kinds, too, or so I will suggest: some versions of despair that are compatible with activism, with courage and tenacity, with proceeding in the battle even when all 'hope' is lost. It is simply not the case that we need to be positively hopeful in order to be determined to fight. Past movements of resistance and activism have indeed been driven by hope and expectancy, but also by despair, anger, grief, and more than anything: by reasons of justice and duty—because it is *what we are called upon to do.*

This is a form of commitment and moral drive that is by no means incompatible with despair—and this should not surprise us, as it appears everywhere in our cultural narratives, though we rarely recognise it for what it is. Thus, in the film adaptation of *The Lord of the Rings,* when in the midst of a desperate situation Frodo asks his companion, 'What are we holding on to, Sam?' the latter replies: 'That there's some good in this world, Mr. Frodo. And it's worth fighting for.'[6] This passage, beloved in online commentaries, is often glossed as a belief in hope against all odds, but like Watts's painting it could as easily be read otherwise: that even when there is no 'hope' to be seen, no reason for believing the tide of doom can be stemmed, still there may be *things worth fighting for.* There is not much hope in this, perhaps, but it is a kind of hope nevertheless. In the absence of any real prospects of success, what can sustain us is not the expectant hope of victory but the desperate knowledge that there are things worth fighting for—a quiet desperation from which hope may wisely spring.

The point is that hope matters, but it needs to be the right kind of hope—the kind that persists when other versions fail. J.R.R. Tolkien saw this, which is why there are two words for hope in Elvish—*Amdir* and *Estel.*[7] I will speak instead of green hope, and blue—and argue that while green hope has dominated our consciousness, it is to blue hope that we must turn.

The hope that stands beside pessimism and walks hand in hand even with despair. The hope that is born of sheer uncertainty. The hope of *hopeful pessimism*.

The Danger

The thing to avoid, then, is not so much pessimism but passivity or defeatism or giving up. Even despair need not be completely avoided, since it too can energise and encourage us to strive for change, but we should avoid the kind of despair that causes us to collapse. These things are not the same as pessimism, which is simply the assumption of a dark view of the present as well as the future and does *not* imply the loss of courage or insistence to strive for better: on the contrary, often these are the very gifts that pessimism can bestow.

Does this mean that authors warning against pessimism or despair are still entirely justified as long as we substitute for these terms others, such as fatalism and apathy? Does it all turn on a matter of semantics?

If it were so, our task would be a simple one. But there is more to be said. For while the hope narrative successfully avoids the Scylla of apathy and defeatism, it sometimes slips into the Charybdis of optimism, whose danger it underestimates.

Hope and optimism: these are concepts tangled up in close knots of association, and often confused or conflated even by those authors who claim to hold them apart. The danger of optimism is one that the old pessimists kept warning us against: that if we overemphasise the power we have over our minds, our lives, our destinies, it is all too easy to stumble into cruelty. That to insist that life is good even in the face of hard, unyielding suffering, or to stipulate that we are in control of our happiness, is to make our suffering worse. It is to add to suffering the responsibility for that suffering; it is to burden the sufferer with a sense of their inadequacy. This is a danger in all ages (as the pessimists have warned us since at least the seventeenth century), but it is especially seductive in dark times such as we live through now. To constantly stress the need for proclaiming hope and optimism is to overburden not only activists but all who are rightly concerned about climate change: it is to add to the worries of this age the burden of asserting one's hopefulness at any cost.

It is all too common for scientists and commentators to discuss the dark moods of climate activists and (sometimes patronisingly) to express concerns about their psychological welfare— and stress the need for optimism or hopefulness to combat their 'eco-anxiety'.[8] But there has been hardly any discussion of the damage that is done by propounding such narratives, which have seeped into the theoretical framework of the climate movement and create a constant pressure to keep focusing on the achievability of success rather than the possibility of failure. The result, indeed, is burnout and disillusionment—and so the narrative seems to prove itself. But all it proves is that if activism is based on optimism it is vulnerable in a particular way, precisely because it fails to equip its participants to deal with setbacks and disappointments, and the possibility of failure.

And so it is perhaps the very tendency to overstress the need for optimism and hopefulness that leads to burnout, disillusionment, and apathy—as high expectations are easily defeated, and activism based on them is easily undone.

There has to be room in the climate debate for negative feelings and attitudes, for discussions of uncertainty and the prospect of disaster—even the possibility that the climate movement itself shall fail. To recognise such dark horizons is not the same as giving in to despair, and it is not the same as giving up. One can be deeply, darkly pessimistic, one can find oneself in the cold hard clutches of despair, and yet not be depleted of the possibility (and it could just be a possibility) that better may yet arrive. This is a kind of hope that is dearly bought, that does not come lightly but is carved out of a painful vision which may just be the acknowledgement of all the suffering that life can and does hold. If anything, the pessimists have taught me this: with eyes full of that darkness there can still be this strange shattering openness, like a door cracked open, for the good to make its entry into life. Since all things are uncertain, so too is the future, and so there is always the possibility of change for better as there is for worse.

This can itself be a moral stance: one that welcomes the good when it is given and urges it onwards on its journey but also acknowledges the bad without explaining it away or overburdening the will of those it crushes in its path. Sometimes we are not in power to change the world as we would like to, and acknowledging this can be the greatest effort as well as the greatest consolation, while not taking away the drive to give our best and hardest labours to the cause.

As Jonathan Lear has written in his book *Radical Hope*, one common phenomenon at times of cultural devastation is that old values lose their meaning.[9] If they are to survive the collapse of the moral horizon, they need new meanings, new concepts to breathe life into them. The most difficult thing of all is to negotiate this change, to start inhabiting new virtues while the old are still among us. And this, I believe, is one way in which pessimism might serve us—as a virtue in itself but also as a way of giving new meaning to virtues that are changing as part of this changing world. To behold with open eyes the reality before us requires courage, and not to turn away from it, forbearance, and yet not to decide that it ends there: this is hope.

Hope—not that everything will be all right in the end but that nothing has ever truly ended; that there is this 'crack in everything' of which Leonard Cohen once sang, in the good as well as the bad, so that neither is ever entirely shut away from us.[10] This is not the steadfast conviction that things are bound to get better—not the crude optimism that can no longer be a virtue in a breaking world, and might prove to be our besetting vice. It may be easier to lend our efforts under such a banner of assured success, but this ease is a deceptive one, for while it is possible to be dispirited by passivity or fatalism, it is possible to be depleted by continued disappointment also. What hopeful pessimism asks instead is that we strive for change without certainties, without expecting anything from our efforts other than the knowledge that we have done what we are called upon to do as moral agents in a time of change. This may just be the thinnest hope, the bleakest consolation—but it may also be the very thing that will serve us best in times to come, as a value, and yes, an exercise of moral fervour: a fragile virtue for a fragile age.

PART I

Pessimism

1

Optimism, Pessimism, Fatalism

Only one thing is more stupid than absolute pessimism and that is absolute optimism.

—ALBERT CAMUS

IMAGINE ENTERING a gallery. You weren't expecting to be here, but here you are. So you start wandering, this way and that. Some pictures you've seen before; others are new to you; one stops you in your tracks. You are drawn to it, and so, for a moment, you leave all thoughts of the world behind to find yourself 'in the presence of a dim canvas with a bowed and stricken and secretive figure cowering over a broken lyre in the twilight.'[1]

Close your eyes, and open them again. What do you see?

According to G. K. Chesterton, your first thought will be that the painting is called *Despair*. But he also thinks that, after reading its real title and staring at it for a while, 'a dim and powerful sense of meaning' will begin to grow on you. Standing before it you will find yourself 'in the presence of a great truth.' You will perceive 'that there is something in man which is always apparently on the eve of disappearing, but never disappears, an assurance which is always apparently saying farewell and yet illimitably lingers, a string which is always stretched to snapping and yet never snaps.' This something may be called *Hope*, as the painting's creator did, but 'we may call it many other things. Call it faith, call it vitality, call it the will to live, call it the religion of to-morrow morning, call it the immortality of man, call it self-love and vanity; it is the thing that explains why man survives all things and why there is no such thing as a pessimist.'[2] Without it, whatever *it* is, we are truly dead.

No such thing as a pessimist! To a scholar of philosophical pessimism, an unsettling thought—and, considering all the self-declared pessimists of the past and present, a hard one to maintain. But what does Chesterton mean? Does he mean there is no one who does not show, by the fact of living, that they value their existence; that philosophical pessimists like Schopenhauer are really optimists in disguise? Or does he mean that there is no one who does not have *some* positive expectation about the future, a belief that there is something better still to come?

In other words: *What is a pessimist?*

A Brief Tour

It depends whom you ask, and when. The terms 'optimism' and 'pessimism' have shifted considerably in meaning throughout the ages. If we turned back the pages of history and asked a person of letters from the seventeenth century, 'What are optimism and pessimism?' we would be awarded a blank stare, and rightly so, as the terms had not been coined yet. But, flipping forward to the mid-eighteenth century, we'd have more luck. We could knock on the door of Voltaire, author of a book that has 'optimism' in the title, and ask him what that strange word means.

'My friends!' he might tell us, smiling mischievously. 'Optimism is a cruel philosophy formulated by the likes of Leibniz and Pope, according to whom *all is for the best* and *we live in the best possible world*. After all, if God could have created a better one, he would have done so! Or so the optimists tell us.'

But we've done our homework. Didn't Voltaire himself admire Leibniz at the start of his career? Didn't he himself agree that, while there are imperfections in the *parts* of creation, the *whole* is very good?

This might annoy him a little. 'A man can change his mind, can't he? Anyhow, that's not the same as optimism. I never said that *all is good* and *all is right*, as Alexander Pope did.'[3]

What then is the problem with optimism? we might ask.

'Haven't you read my famous book *Candide, or Optimism*? "If this is the best of all possible worlds, what on earth are the others like?"'[4]

Yes, we've read *Candide*: that's the book responsible for making *optimism* a household term. So did Voltaire coin it himself?

'I wish!' he says wistfully. 'It was the Jesuits, of course.'

So, let's visit the Jesuits—those clever scholars of the Society of Jesus. They grant us an interview, though we don't know the name of the dark-robed scholar who sits before us; they like to act anonymously.

'Yes,' he might tell us, 'we coined the term *optimism* for philosophers like Leibniz, who paint too positive a picture of the world. Come to think of it, we coined *pessimism*, too, for philosophers like Voltaire and that devious sceptic Bayle, who seem to think the world is very bad and hold the creator accountable! What they both forget is that the world is very bad *now*, because of original sin; but all shall be made well again at the end of times.'

Confused, we would ask more questions, but our time is up and the scholars say no more.

So let's try our luck a century onwards, in the mid-nineteenth, and visit the most famous pessimist of all, perhaps the first one to proudly call himself by that name: Arthur Schopenhauer.

We find him, not scowling over his desk but practising his flute. We politely wait until he is finished, and ask if he will clarify the matter for us.

'Certainly!' he brightly tells us, and takes out a dusty Bible from his shelves, opening it at the Book of Genesis. 'Optimism is best encapsulated by these five words in the Bible: *and all was very good*. Pessimism is the daring challenge to that view: the incredible notion that the world is very *bad*, that suffering is at the very heart of things, that the world is something that *should not be*!' Again he flips through his Bible, reading first from the Book of Job ('Let the day perish wherein I was born, and the night in which it was said, There is a man child conceived'), then from Ecclesiastes ('vanity of vanities; all is vanity').[5]

A little puzzled, we ask him, 'So . . . optimism and pessimism are not about the future?'

'No, my friends!' he cries. 'It is about life, and its meaninglessness, its misery. It is about *the value of existence*!'

Value-oriented

Aha! Now we're getting somewhere. Apparently, for the first centuries after their coinage, optimism and pessimism have to do not with *our expectations of the future* but with the *value of existence*. They are attempts to answer questions such as: Is life worth living? Do the goods of life outweigh the evils? Of course there is much more to be said here, as the answers to such questions can vary enormously even amongst thinkers in the same camp. But for now we can group positive answers under optimism, negative ones under pessimism.

Elsewhere I've called these *value-oriented optimism and pessimism* (sometimes also known as *philosophical optimism/ pessimism*) and argued that they have everything to do with the age-old problem of evil: the question how a good God could allow the existence of evil and suffering in the world.[6] After all, the old optimists of the eighteenth century wanted above all to defend the Creator against attacks by sceptics who asked uncomfortable questions. Such as: If life is not worth living for some creatures, then why did God create them? *Or*: If life on the whole is overwhelmingly bad, how is creation justified?

To ward off such challenges, the value-oriented optimists took different roads. Some argued that life on this earth is indeed pretty bad for most of us but compensated by future bliss in the afterlife (at least, for those who have deserved one). Others went further and tried to prove that even life in this world is very good for most, or even all of us. Some even went so far as to argue that there isn't a single creature for whom life is not worth living (otherwise, God wouldn't have created it).

The most famous of all answers was that given by G. W. Leibniz, in his *Essais de Theodicée*, which is where we get the term 'theodicy' (from the Greek *theo* [God] + *dikē*, [justice])—or the attempt to vindicate God against those who would make him responsible for the (moral and physical) evils of life.[7] Leibniz admitted there is suffering in creation but argued that if we looked at the whole cosmos across time (including possible aliens on other planets and the eternal bliss of the blessed), we would see that we live in the best of all possible worlds.

Leibniz asks us to imagine a great pyramid, in which are contained all the different worlds that God could possibly have created. The pyramid extends infinitely downwards, because there is no limit to possible worlds. But there's just one world at the very top of the pyramid, and that's the world that's *better* than any others. It isn't perfect, but it's superior to all alternatives. This is the best of all possible worlds, and it happens to be the world that you and I are living in. How do we know this? Simple: we know this is the best possible world because it's the world God in fact created. Had there been a better world, then God would have created that one. Had there not been a best option, then God would not have created any.

There were some who fell in love with this dizzying vision of reality, among them the French mathematician and philosopher Emilie du Châtelet (who was also Voltaire's longtime lover and companion). Others were less enthused, and much ink was spent by generations of scholars to either attack Leibniz's uncompromising *optimism* or defend it.

Voltaire attacked. Twice. First, in his famous 'Poem on the Lisbon Earthquake' of 1756, which contrasts the devastation of that natural disaster that struck Lisbon in 1755 with the optimistic philosophies of Leibniz and Pope. And again, in his novel *Candide, or Optimism*, whose characters are put through all manner of suffering and violence, from torture, rape, executions, slavery, plague, and natural disasters, in order to drive home the point that optimism is 'a cruel philosophy hiding under a reassuring name.'[8]

But does this mean Voltaire was himself a pessimist? Hardly. Other philosophers like Pierre Bayle and David Hume went much further in their demonstrations of the badness of existence. For Bayle, and for Hume after him, the point is not just that the evils of life outnumber the goods (though they believe this is also the case) but that they *outweigh* them. A life might consist of an equal number of good moments and bad moments: the problem is that the bad moments tend to have an intensity that upsets the scales. A small period of badness, says Bayle, has the power to ruin a large amount of good, just as a small portion of seawater can salt a barrel of fresh water: similarly, one hour of deep sorrow or intense pain contains more evil than there is good in six or seven pleasant days.[9]

It was against that bleak vision that thinkers like Leibniz and Rousseau emphasised the goods of life, and the power we have to seek out the good in all things, for if we learned to adjust our vision we would see that life is in fact very good: that 'there is incomparably more good than evil in the life of men, as there are incomparably more houses than prisons,' and that the world 'will serve us if we use it for our service; we shall be happy in it if we wish to be.'[10] Just as the pessimists believed the optimists were deceived in their insistence on the goods of life, so too the optimists thought the pessimists' eyes were skewed towards the bad: each side accused the other of not having the right vision.

Fast forward a few centuries, and we find that this version of the debate on optimism and pessimism continues in contemporary philosophy: not just in the philosophy of religion but also in the secular debate on whether procreation is morally justified. After all, if life is indeed overwhelmingly bad, as the pessimists argued, are we justified in creating new persons? At what precise point is life too bad, or too uncertain, to pass on?

But while philosophers still speak of optimism and pessimism in this older, value-oriented way, this is not how the terms tend to be used in everyday life. If we asked a person living today, 'What is optimism or pessimism?' it is likely they would respond that it has to do with expectations of the *future*. And this brings us to the second sense of both optimism and pessimism, which is oriented not on the value of existence as a whole but on the future in particular.

Future-oriented

Consider these uses of the terms 'optimistic' and 'pessimistic' in everyday language:

> I'm optimistic about our chances of developing this
> technology by 2030.
> We are optimistic that we will do well in this tournament.
> I'm pessimistic about my chances of keeping my job.
> I'm pessimistic about the state of the economy.

Nowadays, when say we are optimistic or pessimistic about something, it usually has to do with our expectations of the future or of something happening in the future. For instance, if we say 'I'm optimistic about X', this suggests we think it's likely that some event X will come to pass. Or, if X is a project, it suggests we are confident the project will succeed. Conversely, if we're pessimistic about X, we think that the event will not come to pass, or the project is likely to fail. This is also how newscasters speak about economic projections, or scientists describe scenarios: whereas a 'pessimistic' scenario assumes everything goes wrong, an 'optimistic' scenario assumes everything goes right.

So are these terms just value-neutral descriptions of our expectations about something happening or not happening in the future? Not quite. For instance, consider the following examples:

> I'm optimistic that I will lose money on this investment.
> I'm optimistic that there are hard times ahead of us.
> I'm optimistic that I will fail my exams.

If you think these sentences sound strange, even funny, you are right: no one with a correct understanding of the English language would use the term 'optimistic' in this way (unless they were trying to make a joke). But *why*? If I am confident that X will happen (and X = 'I lose money in an investment'), why would it be inappropriate to say I am *optimistic* about it?

Apparently, even though we think X is likely to happen, we wouldn't say we're *optimistic* unless we also *hope for* it to happen. We reserve the term for things we *want* to come about, things we consider good or useful or beneficial. We wouldn't say we're optimistic about a disaster occurring, even if we're confident that it will; conversely, we wouldn't say we're pessimistic about something unless it's somehow bad for us.

So the terms are not value-neutral after all. Optimism is the expectation of something *good* happening; pessimism the expectation of something *bad* happening. This is also the case when we use the terms more generally. For instance, if we say we are optimistic about the future, it suggests we expect the future (in general, or in some specific way) will be *better* than it is now; if we say we are pessimistic about the future, we expect it will be *worse*.

But in none of these cases does the expectation of something bad happening suggest we *want* it to happen. On the contrary, we use words like 'pessimistic' for things that we *think* or *fear* will happen, though we *hope* they don't. We use them for situations we would like to prevent.

Why, then, would it be better to be an 'optimist' than a 'pessimist'?

A 'Duty' of Optimism?

I ask this question because it's very common to hear the terms 'optimist' and 'pessimist' used in ways that are highly emotionally and morally charged. When we call someone an optimist, it's usually praise: this is why politicians and entrepreneurs are particularly keen to insist that they are optimists, or even to speak, following Karl Popper, of a 'duty of optimism.'[11] Conversely, to call someone a pessimist is usually to deride, denounce, deflate them. 'Pessimism is for losers', as one book title has it.[12]

The result is that the terms are associated not only with expectations or attitudes towards the future but with character traits and moral attributes. Being an 'optimist' is generally considered a virtue, or something to be admired, whereas being a 'pessimist' is closer to a vice. These associations have a long historical lineage: the value-oriented optimists of old were quick to fault the pessimists for ingratitude, weakness, pusillanimity. And no matter how these terms have changed in meaning over the ages, the same suspicion clings to the concept of 'pessimism' today. We still tend to associate optimism with willpower and determination; pessimism with weakness and giving up. Consider this quote often attributed to Winston Churchill: 'A pessimist sees the difficulty in every opportunity; an optimist sees the opportunity in every difficulty.'[13] In fact there is no evidence Churchill ever said this, but it is indicative of the kinds of assumptions that are held about pessimism. Pessimists are 'doomsters and gloomsters', they see the difficulty in everything, they tend to be passive and resigned, and they let their disposition get the better of them instead of 'manning up' and believing in a better future; whereas optimists are active, bold, courageous, doers, and go-getters.

There are several reasons why we should be suspicious about such associations. For one thing, on this view the question of optimism and pessimism is purely a matter of personal temperament or disposition. But if this is true, and some people have an innate tendency to always look on the dark side of things, while others are naturally predisposed to have a cheerful outlook even in the direst circumstances, then it is all the more unclear why the latter disposition should receive our praise and the former our blame. After all, we do tend to appreciate traits such as friendliness and a sunny disposition, but we also value compassion and sympathy, as well as the ability to show emotions like sadness and anger. It is hard, perhaps, to be friends with someone who never smiles, but at least as hard to stay friends with someone who is *always* smiling, even when we share bad news with them—or with someone who responds to our personal tragedies with statements such as *it's all for the best*.[14]

But in fact it is not the case that we conceive of optimism and pessimism *purely* as personal dispositions: this is belied by the way we use these terms, and by the fact that optimism is so positively charged and pessimism so negatively. When we praise someone for their optimism, or when someone praises themselves by saying 'I am an optimist', this suggests that optimism is not simply an innate disposition but a cultivated character trait—something we can train and develop, like a virtue; something we can pride ourselves on if we have achieved it. To speak of a 'duty of optimism' is to suggest that we *ought* to be optimists, that we must *always* believe in the achievability of success, even against all odds.

For instance, it is very common to hear a phrase like the following: 'All evidence points to things turning out badly for X, *but we have to be optimistic*.' But then we still have a problem. Why should it be considered a virtue for someone to declare their optimism *even against the facts*? In fact, would this not be a misuse of the very term 'optimistic', which we usually employ when we *expect* a good thing to come about? If a person told us they were 'optimistic about X' *in blatant disregard of the facts*, would we trust their judgement? Immanuel Kant famously argued that we should never tell lies, because if we universalised our action and imagined a society in which everyone lied, then we could not trust anything anyone ever said. Similarly, if we lived in a society where everyone was optimistic about everything, because the alternative was not socially acceptable, then we would have no reason to believe anyone's expressions about anything.

Of course this is an exaggeration: no one would argue that we have to be optimistic about everything all the time. But then, why this constant insistence on optimism, this pervasive fear that any expression of pessimism is the first step on the road to giving up altogether? Why, at the end of the year 2022, which brought famine to Africa, war to Europe, and searing fires to forests around the globe (not to mention the deepening climate crisis), did several Dutch newspapers choose to present issues themed around 'hope', 'optimism', and 'looking forward to tomorrow', and even to illustrate this 'new perspective on crisis' with a family happily roasting marshmallows on a forest fire?[15]

One reason may be that upbeat, hopeful, optimistic reporting makes us feel comfortable and relaxed, whereas dark news unsettles and discomfits us.[16] But also, I think there is a common confusion underlying the fear of pessimism. When people say that 'even when the odds are against us, we have to be optimistic', what they mean is simply: all evidence is against us, *but we have to try nonetheless.* And perhaps: *if we do our best we might still stand a chance.*

But that commendable attitude is not incompatible with pessimism. It is only incompatible with fatalism.

Fatalism

Fatalism is the belief that the future is set in stone; that our actions cannot change it. This is often conflated with pessimism, on the view that to take a pessimistic stance is to disbelieve entirely in the possibility of success; that all our efforts are bound to fail. But in fact, if pessimism is simply an expectation that some bad thing is likely to happen, or some bad situation is likely to get worse, the equation with fatalism does not follow. To have a pessimistic expectation about the future is not the same as holding that the future is fixed or that nothing can be done to change it. On the contrary: viewing the future as bleak might precisely be a spur to action, a call to arms. Even the perceived unlikelihood of success need not stand in the way of determined action, as long as action is driven deeply by other moral sources than the certainty of victory: such as duty, justice, and the need to fight for those things we hold dear.

That pessimism is not the same as fatalism is also borne out by the fact that most self-declared pessimists of the past do not subscribe to such a notion: on the contrary, they do all they can to resist it. As Dienstag has argued, to be a pessimist is not necessarily to expect the worst but rather *to expect nothing at all*.[17] Pessimism, in philosophy, has to do rather with a limitation of what we can possibly know about what life has in store for us. It is, therefore, not at all a positive belief in decline but rather a negative belief, a refusal to believe that progress is a given.

Thus pessimism as a philosophical and political tradition is precisely opposed to fatalism, since the intrinsic uncertainty of life means we can expect neither progress nor decline. Interestingly, this is a view that some self-declared optimists share. Even Karl Popper, who so influentially declared that 'optimism is a duty', was careful to add that all he meant with this was that the *outcome is not yet fixed* and that we have to distinguish the present from the 'wide-open future':

The future is open. It is not fixed in advance. So no one can predict it—except by chance. The possibilities lying within the future, both good and bad, are boundless. When I say,

'Optimism is a duty', this means not only that the future is open but that we all help to decide it through what we do. We are all jointly responsible for what is to come.[18]

And again:

> The open future contains unforeseeable and morally quite different possibilities. So our basic attitude should not be 'What will happen?' but 'What should we do to make the world a little better—even if we know that once we have done it, future generations might make everything worse again?'[19]

But this combination of openness and activism, as will become clear, is in turn an attitude that many pessimists would heartily endorse. When Popper speaks of 'pessimism' he uses it to describe a 'cynical view of history', according to which 'things always have been and always will be so'—a type of fatalism that makes activism unnecessary and, indeed, impossible.[20] But if pessimism is simply an evaluation about the present or an expectation about the future, *without in any way* holding that the future is fixed, then there would seem to be no reason why pessimists cannot be activists. (That this is correct, and pessimism is in no way incompatible with activism, will become clear in the next chapter.)

Of course there is a version of pessimism we might call fatalistic: if pessimism is defined as the belief that things will *necessarily* get worse, or that some bad event is *destined* to come about.[21] We might call this Fatalistic Pessimism. But there's a catch. If this belief is fatalistic, then so is its opposite: the belief that things will *necessarily* get better, or that some good event is *destined* to come about—in other words, Fatalistic Optimism. If the former belief or attitude is fatalistic in positing the certainty of decline, the latter is no less fatalistic in positing the certainty of progress. To the extent that pessimism can be fatalistic, optimism can be too.[22]

The notion of Fatalistic Optimism may seem strange to us today (though the belief in the certainty of progress is in fact much more common than the belief in necessary decline), but it was one of the reasons why Voltaire was so critical of optimism (as he perceived it). Voltaire thought that Leibniz's insistence that *the system as a whole is good* is a kind of fatalism: if everything is for the best in the best of all possible worlds, that suggests things can never get better; that we can never strive for (social, political, moral) improvement.[23] Why would we act for cultural change if we believe things are fated to get better anyhow?

This was Voltaire's concern: if we go about our lives believing everything *was, is,* and *will be* for the best, then this 'deflates our sense of the possible' (in Marilynne Robinson's words)[24]—it makes us apathetic, it removes any drive we might have to act for change. And the same is true if we believe all *was, is,* and *will be* for the worst. On either end, this is fatalism, and we are right to object to it just as Voltaire did. But we should remember such fatalism can take several guises: it is perhaps more obvious to us in the darker folds of pessimism, but it is no less pervasive when dressed in the bright colours of optimism.

Climate Optimism, Climate Pessimism

The thing to be avoided, then, is not pessimism but fatalism: the belief that the future is set in stone, that there is nothing we can do to change it. Such fatalism, and this is important, can take the form of either optimism or pessimism (as we now define them)—but neither of these is *necessarily* fatalistic. Most uses of both 'optimism' and 'pessimism' suggest not certainty but probability, or the conviction that something is *likely* to come about. This will not surprise us in the case of 'optimism', a term we use correctly when we voice our conviction that some good thing is *likely*, though not *destined*, to occur.

But it is all too often forgotten that there is an open-ended version of 'pessimism' too, a term we use correctly when we voice our belief, which is at the same time a fear, that some bad thing is likely to come about. Thus, a climate optimist might say: 'There is every reason to believe we can turn the tide and prevent the worst impact from climate change. Our efforts to prevent climate catastrophe are likely to succeed.' While a climate pessimist might say: 'There is every reason to believe we cannot turn the tide and prevent the worst impact from climate change. Our efforts to prevent climate catastrophe are likely to fail.'

Both statements are oriented towards the future; both involve the expectation of something good or bad happening; yet neither one is the same as giving up. For instance, the climate pessimist may continue: 'Our efforts are likely to fail—*and we will do what we can nonetheless.*' Because, for all the bleak projections of what will happen if we don't keep global warming to 1.5 or even 2 degrees, there is still a possibility that the worst consequences can be mitigated, the darkest scenarios kept at bay—and even small differences between the scenarios may make the difference between life and death for people at the front line of their effects. 'The fight is, definitely not yet lost,' writes David Wallace-Wells, '—in fact will never be lost, so long as we avoid extinction, because however warm the planet gets, *it will always be the case that the decade that follows could contain more suffering or less.*'[25] And as if these are not sufficient reasons for persistent collective action, here is another: quite simply, *because it is owed*—to people alive now as well as to future generations, and to the many creatures, sentient and nonsentient, with whom we share a world.[26]

From the pessimistic premise the defeatist conclusion does not follow. If one believes the future looks dark, the logical next step is not to do nothing: it may well be to act all the more determinedly, to do what one can in resistance and perseverance against the rising storm. Conversely, if one believes the future to be bright, for instance because technology will save us, or governments will spring into timely action, is this an equal ground of motivation?

I leave this, deliberately, as an open question—one that we, as a culture, have failed to ask ourselves. And I insist upon this point: that pessimism should not be confused with fatalism; that to be pessimistic about something is by no means equivalent to saying 'We may as well give up'. As will become evident in the next chapter, there have been plenty of deeply pessimistic activists already—and it should be clear even from the amount of despair-fuelled resistance visible today that climate pessimism is not the same as fatalism or defeatism and not logically equivalent to an attitude of inaction or resignation. History and popular culture are full of examples of resistance even without any perspective of victory but for reasons of justice and duty—because it is the right thing to do. We just don't recognise these for what they are: an exercise of *hopeful pessimism*.

Now of course there can be degrees and variations and even mixtures between these two alternatives—climate optimism, climate pessimism—and for each, there is a fatalistic version. Optimistic climate fatalists reveal themselves by statements like the following: 'Humanity will *certainly* resolve climate change; our efforts are *destined* to succeed.' While pessimistic fatalists might tell us: 'Humanity will *certainly* not resolve climate change; our efforts are *doomed* to fail.' Climate fatalism thus has two varieties: an optimistic and a pessimistic kind. Among the former we might count certain varieties of techno-optimism, which stakes such a conviction in technological solutions that it deflates the need for either individual or collective change, while among the latter, we may include the advocates of what some have called 'climate stoicism' and 'deep adaptation'—the belief that instead of acting to minimise human suffering we should 'learn to accept and adapt': accept that 'we're doomed', and adapt by means of a 'daily cultivation of detachment.'[27]

Strictly speaking, even these fatalisms do not equate inaction or passivity, as will become clear—but there is a real risk in such views, and it is this risk that writers emphasising the need for hope or optimism are getting at when they warn against pessimism or despair. Namely, the risk of believing *that there's no point in acting*, as either the crisis is unsolvable or it will be solved for us. This is a risk worth combatting and a battle that must be waged on two fronts. Optimistic fatalism poses as much a risk as pessimistic fatalism; the danger of deflatedness threatens on both sides. In the words of novelist China Miéville, 'There is bad pessimism as well as bad optimism.' Against those who would tell us there is no point in acting, 'there are sound scientific reasons to suggest that we're not yet—quite—at some point of no return. We need to tilt at a different tipping point, into irrevocable social change, and that requires *a different pessimism, an unflinching look at how bad things are.*'[28]

We should never pretend that there is no use in acting. Even if in some way the disaster is already upon us, our actions now can prevent some of the worst outcomes and have a direct and measurable impact on those alive and suffering *now*. But neither should any of us feel pressured to tone down our concerns about the future or the nature of the very real threat that is upon us.

This is especially important to remember in the debate on climate change, where it is all too common to hear questions such as 'Are you optimistic or pessimistic about the future?' or statements such as 'We have to be optimistic, at all costs.' For while there is nothing wrong in principle with saying we are optimistic or pessimistic about something—in so far as we are describing our personal expectations, our hopes and fears—something goes awry when a culture requires its members to express optimism at any cost, whereas pessimism is considered so suspect as to be shunned, as if it were a vice, a dereliction of duty.

And this is where the cruelty of optimism reveals itself: not only in imposing the burden of having to express one's optimism or hopefulness, even when it is not felt, but in overemphasising the amount of control we can have over our own affects and attitudes. 'If we let ourselves be negatively affected,' it simply means we have achieved 'insufficient reorientation in our ways of thinking and attitudes towards ourselves and our relationship with the world,' as one scholar tells us. 'The experience of harm—having been negatively affected—simply means that we are to be blamed for not yet having become sufficiently aware of our attachments.'[29] But, as the pessimists of the past would be the first to remind us, to deride pessimism, or to dismiss people who are in the depths of despair, is to pile suffering upon suffering: it is to add to this despair the burden of being responsible for it.

In an age when entire islands are sinking into the sea, vast stretches of land and wood are swept away by storms of wind or fire, and cities by floods; when we are losing species more quickly than we can count them, and people young and old stand weeping in the streets—it is crucial that all of us living through these times are able to express, freely and sincerely, our beliefs and attitudes, even (and perhaps *especially*) when these moods are dark. The insistence on positive, optimistic, hopeful narratives comes with its own risks and burdens, whereas the repression of negative, pessimistic, even desperate counternarratives is truly dangerous, as it charges the already burdened with the duty of optimism.

And so it seems that something is to be gained in encountering these terms again, reacquainting ourselves with them as if for the first time, and asking ourselves: Why are they so important to us? What do we mean when we speak of *optimism* or *pessimism*? Is it true that we feel comforted by optimism, whereas pessimism threatens our repose? And if it is true, is it also right?

Whatever our answers to such questions, one thing is clear: in an age of climate crisis and ecological devastation, pessimism has a role to play.

2

Pessimism and Activism

The only cowardice is to get down on one's knees.... It is our
duty to do what we know to be fair and good.

—ALBERT CAMUS, 1943

SO CHESTERTON was wrong when he said that 'there is no
such thing as a pessimist.' But is there also such a thing as a pessimistic activist, or an activistic pessimist?

To some, this may seem like a contradiction in terms, considering the common view that activism has to be optimistic or
even utopian[1] and the tenacious association of pessimism with
defeatism or fatalism. The alternative may even seem absurd: if
you're a pessimist or think a dystopian future is likely, why
would you still fight for change? Surely activism's slogan should
be 'We can do it!' and not 'We're doomed!' Recall Noam
Chomsky's statement that we can either 'be pessimistic, give
up, and help ensure that the worst will happen' or 'be optimistic, grasp the opportunities that surely exist, and maybe help
make the world a better place.'[2] In one sense, this is surely right:
if we 'give up' we aid the worst outcomes; if we commit to

action we 'maybe help make the world a better place.' But, as I have argued, the dichotomy *optimism/pessimism* is unhelpful in this context, as it suggests that anyone who is less than confident in the achievability of success is thereby *giving up*—even when their actions belie this. Not only is this unfair to those who find themselves in despair *and yet* are resolutely activistic; it is potentially discouraging to many who want to act but can't muster the 'optimism' that seems to be required. And one might ask as well: if to be pessimistic is the same as giving up, why do climate activists hold up banners saying, 'I am hopeless'; 'I am afraid to grow old because of the climate crisis'; or (quoting David Wallace-Wells), 'It's worse, much worse, than you think'?[3]

Now, to be fair, there have been pessimistic arguments for resignation, both in the philosophical tradition and in the climate debate—and indeed such arguments have been used as excuses to do exactly nothing, to sit back and draw a quietist pleasure from the fact that 'we're doomed'.[4] But so too have optimistic views—as in the case of certain techno-utopian ideologies which deprioritise climate change out of a misplaced confidence that technology will solve the problem for us. To argue therefore that activism can only be optimistic or utopian is to conjure up a dual risk: not only does it suggest that anyone who is pessimistic about the future *has already given up* (thus furnishing the passive with an excuse for their inaction), but it also suggests that anyone who is optimistic is by definition also activistic. This, however, is not the case. Optimism can be just as deflating, or even more so, than pessimism. If you hear someone say brightly 'I trust humanity will solve this problem', this usually means they think they do not have to take *any* action, whether individual or collective—it means the climate problem is not a problem *for them*.

We should, in other words, not be blindsided by the wrong use of either optimistic or pessimistic arguments. The question should

FIGURE 2. Trafalgar Square March and sit-down protest by Extinction Rebellion (XR) on the first day of their April Rebellion, 9 April 2022. © Crispin Hughes.

not be whether one is optimistic or pessimistic—but whether one is active or passive; whether one is determined or resigned. And if the real enemy is inaction or passivity or resignation, then this danger (as we have seen) looms on both sides. So let's put aside all such assumptions for a moment and ask a different question: Have there in fact been activists or activistic movements that have been outspokenly pessimistic in their outlooks?

The answer is yes.

Albert Camus

In his book *Pessimism: Philosophy, Ethic, Spirit,* Joshua Foa Dienstag has argued not only that there is a pessimist tradition of political thought but that pessimism can be a source of powerful political engagement.[5] As counterexamples to 'the common conception of pessimism as issuing in political detachment,' Dienstag points to Albert Camus and Miguel de Unamuno, whose 'philosophical interpretation of pessimism pointed toward an engagement with, rather than a retreat from, politics.' To which Dienstag adds that 'it certainly *ought* to disturb the ordinary interpretation of pessimism to realize that two of the most active, politically engaged intellectuals of the twentieth century fall within its ranks.'[6]

Camus's name should need little introduction, if only because during the Covid-19 pandemic so many of us read *The Plague*, the 1947 novel that won him the Nobel Prize (which Jean-Paul Sartre mocked him for accepting).[7] Aside from a novelist, Camus also came to be known as an existentialist philosopher—though he himself disavowed the label—and, as Dienstag argues, a pessimistic one. Camus did not call himself a pessimist—a word which was already a condemnation in his time—but his philosophical writings on 'the absurd' and on the tragic condition of humankind do seem to place him squarely in that tradition.[8] As Camus writes in *The Myth of Sisyphus* (1942), it is the destiny of humankind to long for purpose and clarity in life when the world itself is devoid of meaning: 'The absurd is born of this confrontation between the human need and the unreasonable silence of the world.'[9] The absurd is an inalienable condition of humankind as locked in linear time and confronted with the certainty of death. If many people are not aware of the absurd, it is because of the tactic of *l'esquive*—the eluding of the challenges of existence, for instance by means of hope (that is: hope for another life, or for 'some great idea' that will give life meaning). 'Eluding is the invariable game.'[10]

As an alternative response to the absurd (an alternative, that is, to either hope or suicide), Camus provides us with the image of Sisyphus, the mythological king who was condemned by the gods 'to ceaselessly rolling a rock to the top of a mountain, when the stone would fall back of its own weight.' While Sisyphus is fully conscious of the uselessness of his task and his condition is therefore tragic, Camus asks us to imagine Sisyphus, not resigned and defeated but scornful and rebellious and even joyful at times, as someone who has said 'yes' to his fate: 'the absurd hero.' 'One must imagine Sisyphus happy.'[11]

How could this possibly be a principle for activism? It should be noted, first of all, that *Sisyphus* was written before World War II, a time during which, after being tempted to seek refuge in Algiers, Camus became active in the French Resistance and edited the resistance journal *Combat*. After the war, as Europe staggered through the ravages, Camus was concerned to confront his generation with the danger not just of active monstrosity but of compliance and complacency. As Dienstag writes, 'The dangers of absurdity he now considers to be importantly social and political—*l'esquive* is not just a personal failing, but . . . one that can lead to compliance with monstrous evil.'[12] Thus, in postwar writings such as *The Rebel* of 1951 (*L'Homme Révolté*: 'the human in revolt'), Camus 'strove to connect the situation of absurdity to a defense of vigorous political participation.'[13] Rebellion or revolt is to be sharply distinguished from revolutions that turn to murder and oppression; it is to be based not on ideologies that crush the lives of other humans beneath their utopian dreams but on principles of justice, solidarity, and human dignity. As Camus writes in the final chapter of *The Rebel*:

The words which reverberate for us at the confines of this long adventure of rebellion, are not formulae for optimism, for which we have no possible use in the extremities of our unhappiness, but words of courage and intelligence which, on the shores of the eternal seas, even have the qualities of virtue.[14]

What is required for revolt is not outright optimism, as there will always be misery and injustice in the world and optimism *always* jars with the experience of those who suffer. What is required, instead, is 'courage and intelligence' and determination to act even if there is no prospect of success: this is the meaning of our justice and our freedom. Such determination is *in no way* incompatible with pessimism. 'The idea that a pessimistic philosophy is necessarily one of discouragement is a puerile idea,' Camus writes in the September 1945 issue of *Combat*: any objective mind taking the *facts* into consideration would conclude that 'a negative philosophy was not incompatible, in actual fact, with an ethics of freedom and courage.'[15]

These are not empty words. In his editorial for the issue of *Combat* that was published on the night Paris was liberated from German occupation,[16] Camus writes:

> Nothing is given to men, and the little they can conquer is paid for with unjust deaths. But man's greatness lies elsewhere. It lies in his decision to be stronger than his condition. And if his condition is unjust, he has only one way of overcoming it, which is to be just himself.[17]

As Dienstag interprets this passage, the actions of Resistance were not justified by their eventual success but because they 'simultaneously gave dignity to individual life under occupation while allowing those who respected such dignity to create a common space where they could have the experience of freedom. . . . Resistance, rebellion, if they are genuine, validate themselves in the moment of their occurrence, not by reference to some desired outcome, no matter how noble.'[18]

Dienstag, following others,[19] links Camus's theories to those of Hannah Arendt: 'Both took as their model the activities of the French Resistance, which were, in this view, not undertaken in the belief that they would necessarily be efficacious or success-ful, but simply with the thought that they were the necessary human response to tyranny.'[20] Rebellions, in other words, are not justified by the expectation of success, nor by reasons of op-timism or efficiency, nor even by the image of a Sisyphean hero rebelling in a scornfully individualistic way—but by reasons of *justice* and, crucially for the later Camus, *solidarity*. As Camus wrote to Roland Barthes, compared to his earlier novel *The Stranger* of 1942, *The Plague* represented 'the transition from an attitude of solitary revolt to the recognition of a community whose struggles must be shared. If there is an evolution from *The Stranger* to *The Plague*, it is in the direction of solidarity and par-ticipation.'[21] According to Dienstag this view of rebellion not only shows 'the existence and seriousness of a pessimistic tradi-tion in political philosophy' but also 'answers one of the most persistent criticisms of pessimism, namely, that it cannot be ef-fectively political. . . . Camus' ethic at least allows us to see how such a philosophy can orient us toward the political arena.'[22]

It also allows us to make sense of historical examples of 'des-perate resistance'[23]—of rebellions in the certainty of defeat. Thus on 23 April 1943 Mordecai Anielewicz, the commander of the Jewish revolt in the Warsaw ghetto, wrote to Yitzhak Cukierman:

I feel that great things are happening and what we dared do is of great, enormous importance. . . . It is impossible to describe the conditions under which the Jews of the ghetto are now living. Only a few will be able to hold out. The remainder will die sooner or later. Their fate is decided. . . . With the aid of our transmitter we heard the marvelous report on our fighting by the 'Shavit' radio station. The fact that we are remembered beyond the ghetto walls encourages us in our struggle. Peace go with you, my friend! Perhaps we may still meet again! *The dream of my life has risen to become fact. Self-defense in the ghetto will have been a reality. Jewish armed resistance and revenge are facts. I have been a witness to the magnificent, heroic fighting of Jewish men in battle.*[24]

On the view that resistance or activism must be based on considerations of optimism or efficacy, such acts of resistance seem tragic, *and nothing else.* But on the view of Camus and others (such as Arendt, Foucault, and Adorno),[25] such actions are truly *justified* in a critical sense—for reasons of justice, dignity, and solidarity, if not victory.

This is all the more poignant because examples of Jewish resistance against the Nazis have been cited as an inspiration in the climate debate—to make the point that *even if* victory is unlikely, resistance is *still* justified. Towards the end of his book *How to Blow Up a Pipeline,* Andreas Malm quotes the following passage from the book *Revolutionary Yiddishland* by Alain Brossat and Sylvie Klingberg:

> In the ghettos, as in the extermination camps to which they were the antechamber, the *résistants* embarked on a race against death. To struggle and resist was the only lucid choice, but this most often meant for the fighters no more than choosing the time and manner of their death. Beyond the immediate outcome of the struggle, which most often was inevitable, their combat was for history, for memory. . . . *This affirmation of life by way of a sacrifice and combat with no prospect of victory* is a tragic paradox that can only be understood as an act of faith in history.[26]

To which Malm comments:

> Precisely the hopelessness of the situation constituted the nobility of this resistance. The rebels affirmed life so extraordinarily robustly because death was certain and *still* they fought on. It can never, ever be too late for that gesture. If it is too late for resistance to be waged within a calculus of immediate utility, the time has come for it to vindicate the fundamental values of life, even if it only means crying out to the heavens. To make that statement would require some forceful type of action. This is the moment for the cliché from Emiliano Zapata: 'It is better to die on your feet than to live on your knees.'[27]

Another person who liked to quote that last sentence was Albert Camus.[28] So-called 'realists', he tells us, will act only in efficacy: 'They are willing to undertake only tasks that succeed.'[29] We must be braver than that, in the knowledge that where complete success is unachievable, it is always possible 'to diminish the pain of men',[30] and so it is always our duty to try.

Thus the people combatting the plague in his novel are not to be considered heroic or extraordinary: 'In reality, it was no great merit on the part of those who dedicated themselves to the health teams, because they knew that it was the only thing to be done and not doing it would have been incredible at the time.'[31] This message is repeated again and again in *The Plague*—which many of us read in the context of the pandemic but should reread in that of climate change—the question is not *Why should we act?* but *How could we not act?* As Dr. Rieux says, 'when you see the suffering and pain that it brings, you have to be mad, blind or a coward to resign yourself to the plague.'[32]

Published in the aftermath of World War II, *The Plague* was criticised by some for seeming to use pestilence as a metaphor for fascism—as though the latter were an impersonal, natural force. On a closer look, however, the plague does not stand for either fascism or the Vichy regime but for the temptation to comply with any moral evil: the temptation to give in to it, to not have resisted enough. As Tarrou says towards the end of the book, 'everyone has it inside himself, this plague, because no one in the world, no one, is immune.' The plague confronts the citizens of Oran with a decision: whether or not to act, or rather which side to be on (as not acting is itself an act: it is to opt for the side of 'pestilence'). 'All I say is that on this earth there are pestilences and there are victims—and as far as possible one must refuse to be on the side of the pestilence.' For Tarrou, having understood this was itself a first step to action: 'So I decided then to speak and act clearly, to put myself on the right path.'[33]

Tarrou makes one decision, Cottard another. Confronted with Tarrou's argument 'that too many people were not doing anything, that the epidemic was everybody's business and that they all had to do their duty', for instance by joining the health teams, Cottard replies that 'it won't do any good. The plague is too strong.' Asked again if he won't join them, he adds, 'It's not my job.' And finally, because he knows that if the plague ends the police will remember to arrest him for a previous crime, 'In any case, this plague is doing me a favour, so I don't see why I should be involved in getting rid of it.'[34]

It's no use, it's not my job, it's doing me a favour. Three arguments, not quite incompatible with each other but suspicious precisely in their compatibility, as if Cottard recognises none of them is good enough, so he needs to heap them up. In the climate crisis, too, there is no shortage of people who believe that *it's no use* acting, as 'we're doomed' anyway, or that *it's not my job*, or even that *it's doing me a favour.* (We know that there are parties who profit from climate change, and have spent ample time and money to stridently prevent it from being combatted.)[35] This is the great danger to be resisted by any means—that of adaptation and resignation and inertia in the face of evil and injustice—what one of Camus's most famous characters calls *the habit of despair*:

> The townspeople had adapted, *they had come to heel*, as people say, *because that was all they could do*. Naturally, they still had an attitude of misfortune and suffering, but they did not feel its sting. Dr Rieux, for one, considered that the misfortune lay precisely in this, and that the habit of despair was worse than despair itself.[36]

And this points us in the direction of a different kind of risk—which may perhaps be best introduced by a different pestilential tale.

Climate Barbarism

In Edgar Allen Poe's story 'The Masque of the Red Death' a certain country is devastated by a plague, the 'Red Death' of the title, which kills all who catch it within a terrible half hour. 'But the Prince Prospero was happy and dauntless and sagacious.' This jovial ruler chooses, while 'his dominions were half depopulated,' to invite 'a thousand hale and light-hearted friends' to a secluded castle with thick walls and iron gates. Inside, the prince 'had provided all the appliances of pleasure': 'There were buffoons, there were improvisatori, there were ballet-dancers, there were musicians, there was Beauty, there was wine. All these and security were within. Without was the "Red Death."' After all, thought Prospero: 'The external world could take care of itself. In the meantime it was folly to grieve, or think.'[37]

In his climate novel *The Ministry for the Future*, set in the near future, Kim Stanley Robinson features a fictional scientific article discussing the various possible negative reactions to 'global climate catastrophe.' One of these has been called, after Poe's story, 'The Masque of the Red Death Syndrome', which hinges on 'an assertion that the end being imminent and inevitable, there is nothing left to do except party while you can.'[38] But perhaps this 'syndrome' should be conceived differently. After all, the problem in the story is not that Prospero withdraws *to party* instead of (for instance) holding a wake or vigil: to the people suffering outside his walls, it makes little difference whether he feasts or mourns. The problem is that Prospero withdraws *at all*. The problem is that he, a ruler, seeks shelter in the confines of his castle, shutting out the people he is duty bound to protect. As Tarrou would have put it, by hiding away in his castle, Prospero paradoxically chooses to be 'on the side of the pestilence' when he should be on the side of the victims.

Note that Prospero does not *deny* that the plague exists. On the contrary, his bright feast is premised on the presence of the darkness outside. Prospero and his fellow party-goers know full well what is happening outside the gates. But knowledge is not the same as action; mere awareness is not enough.

This is a point that has also been made in the climate debate. While philosophers and activists keep stressing the need for climate awareness, under the assumption 'that genuine awareness and acceptance of the existence of anthropogenic climate change (as opposed to either ignorance or denial) automatically leads one to develop political and moral positions which advocate for collective human action,'[39] several authors have argued that this assumption is false, as awareness can easily be accompanied by inaction. As James Butler has noted,

belief in the saving power of climate awareness is obdurate in climate activism, as shown by the *Guardian*'s eschatological headlines or Extinction Rebellion's exhortation for us all to acknowledge the emergency. If only we knew, we would act in the right way. But there is no obvious point at which knowledge tips into action; in an increasingly mediatised political sphere, spreading awareness ends up as a substitute for action itself.[40]

And the problem is worse than this: not only can awareness end up as a *substitute* for collective action; it can also trigger action *of the wrong sort*, leading to a different and more present danger, that of *climate barbarism*.

The latter is a term used by Naomi Klein and others to describe a specific form of climate adaptation which accepts the reality of climate change yet draws from this the wrong principle of action: namely, to replace talk of climate justice with a different ideology, *each nation for itself*. Just as Prospero accepts the reality of the plague and *as a consequence* chooses to withdraw behind the walls of his own castle, so the tactic of climate barbarism is for countries to withdraw behind the walls of their own making, shutting out those whose own homes have been made uninhabitable *by those very same countries*, while continuing to emit the greenhouse gases that cause death by drought and flood and fire. 'Let there be no mistake: this is the dawn of climate barbarism,' writes Naomi Klein in her book *On Fire*. 'And unless there is a radical change not only in politics but in the underlying values that govern our politics, this is how the wealthy world is going to "adapt" to more climate disruption: by fully unleashing the toxic ideologies that rank the relative value of human lives to justify the monstrous discarding of huge swaths of humanity.'[41]

This is a hard shift of perspective to make, as for the past decades the great challenge for scientists and activists alike has been to combat the wildfires of climate denial even as Big Oil

fanned the flames. While this campaign was in many ways successful (albeit at the cost of decades of delay, which allowed
fossil-fuel companies to comfortably change tack by way of greenwashing),[42] it has overstressed the saving power of awareness,
under the optimistic assumption that vision necessitates action.
Climate barbarism disturbs this logic, as it confronts us with
'the possibility of a cruel adaptation to climate change.'[43] In the
words of Jacob Blumenfeld, the problem is that 'climate denial
is no longer socially acceptable, and moreover, no longer *necessary*. One can now accept the irrefutable truth of climate change
without giving up one's love of fossil fuels or hatred of immi-
grants.' This is the spectre of climate barbarism, which 'recog-
nizes climate change and adapts to it by withdrawing from any
obligations to others, outside of one's own preferred in-group,
the boundaries of which can always be narrowed further and
further in cascades of violence and disregard.'[44]

This is not to say that awareness is not important: in an age
of obfuscation and disinformation it is crucial to get the facts
and the science straight. It is just to make the manifest point
that awareness itself is not enough, just as mere hope or grief is
not enough unless it hardens into action and resolve.[45]

In Poe's story, it does not end well for Prospero or his fellow
feast-goers. But we do not live in stories. And so the question
we must ask ourselves and our governments is how much like
Prospero we want to be. To quote, again, Naomi Klein:

The rapidly escalating cruelty of our present moment cannot
be overstated; nor can the long-term damage to the collective psyche should this go unchallenged. Beneath the theatre
of some governments denying climate change and others
claiming to be doing something about it while they fortress
their borders from its effects, there is one overarching question

facing us. *In the rough and rocky future that has already begun, what kind of people are we going to be?* Will we share what's left and try to look after one another? Or are we instead going to attempt to hoard what's left, look after 'our own', and lock everyone else out?[46]

Or as Tarrou would have put it—are we going to be on the side of the pestilence?

The Dangers of Optimism

Long before the age of climate change, Camus saw the dangers of inertia and adaptation, and warned against them. We find in his pessimism a clear-sightedness that cuts through all the subterfuges and evasions available in his time to the beating core of his activism: that we must do what must be done, for reasons of justice and solidarity—because we owe it to our fellow humans to prevent their suffering as best we can. Against the temptation of inertia, of hiding away in our fortresses like Prospero, of turning our backs to suffering like Cottard, Camus proposes a fierce philosophy of action that is as bold as it is stark, stripped from any confidence of victory.[47] As Tarrou says to Rieux, 'your victories will always be temporary, that's all.' To which Rieux answers, 'Always, I know that. But that is not a reason to give up the struggle.' The plague means for him an 'endless defeat'; but he will not stop trying, he who has been 'taught' by suffering.[48] In a similar vein Adam Tooze has pointed out that Andreas Malm draws on 'the dramas of 20th century European history . . . not as an inspiration to revolution, but as a way of giving meaning to resistance that may ultimately be in vain.'[49]

Camus, of course, is just one writer; his is just one philosophical perspective among many. And the point will be made at this stage that there have also been activists and activistic theories that have been outspokenly optimistic—including in the climate movement. But it is not my aim to argue that activists *must* be pessimists. Rather, I want to make a more modest, two-fold point. First, that pessimism is not the same as defeatism, and is not incompatible with activism—indeed, pessimism in a certain mode can be especially empowering. Second, that optimism, while potentially a powerful drive to action, also has its dangers.

These dangers have recently been described by philosopher and climate activist Anh-Quân Nguyen, who notes that while optimism 'is present almost everywhere in the climate movement' and is 'often thought to be a necessity for maintaining climate activism,' this is a mistake: 'Clinging to optimism is understandable, but in the end leads the climate movement to more despair, burnout and withdrawal.'[50] The main reason for this is that climate optimism in several variations places 'an unreasonable mental burden on activists, with overwhelming expectations that are supposed to mobilise and motivate activists leading to bad effects on mental health, burnout, and eventually, withdrawal from climate activism.'[51]

This is a striking claim, as it has become common for academics and media to express concerns about climate activists experiencing eco-anxiety and other dark moods associated with climate crisis. But Nguyen thinks it is precisely *climate optimism* that 'leads to bad effects on the mental health of climate activists.' He cites a 2019 study of climate activists in New Zealand by Karen Nairn, who points out that participants 'framed their experiences of burnout as though they were somehow responsible for "burning out."' For instance, one activist who blames herself for having been too optimistic draws a direct link between her optimism and her subsequent burning out:

Well for a really long time, I guess I assumed that you had to have *some kind of optimism about the future*, that is, the ability for us to create a situation where climate change wouldn't ruin the world ... but I had a friend who is incredibly cynical and pessimistic, actually a couple of them, both involved in [a climate activist group] and both of them not burnt out, surprisingly which I find quite interesting ... *I'm just thinking about how I could've not burnt out and if I hadn't been so blindly optimistic*, maybe I would've been able to temper my engagement in things so I didn't just go all out and try and do as much as I could and just realizing what's actually a bit more realistic.[52]

This, Nguyen argues, is precisely the danger associated with optimism: 'Under future-oriented climate optimism, activists are responsible for their own hope, and conversely also for their own despair, on the journey towards climate justice.' He concludes that climate activists should reject climate optimism 'due to its tendencies towards success-washing, explaining away dark emotions, and mentally overburdening climate activists in their struggle,' and suggests they should instead embrace 'a courageous pessimism that can make sense of the absurdity of activist struggles.'[53]

There is also another danger, which has to do with the tendency of climate optimism to create expectations *it is then pressured to fulfil*. This may be an effective way to rally first-time activists to the cause, but it leaves the climate movement, and activists, ill-equipped to deal with disappointment and failure. According to Nguyen, this pressure to maintain, at all costs, 'the belief that we will win' results in a tendency for the climate movement to engage in what he calls 'success-washing': 'Future-oriented climate optimism is so embedded in the movement that it ignores or explains away failures and engages in *success-washing* actions taken by climate activists,' for instance by claiming certain actions have had an impact *even if* their goals were not reached. He comments:

> The temptation towards success-washing is understandable if we accept that we need climate optimism to maintain hope and agency for the climate movement. Telling millions of activists that mass mobilisations, protests and strikes have achieved next to nothing to stop catastrophic climate breakdown is not easily done, and the worry that this could overwhelm activists with despair, grief and hopelessness is understandable.[54]

He then adds an important point: '*But most activists already know this*, and some movement leaders such as Greta Thunberg have already spoken out on it'—for instance, by stating (in contrast to UN secretary-general António Guterres and others who were filled with optimism by the actions) that the worldwide 2019 Fridays for Future school strikes 'achieved nothing.'[55] 'Facing the inefficacy of many of their climate actions, the climate movement needs an honest assessment that avoids bad answers, which only generate false hopes that eventually lead to even more despair,' Nguyen argues. 'They should embrace a stance that enables a kinder, more sustainable way of viewing and assessing their activism.' In other words: 'They should be pessimists.'[56]

To this we may add a further consideration. One thing that is striking in discussions of optimism and pessimism in the climate debate is that these seem to be taken not just as questions of how we expect the future to unfold but as stand-ins for specific sets of positive and negative emotions. 'Pessimism' is associated with 'dark' moods or emotions, such as grief, anger, and despair; 'optimism' rather with positive emotions such as hope, joyfulness, and sometimes courage or perseverance. The commonsense notion, or rather the gut feeling, of many seems to be that negative emotions deflate or de-energise us, whereas positive emotions are a better source for action.[57] But there is some evidence that such associations may be culturally mediated.[58]

One study from 2017 by Jochen Kleres and Åsa Wettergren (which Nguyen also cites) has compared patterns of emotional responses in activists of the global north and south. The researchers note that northern activisms tend to share a 'very strong emphasis on mobilizing with *hope in collective action*.'[59] As the Danish Eco-Council put it in September 2013: 'Prospects do not look good. . . . But hope and positive actions and problem solving is much better than painting all in black.'[60] Or the U.S.-based Sierra Club in 2014: 'What our committee is trying to do is send positive messaging, like *Yes this is bad but we can overcome it*, and *You should be optimistic about what we can achieve*, *You should be excited about working on this with us*.'[61] Such endorsements of positive emotions as against a suspicion of negative emotions (such as anger, guilt, and despair) were echoed across many interviewees—at least from countries in the global north. 'We found that our northern interviewees embrace fear but emphasize hope, reject guilt, and treat anger with caution,' as the researchers commented. By contrast: 'Our interviewees from the global south are instead more acutely frightened, less hopeful, and more angered, ascribing guilt—responsibility—to northern countries.'[62]

Consider, for instance, this statement by an activist from an (unspecified) African country:

Climate change is changing our world already now. Like I said, the impact is more felt in the Global South because we don't have what it takes to adapt—for example our houses, the way we build houses [they] float easily, [the rain] washes them away. [. . . It is different] because of the issue of development. This is why we are so affected by climate change, that's why when rain is falling *we always panic* because at times students don't go to school, because waters wash away their school. [. . . It's] *like inside a fire* . . . that's why we are so passionate about the issue of climate change, because it is affecting us more.[63]

It's like inside a fire. These words were spoken four years before Greta Thunberg exhorted the political and economic leaders at Davos to 'act as if our house is on fire. Because it is.' Whereas the global north had to be urged 'to act as you would in a crisis,'[64] little need for such reminders in countries where climate change is already wreaking ravages: where the threat is not somewhere in the future but has already crossed the threshold. As Kleres and Wettergren comment:

> Here the 'passion' of activism derives from an experience of climate change as *an already manifest reality* with devastating consequences—a stark contrast to the abstract fear of climate change in the north. The outstanding emotional element is acute fear. There is explicit reference to *panic*, as when rain falls and floods houses. The quote describes the pain of living in this fear as 'inside a fire'. Hope is less emphasized.[65]

It is not that hope for change is not present but that it is articulated through the need for action and a powerful sense of urgency, since the disaster is already here—and instead of being held apart from dark emotions such as fear and anger is powerfully combined with them. As one activist from a sub-Saharan country frames her activism:

> We don't stop, activists don't stop, we keep going we keep going, that's activism, you won't stop until you [achieve mission] so we'll keep going. . . . We want to see the change in

this [area] we want to stop climate change and we need climate justice, so why should I stop, considering where I came from? If you start then you have to. . . . If you get [hurt] you can rest when you get up, you keep going, that's activism.[66]

What is striking is that while northern activists (encouraged in this by media and academia alike) are led to worry that dark emotions will lead to burnouts, this concern seems not to be as present in activists of the south, where the urgency is felt to such an extent that giving up is not an option, you just 'keep going.'

This is all the more salient in that some northern activists grapple with the problem of burnout as a direct result of punctured optimism. In the words of one Swedish activist, there is nothing more deflating than one's hopes being built up and subsequently disappointed:

> I've always had this huge climate anxiety attack when I come home from a COP, *I'm always so hopeful before I go to a COP*, I'm like 'oh my god we'll save the world', and then when I get home I realize I didn't, I always fall apart, *and it's the worst feeling ever*, feel like why am I doing and I always get this feeling . . . like I'm gonna quit everything and move in the forest and build my own cabin, live sustainably by my own and leave society.[67]

Thoughts of withdrawal, in this case as in others, seem to have been prompted not by sustained pessimism but by one's hopes being disappointed. Considering such statements, one wonders where we get the idea that pessimism deflates us. After all, if this activist had not had such high hopes—if they had espoused a kind of sustainable pessimism as Nguyen recommends— would they have been as de-energised?

There is therefore some evidence that the resistance to dark moods in activists of the global north is refracted through cultural assumptions as well as regional preoccupations: where the danger is perceived as belonging to a remote future, the source of fear is seen as abstract in a way that is unthinkable to those for whom the disaster has already arrived—for whom 'the source of fear is not imagined but present and acute.'[68] Such assumptions should be questioned accordingly, not because they are illegitimate in themselves but in an awareness that the stressing of hope and optimism *at the expense of* dark emotions such as grief, anger, and despair may itself have its dangers. These dangers, furthermore, are not just psychological but potentially political. As Kleres and Wettergren also warn us, the differences in emotional responses between northern and southern activisms may have concrete political consequences: 'These differences may indicate a relatively depoliticized activist approach to climate change in the north, as opposed to a more politicized approach in the south.'[69]

The Value of Pessimism

'Pessimism has a bad rap among activists, terrified of surrender,' as the novelist China Miéville writes. 'But activism without the pessimism that rigor should provoke is just sentimentality.' These words were published in the left-wing journal *Salvage*, founded in 2015 by a group of London-based writers, Miéville among them. In striking opposition to most activistic narratives, which emphasise hope and optimism, the authors associated with *Salvage* are adamant that pessimism has a role to play. While it is true that there is 'bad pessimism as well as bad optimism', there is something in this vision that is indispensable to any age in crisis: 'We need to tilt at a different tipping point, into irrevocable social change, and that requires a different pessimism, an unflinching look at how bad things are.'[70]

That piece was published on 1 August 2015. The editors of *Salvage* had a chance to put this ethos into practice one month later, when Jeremy Corbyn was elected leader of the Labour Party, arousing the hopes of many on the left. 'For the first time since George Lansbury, the Labour Party has a leader who is both a socialist and an experienced activist,' as the editors described the shock of Corbyn's win. Nevertheless their response was one of a 'hard-won pessimism' that is 'neither cynicism nor hopelessness':

> We will not be equal to the challenges to come if we once again lurch from despondency to bad hope—we have seen where this ends. *Salvage*'s answer to such unproductive careening remains a hard-won pessimism. This is neither cynicism nor hopelessness: it is about our clear-sighted analysis—of capitalism, of the class system, of the centrality of this antagonism to our lives—that we refuse to gloss over the scale of the difficulties we continue to face.

They note that 'Bad Hope,' which they equate with a 'philistine and panicked "optimism,"' 'is prone to instant phase-shift into Bad Despair' and, like Nguyen and Nairn, connect optimism with the danger of burning out: 'one of the worst aspects of traditional Left boosterism is that, in failing to acknowledge the scale of our previous defeats and their legacy, it prepares every hopeful new recruit not for years of patient work, but for *rapid burn-out and demoralisation*.' Straightforward optimism is thus seen as a real danger for activism: 'There is no point in surging to life, only to fall back more permanently and numerously into the sepulchres.' Instead the editors declare a full-blown pessimism that is not deflating but 'energising':

> *Salvage* cleaves to the necessity of a pessimism that is not a nostrum but a result of analysis, and urges others on the left

to approach this battle with the same sober caution. Aspiring to such rigour is not merely a responsibility in these circumstances, it is *energising. Salvage* counsels a pessimism that has the humility to be surprised, to celebrate the shocks of our victories without surrendering the caution we—all—need. And we proceed in the utter and committed desire—the *Sehnsucht*—to be proven wrong.[71]

Whether or not we not agree with the politics of the *Salvage* collective, the analysis of the energising power of pessimism is, I think, correct. This notion that pessimism does not have to be discouraging, that in a certain mode it can even be empowering, is precisely the point made by Dienstag and the pessimists of old, who have shown us again and again that pessimism is not to be equated with defeatism or passivity: on the contrary, that this is a philosophy charged with ethical and political potential; with moral fervour and motivational force.

The real enemy to be combatted, I argue, is not optimism or pessimism, perhaps not even despair (as examples show there can be solid grounds for resistance even beyond all hope of success), but any stance of *looking away* or *giving up*. This stance can walk the world in different guises, from 'it's all going to be fine' to 'we're doomed' or 'every nation for itself'. Such slogans, however diverse, all point towards a common source: what Camus once called 'man's strongest temptation': 'the temptation of inertia.'[72] As Camus said in an interview in 1957:

> We have nothing to lose except everything. So let's go ahead. This is the wager of our generation. If we are to fail, it is better, in any case, to have stood on the side of those who choose life than on the side of those who are destroying.[73]

3

Losing the Future

... There isn't much to see
Beyond that, for the important questions,
The questions to which one constantly comes back,
Aren't about their lost, undepicted home,
But the ones framed by their distorted mouths:
What are we now? What will we become?

—JOHN KOETHE

THE WORLD ends in 2100. But it isn't climate change that does it: it is the plague.

Such, at least, is the premise of a strange rambling novel published in 1826 by Mary Shelley, who just a few years earlier had brought the world *Frankenstein*. Shelley was only the last in a string of authors and artists to take up the theme of the world ending, as the literary scene of the time was swept up by an unlikely craze: *lastness*. If the world were to end, Shelley and her contemporaries asked themselves, what would life be like for the last person standing?[1]

Set in the second half of the twenty-first century, *The Last Man* is part romance, part dystopia; a tangle of love stories against the backdrop of humanity's demise. In one sense it is about love and friendship in times of plague; in another, about things ceasing to matter, or mattering in different ways. As the plague rages on and hope dwindles, most normal activities are rendered futile; even time takes on a different meaning. As the main character Lionel Verney reflects, during a winter that sees a temporary lull in the plague's onslaught:

> The experience of immemorial time had taught us formerly to count our enjoyments by years, and extend our prospect of life through a lengthened period of progression and decay; the long road threaded a vast labyrinth, and the Valley of the Shadow of Death, in which it terminated, was hid by intervening objects. But an earthquake had changed the scene— under our very feet the earth yawned—deep and precipitous the gulph below opened to receive us, while the hours charioted us towards the chasm.[2]

Beyond this, there is a general weariness that enters into every hour and every pastime, a sense of the 'utter inutility' of things. 'I longed to return to my old occupations, but of what use were they?' Verney tells us. 'To read were futile—to write, vanity indeed.'[3] This experience intensifies once it has become clear that Verney has become the *last man*, the 'sole survivor of my species.' For a moment he compares himself to Robinson Crusoe: 'We had been both thrown companionless—he on the shore of a desolate island: I on that of a desolate world'—but he quickly sees that they could hardly be more different, for Crusoe 'could hope, nor hope in vain,' that one day he might be delivered; whereas, 'no hope had I.'[4] And so he wanders through Rome in solitude, and marks the new year on the topmost stone of St Peter's: '2100, last year of the world!'[5]

There is something ominous in reading such words in this early twenty-first century, when the year 2100 features so often in predictions and projections about climate change and with the ashes of a global pandemic still smouldering.[6] But it is just a novel after all, and a dystopian one at that. And we are no newcomers to dystopia. The genre became well-established in the century between ours and Shelley's, which eagerly projected dates into a future just near and just distant enough to feature as a canvas for our hopes and fears. But time marches on, and as the twentieth century fled towards the twenty-first we have seen a number of curious anniversaries, as dystopian futures were caught up by the present. Thus George Orwell in 1949 placed his totalitarian dystopia in 1984, while 1982's *Blade Runner* targeted 2019 and 1973's *Soylent Green* projected overpopulation concerns onto 2022. And in 2021 we met the year central in a novel published in 1992 by the British author P. D. James: *The Children of Men*.[7]

Like Shelley's *Last Man* and many other apocalyptic films and novels, James's novel offers us a vision of lastness but under a different premise: in her imagining, it is not a plague or a meteorite that strikes humanity but a wave of worldwide infertility. There is, in other words, no single or acute event that disrupts day-to-day existence, no collective dying: for the time at least, life goes on, people go about their jobs and activities, with the only difference that no children are born.

What would it be like to live in such a world? According to Theo Faron, the novel's central character, the main result was an onset of 'almost universal negativism,' as things ceased to matter in the way they did before. Pleasures, whether sensual or intellectual, are all that can counter the *ennui universel*:

But those who lived gave way to the almost universal negativism, what the French named *ennui universel*. It came upon us
like an insidious disease; indeed it was a disease, with its
soon-familiar symptoms of lassitude, depression, ill-defined
malaise, a readiness to give way to minor infections, a per-
petual disabling headache. . . . The weapons I fight it with are
also my consolations: books, music, food, wine, nature.[8]

What is interesting is that while Shelley's Last Man faces the
prospect of his own death as well as the suffering and deaths of
his loved ones, for James's Last Humans the tragedy takes a very
different shape. There is no plague, no looming meteorite or
comet set on a collision course with earth; and indeed there is
in a sense no concrete disaster. It is true that people cannot have
children, but many who are alive now live meaningful and
happy lives without children, and so there seems to be no reason in principle why *some* humans at least could not continue
to do so, even in a world of lastness. This is what Theo Faron
and others in the novel attempt to achieve. And yet, as he tells
us, there is everywhere this erosion of meaning:

We can experience nothing but the present moment, live in
no other second of time, and to understand this is as close
as we can get to eternal life. But our minds reach back
through centuries for the reassurance of our ancestry and,
without the hope of posterity, for our race if not for ourselves, without the assurance that we being dead yet live, all
pleasures of the mind and senses sometimes seem to me no
more than pathetic and crumbling defences shored up
against our ruin.[9]

Again, this is fiction: we do not live and have never lived in such
a world. But we can imagine, perhaps, what living in such a

world would be like. This, at least, is what philosopher Samuel Scheffler has argued in his now classic 'Afterlife' lectures.[10]

In these lectures, and the book that followed, Scheffler tries to answer why and how the 'afterlife' of humanity (by which he means 'the continuation of human life on earth after our own deaths') matters to us.[11] He does so by way of two hypothetical scenarios. First, in the 'doomsday scenario,' he asks us to imagine that 'although you yourself would live a normal life span, the earth would be completely destroyed thirty days after your death in a collision with a giant asteroid.'[12] Second, in the 'infertility scenario,' he asks us to imagine a future akin to that painted by James in *The Children of Men*: a world in which all humans have become infertile, so that humankind 'faces the prospect of imminent extinction as the last generation born gradually dies out.'[13] In this case, no one dies prematurely, or faces the loss of loved ones, but the end of humanity looms as a dark certainty on the horizon.

For each scenario, he asks us to consider how we would react, and more specifically: 'How would this knowledge affect your attitudes during the remainder of your life?'[14]

In the case of the doomsday scenario, Scheffler imagines that most of us would probably respond with something like 'profound dismay.'[15] Beyond that, he suggests that some and possibly many of our most valued projects and activities would no longer seem worth doing—for instance, finding a cure for cancer or having children and raising them. For some projects this is not so clear: would writers still write books if soon there will be no one left to read them? Perhaps; perhaps not. What is interesting to Scheffler is that for many activities the prospect of our *own deaths* would not be a reason to stop doing them (on the contrary: we might do many things in the knowledge that posterity will benefit from them; and in any event we all know we are going to die someday). But the prospect of the death of *everyone else* could be a reason to stop doing them. What this suggests, according to Scheffler, is that the afterlife of the rest of humanity seems to matter *more* to us than 'our own continued existence.' And the reason it matters more to us is that the afterlife of others is 'a condition of other things mattering to us. Without confidence in the existence of the afterlife [of humanity], many of the things in our own lives that now matter to us would cease to do so or would come to matter less.'[16]

And Scheffler thinks the same would hold for the infertility scenario: 'I find it plausible to suppose that such a world would be a world characterized by widespread apathy, anomie, and despair; by the erosion of social institutions and social solidarity; by the deterioration of the physical environment; and by a pervasive loss of conviction about the value or point of many activities.'[17] In other words, by precisely the kinds of characteristics sketched by P. D. James and, indeed, by Shelley before her. While acknowledging that it is hard for us to imagine what such a world would actually be like, Scheffler thinks it likely that 'the imminent disappearance of human life would exert a generally depressive effect on people's motivations and on their confidence in the value of their activities—that it would reduce their capacity for enthusiasm and for wholehearted and joyful activity across a very wide front.' In fact we cannot 'even be confident that there is something that we would be prepared to count as a good life' in such a world.[18]

The point is that there seems to be a difference in kind between the tragedy of our own deaths and the demise of the rest of humanity: the latter threatens an erosion of meaning from all our activities that the former does not. According to Scheffler, this asymmetry has something to do with the future and how we relate to it. When we live in societies and social groups or families, we are participants 'in a larger or smaller network of valuable personal relationships': and this means that, while we are alive, we can imagine what will happen when our deaths 'wrench' us out of such networks.[19]

By virtue of this connectedness, death is not pure uncertainty: we can imagine the lives of our loved ones continuing, as well as the places we used to frequent, and so we have an idea of what the world will be like once we're gone. 'Rather than looming simply as a blank eternity of nonexistence, the future can be conceptualized with reference to an ongoing social world in which one retains a social identity.'[20] In other words, our interwovenness with other people 'personalizes' our relation to the future after we are gone: 'the fact that there are other people who value their relations with you and who will continue to live after you have died makes it possible to feel that you have a place in the social world of the future even if, due to the inconvenient fact of your death, you will not actually be able to take advantage of it. The world of the future becomes, as it were, more like a party one had to leave early and less like a gathering of strangers.'[21] Traditions and social groups thus ensure that, even if it does not remember us personally, 'the world of the future is not an altogether alien place.'[22]

All of this would be threatened by the knowledge that the world would end thirty days after our own deaths (or, indeed, at any point in the not-too-distant future):

> One reason why we react so strongly to the doomsday scenario is that it seems to render our own relation to the future incurably bleak. We are used to the idea that we ourselves will not be a part of the future after our deaths. In the doomsday scenario, we must reconcile ourselves to the fact that nobody we care about will be a part of the future either, and

that fact, I have suggested, makes the future itself seem more alien, forbidding, empty.[23]

What is more, it would be threatened equally by the infertility scenario, which suggests not only that the survival of humanity matters to us more than our own survival but that 'the coming into existence of people we do not know and love' matters more to us than our own survival: 'In certain concrete functional and motivational respects, the fact that we and everyone we love will cease to exist matters less to us than would the nonexistence of future people whom we do not know and who, indeed, have no determinate identities.'[24]

Of course much more can be said about this discussion, and we may not agree with all of Scheffler's suggestions *or* conclusions.[25] But our intuitive reactions to dystopian scenarios as those sketched by Scheffler do seem to confirm his point that the afterlife of humanity and the extension of our world into the future matter to us, not only because we value the lives of others but as *grounding goods*: as conditions for other things to matter at all.

Let's hold that thought.

Encountering the Abyss

The above are philosophical musings, important perhaps for our understanding of ourselves but all safely hypothetical: *safely*, because they were all written from a place of safety, before the climate crisis emerged on the horizon as a great collective darkness hotly blocking out the sun; as the thing that 'changes everything'.

But to us, standing on the other side of that watershed, this safety is no longer as self-evident; and the thoughts and experiences once darkly imagined by authors of the past are no longer so alien. Verney and Faron speak of the slow but steady seeping-away of meaning from their lives, and we hear similar things from young people today—at least from those who have opened their eyes to climate change. In the words of one twenty-one-year-old activist:

> When you see by how many degrees we're probably going to warm up and the consequences that are attached to such warming, you just genuinely panic. Especially because you eventually realise that *the way you thought your future would be is not the case anymore.* And what you thought was important, suddenly becomes less important. If you don't take action then, you just feel completely hopeless.[26]

Seeing this, it becomes hard to see anything else—least of all a future in which to place one's trust. As Greta Thunberg said in her 2019 speech to the Houses of Parliament in London, voicing an experience of many:

> In the year 2030 I will be twenty-six years old. My little sister, Beata, will be twenty-three. Just like many of your own children or grandchildren. That is a great age, we have been told. When you have all of your life ahead of you. But I am not so sure it will be that great for us.
>
> I was fortunate to be born in a time and place where everyone told us to dream big; I could become whatever I wanted to. I could live wherever I wanted to. People like me had everything we needed and more. Things our grandparents could not even dream of. We had everything we could ever wish for and yet now we may have nothing.
>
> Now we probably don't even have a future any more.
>
> . . . You lied to us. You gave us false hope. You told us that the future was something to look forward to.[27]

Such words are echoed everywhere. 'I am an art student,' said one twenty-one-year-old woman who glued herself to the frame of a copy of Da Vinci's *Last Supper*, 'but there is no place for me to follow my calling as an artist in a world where I have no future. . . . I am outraged, and you should be too.'[28] 'In the course of a decade,' writes activist Daniel Sherrell, 'it's become vaguely absurd to build our future in the world like we would a house on some land, just erect it and trust it to stand. Increasingly, the only viable future seems to be in shoring up the future itself. And so the world transforms from a premise into a question, and we work desperately to answer it in our favor.'[29]

Where the future was is now a gap, an absence—but it is a 'gap that is intensely active': it exudes darkness, a quiet or not-so-quiet sense of desperation.[30] 'I live with a quiet dread,' says writer and activist Yotam Marom, 'a constant sadness at the loss people around the world are already facing, a nagging fear of what's to come and a sort of ashamed hopelessness about what we can do to stop it.'[31] Or, as Icelandic author Andri Snær Magnason describes his response to hearing about the prospect of rising sea levels and the many other effects of climate change: 'I sense a buzzing inside me, the way all these words form a black hole I can't directly perceive because its quantity absorbs all its meaning.'[32] This is an experience that transcends generations—but to those of us who have already built (or are building) a life for ourselves, including a home and a career, the threat is of a fundamentally different kind compared to those who have yet to imagine what and who they will become. To envision a meaningful life for ourselves we need to be able to imagine the future and our place in it. But this very possibility, this very *imaginability* of a future in which we might feel at home, is precisely why the young feel so threatened by climate change.

It is all too easy to miss the fact that many in this generation—the first to grow up in a world where a climate emergency is not just on the horizon but a stark reality—are haunted by a real sense of losing the future, as all the things they have been told give life meaning are rendered either pointless or problematic. Things like: *study, get a good job, settle down*—but what jobs are still certain? Where will it be safe to settle down? As Greta Thunberg said in Parliament Square in London in 2018: 'And why should I be studying for a future that soon will be no more, when no one is doing anything whatsoever to save that future?'[33] Things like: *start a family*—but if the future is so uncertain, is it still OK to have children? Even more trivial things, like developing oneself by travelling, are no longer straightforward: for how important is self-development when weighed against the carbon cost of modern travel?[34] This is a pervasive collapse of meaning that is only now becoming clear to us. There is a very real sense in which young people are experiencing not only the loss of concepts but the loss of the future itself, as all the usual answers to the question of what makes life worthwhile become increasingly uncertain.

And this uncertainty itself is key. For while the climate crisis is often framed as having to do with the certainty or probability of disaster, *uncertainty* is at least as great a part of it. By this I don't just mean the scientific problem of feedback loops and tipping points, which mean that we don't know exactly when points of no return are passed; or even the hard fact that what the future will be like depends to a great extent on our collective actions and decisions today. I mean that there is something in the nature of this crisis that blocks our vision: we can see there is a darkness but cannot see *through* the darkness; we cannot see exactly what shape it will take, or what life will be like on the other side. As arctic scientist and IPCC member Robert

Corell said at a symposium in Greenland in 2007, 'For the last 10,000 years, we have been living in a remarkably stable climate that has allowed the whole of human development to take place. In all that time, through the mediaeval warming and the Little Ice Age, there was only a variation of 1C. Now we see the potential for sudden changes of between 2C and 6C. We just don't know what the world is like at those temperatures. We are climbing rapidly out of mankind's safe zone into new territory, and we have no idea if we can live in it.'[35]

It is this uncertainty, and the dizzying awareness of it, that young people experience when they speak of losing the future. Of course this experience is also relative: there is no time to worry about meaning or uncertainty when you are fighting for survival; no time to think about being alienated from the future when you've been driven from your home by flood or drought. The sense of losing a future one can relate to may well be particular to those who live in countries where the disaster has not yet struck—and so it should not be overstressed.

But neither should it be discounted. The certainty of disaster *combined* with a radical uncertainty about what form it will take creates an uncommonly dark scenario—or perhaps not dark but *abysmal*: *something beyond which we cannot see*. And this is why people who are climate-aware experience this storm as not simply one crisis or emergency among many but as *the* crisis, *the* emergency, *the* storm of a lifetime.[36] The crisis is experienced as truly existential not because it threatens the end of all of humanity (as some philosophers narrowly define an 'existential threat') but because it threatens the meaning and mattering of things. Like the strange unstoppable 'Nothing' of Michael Ende's *Neverending Story*, it looms over everything, not only physical places and ecosystems but how things matter to us, and why.

Philosopher Glenn Albrecht has defined *solastalgia* as: 'The pain or distress caused by the loss or lack of solace and the sense of desolation connected to the present state of one's home and territory. . . . It is the homesickness you have when you are still at home.'[37] Something of this is echoed by young and old people when they speak about the future. It's not just the fear of not having a future at all, in the sense of having a shortened lifespan, or of not having opportunities that they would have liked to have. It's that they are unable to relate to the future in a grounding way. Like Albrecht's solastalgia, there is a sense of homelessness, of being uprooted and temporally adrift—it is the experience of losing a future *in which one might feel at home.* The future has itself becomes a foreign and hostile and above all *uncertain* territory; it has become, in Scheffler's words, 'an altogether alien place.'

This raises questions for the youngest generations that may be hard to understand for those who are already grounded in their lives. Such as: How do we build a life for a future we cannot relate to? What careers will stand up to the test? How do we envision the good life, a life of joy and meaning, if (as Scheffler warned us) we cannot 'even be confident that there is something that we would be prepared to count as a good life' in a deeply broken world?[38] And, if we cannot see what the future will be like, how can we know whether we will want to bring children into it?[39]

To those forced to struggle with such questions, any crude statements of optimism would be more than misplaced: it would be the kind of lie that deceives no one, least of all the sharpened moral senses of the young, who see through the empty promises and reassurances of politicians with an anger we know is justified. If we told them that everything will be OK, these are less than empty words: they are a failure to take their experience seriously, and that, as the pessimists of old would tell us, is the one thing guaranteed to make their suffering worse. Aside from callous, such statements would be unhelpful. Straightforward optimism can only serve as a guide where the future is clear, visible, conceivable; where the road lies open—there may be challenges on the way, but at least we can *see* the challenges, and we can *see* the way. Where the road ahead is dark and the future deeply uncertain, such optimism is meaningless: it either falls apart in this strange and alien territory or weighs as a burden on those whose eyes are full of the abyss.

This may in part explain why there is so much talk about *hope* in the climate debate. Alienated from a future that we once relied on to ground our aspirations, many turn to the same question once asked by Immanuel Kant—*What may we hope for?*— adding only the predicament of our times—*What may we hope for in the age of climate change?* For some, to ask the question is to answer it, for instance by stating that 'there is always hope' or that 'to give up hope is to give in'. But this rings false to many ears, as hope has become so overused in our discourses as to lose its power to convince. Better, perhaps, to leave this question open for a while: to encounter the possibility that hope itself hangs in the balance, and that this encounter, too, is part of what it is to be alive today.

The challenge, then, is not to predict the future with certainty but to learn to live with this uncertainty, and most importantly: to treat it not as an excuse for resignation but as a *principle of action*—in the knowledge that, as Catriona McKinnon writes, 'the context for hope is radical uncertainty.'[40] And so it lies before us as a challenge and a test. It is now for all of us to consider what it would be like to lose the future, as this sense of loss may turn out to be not only a pivotal experience of the climate crisis but part of the moral coming of age of not just a generation but a culture. The abyss must be encountered—for the true risk lies not in this encounter but in its avoidance.

The Labyrinth

Finally, a warning.

There is a tendency in much writing on climate change to suggest that the core of problem is an inability or unwillingness to look past the immediate present and into the (far) future. We are urged, by philosophers and activists alike, to take into account the interests of future generations, to shift our focus from the short to the long term, lest we, living in the present, be guilty of colonising or even 'enslaving' the future. What such discourses have in common is the assumption that the fundamental problem of climate crisis is that of *temporal myopia* or *temporal near-sightedness*: that we see only the here and now and prioritise our (selfish) short-term interests over the long-term concerns of future generations. And the implication is that, as soon as we take the future into account, as soon as we adopt a long-term perspective, the crisis can be resolved.

There is good reason for all of this. The future matters—future generations matter—and the question of how to weigh their interests against our own deserves our most careful attention.[41] But there is also a risk here, and it is to forget the stark fact that climate change is *not* simply a problem of the near or distant future—that many people are suffering and dying *now*, and species rapidly becoming extinct.

Considering the recent disasters worldwide, from drought and fire to flood and storm, it is baffling that this even needs to be stated—but as others have noted, there is a tendency for the global north to forget how climate change is already causing deaths and suffering *in this present time*. In the words of activist

Vanessa Nakate, disappointed by the media coverage of climate change, 'They keep talking about climate change being a matter of the future, but they forget that [for] people of the Global South, *it is a matter of now*.'[42] Greta Thunberg, similarly, sees the danger and warns us: 'This is a humanitarian catastrophe *for those who are living*, not just for those who come after us.'[43] 'By using up the remains of our carbon budgets, the Global North is stealing the future as well as the present,' she writes in *The Climate Book*, 'not only from their own children but above all from those people who live in the most affected parts of the world, many of whom are yet to build much of the most basic modern infrastructure that others take for granted.'[44] Or, as she warned world leaders in 2019, shaking with indignation: 'People are suffering. People are dying. Entire ecosystems are collapsing.'[45] Note that her words are adamantly *present tense*: this, she was saying, is something that is happening not in the distant future but *now*.

Many climate activists are fiercely aware of this presentist inflection of the crisis—hence the shift in emphasis towards *climate justice*, which stresses the interests of those who are already struggling *as well as* the suffering of future generations. But it remains a blind spot for many in the global north—as if it is easier for writers in countries not yet threatened by climate change to relate to future generations (which they can imagine as their own descendants) than to people alive and suffering now, on the other side of the planet. The risk, then, lies in focusing so much on the future that we forget what is happening here and now. 'They forget the present for the future,' as Camus wrote of the utopians of his day, and his caution to them might serve us still: 'Real generosity towards the future lies in giving all to the present.'[46]

This is not to say we should not take the future into account—on the contrary. Future generations *do* matter; myopic short-termism *is* a problem. It is only to show that while taking the future into account is part of what is needed, it cannot be the whole story; in fact it comes with dangers of its own. Climate change must not be framed as *primarily* or *solely* a question of caring about future generations: as it is not just a problem for the future but a problem for people living now.

In his essay about technology, Heidegger famously quotes the poet Hölderlin's line: 'But where danger threatens / That which saves from it also grows.'[47] But it occurs to me that in the case of climate change, often the inverse of Hölderlin's dictum holds true: *where the saving power grows, the danger is also.* Everywhere there are temptations on the way; false turns that seem to help us further but instead serve to tangle us further in a web of our own making. It is as if we were in a great labyrinth, full of constantly forking paths, some of which look promising but are dead ends, while others will lead us back to where we started, and others yet (and these perhaps are the most dangerous ones) seem to lead us firmly onwards through the maze. With every step we take, the walls tighten around us and the road lengthens before us so that the further we walk, the further our destination recedes from view—and all the while we run out of air. As Naomi Klein has written wisely, 'climate change will test our moral character like little before.'[48] Yes—and it will tempt us too. Sometimes the paths that look most promising have hidden traps and falls, and it is no different here—for while neglecting the future has its dangers, so too has overstressing the future at the expense of the present.

And it is the same with hope.

PART II

Hope

4

The Ambiguity of Hope

I said to my soul, be still, and wait without hope
For hope would be hope for the wrong thing

—T. S. ELIOT

FIGURE 3. G. F. Watts, *Hope*. Second ('blue') version,
1886; see book cover.

IN DECEMBER 1885 the painter G. F. Watts wrote to his friend
Madeline Wyndham with an idea for a new project: 'Hope sitting on a globe, with bandaged eyes playing on a lyre which has
all the strings broken but one out of which poor little tinkle she
is trying to get all the music possible, listening with all her
might to the little sound—do you like the idea?'[1] The painting
in question, of course, was *Hope*—a depiction so ambiguous
that Chesterton thought it might as easily be called despair.[2]
And Chesterton was not alone. 'Its title "Hope" is, as it were, a
courtesy title,' thought James Manson, the director of the Tate
Gallery, in 1930. 'It might be called, with equal propriety, many
other things. It is a sort of pretension in which the spectator
plays a necessary part.'[3]

In his book about Watts's iconic painting, Nicholas Tromans
suggests that *Hope* resisted any straightforward interpretations,
in part because it subverted traditional iconography. For instance, Watts neglected to portray an anchor, which was the
standard attribute for Christian hope, the 'anchor' of the soul:
instead he gives Hope a lyre with broken strings, which was
usually associated rather with lost love or separation (the poet
John Keats used a lyre with broken strings for his personal seal,
and a similar image came to adorn his gravestone).[4] So why
would Watts use such an image for *Hope*? Was he aware, perhaps, that the Hebrew word for hope, *tikvah*, literally means
'cord' or 'rope'?[5]

The bandaged eyes are also curious, as it was common to
portray fortune as blindfolded, and sometimes love, but never
hope. Was Watts alluding to the 'blind hope' that Prometheus
gives to humankind in Aeschylus's tragedy *Prometheus Bound*,
where it remains unclear if this hope is 'a blessing or curse'?[6]
And, by showing Hope in isolation, without the 'flanking but-
tresses of Faith and Love', the other theological virtues, did

Watts envision a return to 'Greek ambivalence about Hope itself'?[7] And what, finally, is the meaning of the star faintly visible in the background of the painting? 'Does the fact that the star is unobserved by the figure add to her tragedy, or does it console the viewer that things are not so bad for her as she might think?' asks Tromans.[8] Again and again, the same question presents itself, and we are kept on the edge, wavering between ways of answering it: how hopeful is *Hope*?

This ambiguity may well have been Watts's intention. In the same letter to Madeline Wyndham where Watts sets out his plan for *Hope*, he mentions that his adopted daughter Blanche Clogstoun 'had just lost her infant daughter' and writes that 'he himself was more than resigned to death': 'it seems to me that I see nothing but uncertainty, contention, conflict, beliefs unsettled and nothing established in place of them.'[9] He thus found himself in an ambiguous state of mind; and if his purpose was to make *Hope* intrinsically equivocal, then he was successful, as opinions were divided from the start—about both the composition and the message.

Even within the Christian reception of *Hope*, readings were as different as night and day. Some Christian interpreters saw Watts's *Hope* as delivering a positively hopeful, even optimistic message, such as the Welsh poet Emily Pfeiffer, who thought the 'unbroken midmost chord' of *Hope* might offer a celestial vision:

Oh win for us the secret of that tense
Unbroken midmost chord! It may recall
The scattered tones, nay, haply may surprise
Thee with a vision to inform the sense;
And gift thee out of wreck and wrong withal
To see the city of God to music rise.[10]

By contrast, the Scottish theologian Peter Taylor Forsyth offered a tragic reading of Watts's image—the danger of separating hope from its spiritual dimension. 'Do not think that the loss of Faith develops the strength of Hope,' he cautioned in a lecture series in 1887. 'It throws more strain upon Hope alone, and Hope is not infrequently overtasked.'[11] As Tromans explains, in Forsyth's view the figure bending over the lyre is 'not Hope itself, but rather the soul of humanity who, having gained the world through science, sits atop nature in a spiritual dead end. Confronted with the godless universe that modern technology appears to have revealed, the soul can no longer bear to look and has blindfolded herself.' On this view, what Watts has painted is not an uplifting image of hope in the dark but the pathetic state of humanity cut off from all spiritual solace.[12]

Similarly, the Reverend James Burns argued in 1908 that 'the figure seated upon the globe is not Hope at all, and was not meant by the painter to represent Hope. The figure is the Spirit of the Age, of an age that has climbed to the mastery of the material world, but has lost faith in itself . . . whose eyes are bandaged so that she cannot see God and live.'[13] Another commentator thought the bandages were a sign of wilful blindness: 'The eyes are bandaged, because, if the facts were faced, hope would cease.'[14]

What didn't help in clarifying the painting's message was that Watts painted *Hope* not once but twice in the same year, and both versions differed in colour as well as tone. If the first version of *Hope* was mostly green and infused with a strange translucent glow, the second version (which Watts himself preferred) was 'darker and more melancholy'—and more blue than green.[15] It was this second, bluer version of *Hope* that became 'the public face of the image' (see plate 1 and book cover).[16]

And it was this version that was loaned to the Melbourne International Exhibition of 1888, 'where it was reported that the painting "has been puzzling the art-critics" with its apparently pessimistic message "that the world is rather in a bad way at present."[17] It is not hard to see why. Even more so than the first version, the second lends itself to a variation of Chesterton's 'desperate' reading: if we did not know the name of the painting, we might as easily have labelled it *grief, mourning, resignation,* or *despair.* If Watts had wanted to depict the final moments of the world—the last breath drawn by creation before the end—*Hope* would have had to be no different.

But even this more 'pessimistic' reading was not consistent. Chesterton, as we have seen, thought that while a first-time viewer might initially be tempted to think of despair, a second glance would afford a different experience, having to do rather with an indomitable endurance, something akin to 'faith', or 'vitality', or 'the will to live.'[18] Years later, the American pastor Jeremiah Wright similarly thought that Watts had depicted spiritual fortitude even amidst all darkness; that the painting showed a woman's 'audacity to hope':

> See, in spite of being on a world torn by war; in spite of being on a world destroyed by hate; in spite of being on a world devastated by distrust and decimated by disease; in spite of being on a world where famine and greed were uneasy bed partners; in spite of being on a world where apartheid and apathy fed the fires of racism . . . her harp all but destroyed except for that one string that was left—in spite of all these things, the woman had the audacity to hope. She had the audacity to hope and to make music and to praise God on the one string she had left.[19]

What to make of this ambiguity? Is it a weakness for a painting that it could feature on the cover of a book about hope as easily as on a book about despair; that it could be taken to portray perseverance as well as resignation? There have been subtler, richer, deeper works of art in art's history—but few excel so readily in remaining *perfectly poised* between competing interpretations. If there is a core to *Hope*, it must be this ambiguity, this resistance to closing off interpretation—and this very ambiguity is perhaps what gives the painting its force. And if I return to it in this book, repeatedly, after so many have already done so, it is not because the painting gives a clear-cut view of what hope is or what it means—this, after all, is clearly not the case—but because it may restore to us an aspect of hope that is too often neglected. And that is, of course, its ambiguity.

Hope's History

For all our anxious quests for hope, it is all too often forgotten that hope, too, has a history—and that for much of it hope was seen as something duplicitous, even treacherous. The classical Stoic tradition, possibly influenced by Eastern traditions, saw hope as a species of desire, and consequently problematic—not only because it attaches us to things we can't control but because, along with fear, hope was 'conceived as an immobilizing power.'[20] So too the first Western historians, Thucydides and Herodotus (both 5th century BCE), saw hope as a 'two-edged emotion' that on the one hand drives us to action but on the other hand tempts us to rash decisions. As one scholar argues, these 'past investigators of the dangers of hope' cautioned against the risks of hope run wild, especially in cases of warfare, and thus followed Hesiod and Homer in 'recognizing that *hope is not a strategy*.'[21]

The ancient Greek poet Hesiod (c. 750–650 BCE) was the source of one of the most famous and ambiguous stories involving hope—or at least, *elpis*.[22] It involves a woman, Pandora, and a jar or vessel (not a box):

> She [Pandora] devised anxious miseries for men.
> Hope alone remained in the unbreakable prison-house,
> within the great jar, under the lip, and did not
> fly out the opening. Before that, Pandora set on it a
>   lid ... [23]

All we know for certain is what Hesiod tells us: that Pandora opens the jar, 'anxious miseries' spread into the world, but one thing remains behind, and that is hope. From this point, interpretations diverge wildly. 'Is hope another evil, perhaps the greatest of evils—or the last remaining good, an antidote to evils—or, somehow, both?' asks Adam Potkay in his book on hope. 'Is Zeus here punishing humans, or showing them mercy?'[24] While modern readers tend to glean a positive message from the story, classicists have often pointed out that negative connotations were common with *elpis*—and so, at the very least, this myth encapsulates 'the ambivalence of hope in Greek thought.'[25]

In the Roman tradition hope or *spes* bore more positive connotations—Spes was even worshipped as a goddess and had her own temple on the Esquiline Hill in Rome.[26] But hesitations remained, as in both the Stoic and Epicurean schools *spes* continued to be a mainly negative concept.[27] The one thing consistent across the ancient world, perhaps, is an awareness of the shadow-side of hope: that at the very least it is not an *unadulterated* good, and not *by default* positively charged. Various scholars have pointed out that the Greek *elpis*, which comes closest to the modern 'hope', had to be complemented with a positive epithet such as 'good' (*agathē elpis*) to be positively charged. (And conversely, negative epithets such as 'blind' and 'empty' were 'conventional'.)[28] As Potkay notes, only with St Paul does this kind of positive gloss on hope become superfluous: only with the Christian tradition does hope become an 'unqualified good'—even a virtue.[29]

But this does not mean that hope, if it is to be *true hope*, is not subject to very strict conditions in the Christian tradition. For instance, hope can only be a virtue if it is oriented on a 'very specific object of desire'—namely, the 'eternal life in Christ'.[30] 'It would never occur to a philosopher, unless he were also a Christian theologian, to describe hope as a virtue,' the Catholic philosopher Josef Pieper wrote in 1935. 'For hope is either a theological virtue or not a virtue at all. It becomes a virtue by becoming a theological virtue.'[31]

It was the thirteenth-century philosopher and theologian Thomas Aquinas who cogently made the case for the virtue of hope, while at the same time stressing that the goodness of hope stands under very strict conditions. Like the ancients before him, Aquinas was aware that, as flawed yet hopeful creatures, we can hope for the bad as well as the good—so how can hope be a virtue? 'Virtue does not relate to both what is good and what is bad, but only to what is good,' he imagines an interlocutor objecting to him. 'But hope is related to both good and bad, as some people have good hopes and some have bad hopes. Therefore hope is not a virtue.'[32] 'Natural hope lacks the distinctive quality of virtue,' Pieper explains: namely, that it can never be the principle of a bad action.[33] A tyrant might *hope* to subjugate his people once and for all, a criminal might *hope* to succeed in some vicious act, yet we would not call these *virtues*. Aquinas readily admits that, on his own principles, hope cannot be a moral virtue like justice, which always tends towards the good—for 'whatever perfects a capacity ought to be the principle of a good action in such a way that it could never be the

PLATE 1. G. F. Watts, *Hope*. First ('green') version, 1885–86.

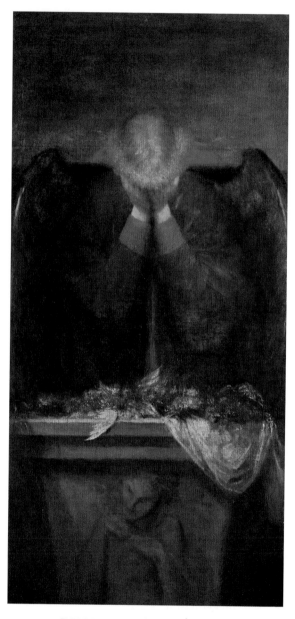

PLATE 2. G. F. Watts, *A Dedication (To all those who love the beautiful and mourn over the senseless and cruel destruction of bird life and beauty)*, 1898–99. © Watts Gallery Trust.

principle of a bad one.'[34] And this is exactly why hope can only be a theological virtue: it must be directed towards God and the eternal life to be ensured of its goodness. 'Hope cannot be related to something bad insofar as it holds on to God's help.'[35]

And even then, there are further dangers—for although 'no one can hope too much concerning God,' one can hope *presumptuously* and slip instead into 'the comfortable certainty of possession,' which is just another kind of hopelessness.[36] For hope to be a virtue, it has to be directed to the right object *and* be restricted to its proper bounds: as such natural hope must be guarded by two other virtues, *magnanimity* (which calls the soul to greatness) and *humility* (which reminds it of its limitations).[37] Aquinas thus distinguishes natural hope from theological hope, and argues that hope is not a virtue insofar as it is *purely* an emotion: to be a virtue, hope has to spring from 'the movement of the *mind*,' and this movement has to reach to the divine.[38] This is a far cry from simply elevating an emotion to the status of a virtue: hope according to Aquinas is not a standalone virtue but needs to be held in balance by other virtues and directed towards its proper good.

It is also not clear that hope can be understood in isolation from the other theological virtues, faith and love. 'And now these three remain: faith, hope and love,' as Paul wrote to the Corinthians. 'But the greatest of these is love.'[39] Hope is here mentioned between faith and love, and accordingly Aquinas assigns hope a middle role among the theological virtues: it always comes second, either in the order of perfection or in the sequence of development. When these virtues are gained, hope is the second to be gained; when they are lost, hope is the second to be lost.[40] This view of the relationship is echoed by Dante Alighieri, who in his *Purgatorio* personifies three theological virtues as three gracious women: Faith is dressed in white, Hope in green, and Love in red. They dance together, following the lead of either Faith or Love—Hope is the only one who never leads, always follows.

> the white one seemed to lead them, now the red;
> and from the way in which the leader chanted,
> the others took their pace, now slow, now rapid.[41]

And it is echoed, too, by some of the Christian commentators who saw in Watts's painting *not* an image of hope in the face of darkness but the dismal depiction of what happens when hope is divorced from her sister-virtues, Christian love and faith.

Hope's history is thus deeply inflected by Christian theology—and yet even on the theological interpretation there remains this sense that hope is not *unequivocally* good; that it needs to be guided and guarded by either the 'countervailing' virtues of humility and magnanimity or the sister-virtues of faith and love.[42] This raises a question that Aquinas and many others would have dismissed out of hand: can hope also be a *secular* virtue?

Voltaire for one emphasised the importance of hope for human activity and improvement. 'Man's most precious treasure is this hope which softens our sufferings and depicts pleasures for us in the future in terms of those we possess at present,' he wrote in his twenty-fifth *Philosophical Letter*. 'If men were unfortunate enough to be concerned only with the present, they would not sow, they would not build, they would not plant or provide for anything, and in the midst of this false enjoyment they would lack everything.'[43] So too Samuel Johnson believed that 'Hope is necessary in every condition', as without it the 'miseries of poverty, of sickness, of captivity' would be insupportable, and even the happiest would still be wretched without the expectation of 'some new possession, of some

FIGURE 4. Gustave Doré, illustration to Dante, *Purgatorio*, canto 29.

enjoyment yet behind.'[44] But excessive or unreasonable hopes will lead to disappointment, so that few come away contented from having embarked towards the seat of 'Hope, daughter of Desire.'[45] This-worldly hope is then, after all, a mixed blessing— as the only hope that we may hold with confidence is that of a future life. 'Hope is the chief blessing of man, and that hope only is rational, of which we are certain that it cannot deceive us.'[46] Similarly Jean-Jacques Rousseau dismissed the 'uncertain and vague hope' that Voltaire's writings offered him, which pales in comparison to the otherworldly glow of hope in God and providence: 'you *enjoy*,' he tells Voltaire, 'but I *hope*, and hope embellishes everything.'[47]

Others, however, were less convinced. '*Hope* is confusing the wish for an event with its probability,' wrote Arthur Schopenhauer a century onwards.[48] According to Schopenhauer, influenced as much by pagan thinkers as by Eastern traditions, hope is problematic because it 'distorts the intellect's correct assessment of probability,' tempting us to overestimate the chances of the hoped-for thing coming about. Like Cicero and others, Schopenhauer saw hope as closely tied to fear: both are linked to expectations about the future, which is a capacity we only receive through our humanity. In contrast to 'the enviable carelessness and peace of mind of animals,' who supposedly live purely in the present, humans are doomed to consider the future, and suffer all the more deeply for it.[49] It is more natural for humans to hope than to fear: 'we are instinctively more inclined to hope than to worry, just as our eyes turn by themselves to light, not to darkness'; 'it is natural for a human being to believe what he desires, and to believe it because he desires it.' However, this does not make our condition any better: when our hopes are disappointed, it is very painful, especially when the process is gradual: 'a hopeless misfortune resembles a quick death blow, whereas a constantly thwarted and repeatedly revived hope resembles a slow torturous death.'[50]

In a famous passage, Friedrich Nietzsche too stressed the shadow-side of hope. While humans treasure hope believing it to be 'the greatest piece of good fortune,' they fail to realise that it was in fact the last evil remaining in Pandora's jar, left there not as a blessing but a punishment. 'For what Zeus wanted was that man, though never so tormented by the other evils, should nonetheless not throw life away but continue to let himself be tormented,' Nietzsche wrote. 'To that end he gives men hope: it is in truth *the worst of all evils*, because it protracts the torment of men.'[51] The young Camus agreed with Nietzsche's reading of hope as 'the most terrible' of the evils contained in Pandora's vessel. 'I don't know any symbol more moving,' he added. 'For hope, contrary to popular belief, is tantamount to resignation. And to live is not to be resigned.'[52] The hope rejected here as well as in *The Myth of Sisyphus* (where hope is the 'typical act of eluding' the absurd) is primarily the otherworldly hope and 'supernatural consolation' promised by religion—but Camus equally opposes the ideological hope for 'some great idea' that will give life meaning and thereby 'betray it.' The absurd mind distinguishes itself by a 'refusal to hope' and to expect anything from the future: Sisyphus, recall, is the absurd hero precisely because he refuses to hope.[53]

The later Camus, however, held a more positive view of hope, even founding a book series *Collection Espoir* in the 1950s, which he hoped would help 'denounce tragedy and to show it is not a solution, nor is despair a reason.'[54] 'Great ideas, it has been said, come into the world as gently as doves,' Camus told his audience at a lecture in Uppsala in 1957. 'Perhaps then, if we listen attentively, we shall hear, amid the uproar of empires and nations, a faint flutter of wings, the gentle stirring of life and hope.'[55] Never an optimist, by the end of his life Camus had, in some sense, made his peace with hope.

A Thing with Shadows

Little remains in our modern-day awareness of the shadow-sides of hope. Though there are exceptions, hope is overwhelmingly viewed as something inherently positive, associated with optimism and positive thinking as much as with virtue and courage. If we call someone (or ourselves) *hopeful* it is to pay them a compliment: to be a hopeful person is to possess a positive trait. Aquinas's concerns—that we can only be certain of hope as a virtue if it is properly oriented on the divine—don't seem to bother us, nor do ancient concerns that hope as an emotion is, at the very least, a two-edged sword.

But as hope's hesitant history reminds us, it is not self-evidently an unblemished good. We've seen various reasons why hope should be considered a thing with shadows as well as feathers; of these shadows, two stand out.

First, if someone hopes for something that harms others (or is unjust), then this is hope *for the wrong thing*. A tyrant might hope to finally subjugate his people, or a CEO representing a fossil-fuel company might hope for the climate crisis to rage wildly, the better to profit from it. In such cases, we would not praise the hopers for being 'hopeful'—and we would not respect them if they wrote an opinion piece praising the value of 'hope'. As Terry Eagleton writes in his book *Hope without Optimism*, 'If you reduce hope to a single positive force, it is hard to account for the kind of aspirations that are noxious through and through'—such as hoping to exterminate part of the population.[56] These are not trivial examples: they serve to remind us that good hope is always grounded in good context, and that one person's hope may well be another person's despair. In such cases, where the object of one hope casts a shadow on the hopes of others, it may be better to follow T. S. Eliot and 'wait without hope', as 'hope would be hope for the wrong thing'.[57]

Second, if someone hopes for something and *does nothing* to bring it about, then this hope is flawed. A government official might stare at the wreckage of some disaster and declare she 'hopes' that many people will be saved, while doing nothing whatsoever to save them; a billionaire at Davos might express his 'hope' that emissions will be cut, having just parked his private jet. In such cases, where hope stands in the place of action, we would be justified in asking these self-styled 'hopers' to hope less, and act more.

It is this kind of purely passive hope that is criticised by Roxane Gay in her 2019 opinion article provocatively titled 'The Case against Hope'. 'I don't traffic in hope,' she tells the reader. 'Hope is too ineffable and far too elusive. Hope allows us to leave what is possible in the hands of others. . . . When we hope, we have no control over what may come to pass. We put all our trust and energy into the whims of fate. We abdicate responsibility. We allow ourselves to be complacent.' Instead, she asks us to focus on action and possibility: 'What we really must wish for one another is the power of all that might be possible if we do anything more than hope.'[58]

The perceptive reader will note that this is in fact a quite *hopeful* note on which to end an essay against hope—and indeed what Gay seems to be arguing against is a species of hope that is close to optimism.[59] When Gay writes that 'instead of thinking about hope, I want to continue thinking about possibility,' advocates of hope could respond that *that is precisely what hope is*. 'Hope just means another world might be possible, not promised, not guaranteed,' as Rebecca Solnit writes. 'Hope calls for action; action is impossible without hope.'[60]

But Gay's deeper point stands: *to the extent that* hope is a placeholder for action, then it is not worth much—and this is in turn emphasised by most advocates of hope, such as Jane Goodall, who emphasises repeatedly that hope must be coupled with action. 'Hope is often misunderstood,' she writes in *The Book of Hope*. 'People tend to think that it is simply passive wishful thinking: I hope something will happen but I'm not going to do anything about it. This is indeed the opposite of *real hope*, which requires action and engagement.'[61] Solnit agrees: 'it's important to emphasize that hope is only a beginning; it's not a substitute for action, only a basis for it. . . . Hope gets you there; work gets you through.'[62] As does Greta Thunberg, who (as we will see) is deeply ambivalent about hope: 'To me, hope is not something that is given to you, it is something you have to earn, to create. It cannot be gained passively, through standing by and waiting for someone else to do something. *Hope is taking action*. It is stepping outside your comfort zone.'[63] It thus appears that those making the case for and against hope are in agreement on this: that hope must be coupled with action to be worth its while. Or, to put it differently: *mere* hope is not enough.

To these two shadows we may add a third. If we hope for something that we perceive to be impossible, or if our hope is based on an irrational belief, then this is *false* hope. A person might hope for aliens to solve the climate crisis, or for it to magically solve itself—but we would not take them seriously, and we would be right not to. For hope to be good hope, it doesn't have to be based in certainty (on the contrary, we typically hope for less-than-certain things), but it has to be somehow grounded in rationality and possibility.

Fools and drunkards hope wildly and immoderately, as Aquinas knew even in medieval times: 'all fools, without using deliberation, attempt everything and are of good hope.'[64] Or, as Aquinas scholar Robert Miner brings this into the twenty-first century: 'The drunk person at a party who hopes to jump from the eighth floor to the ground without injury has false hope, as does his drunken buddy who hopes to charm the girl who has always found him repulsive. Both hope to achieve a difficult good, but their hope is not governed by reason.'[65] For Aquinas, all false hope is problematic, and in cases where our natural hope is founded on irrational beliefs, despair (*desperatio*) may be in fact be preferable.

This is important, because there is sometimes a tendency in our culture to suggest that hope is *always* good or appropriate— the very thing that the ancients as well as Aquinas so insistently warned against—or even that 'there is no such thing as false hope. There is only hope.'[66] But in cases where the thing hoped for is strictly impossible, or based on an irrational belief, hope is clearly not the right response. And this, too, is recognised by hope's modern advocates, as making 'the case for hope' is often shorthand for claiming that a certain objective (such as preventing climate catastrophe) is possible or achievable, against those who think it is not. In doing so, sometimes they overstate their case, and instead of simply arguing for possibility try to make the case for high probability—as if hope can only be founded on a high chance of success. But this is a mistake. As Aquinas argued, avoiding false hope does not mean we cannot hope for *improbable* things; what matters is whether it is appropriate or rational to hope for them. In the words, again, of Miner: 'What makes hope rational is not the fact that attainment of the good is *certain* or *probable*, but the rationality of the belief that it is wise for this person to seek this good at this time.'[67] To illustrate this, he supplies another helpful example:

A soldier who attempts to win a battle in which he is out-numbered does not have false hope. Fighting against the odds, knowing that shame is an evil worse than death, belongs to the essence of an excellent soldier. But a general who has the option of improving his position by waiting and gathering additional armies, yet sends his troops into a disastrous situation, is simply thoughtless. If he pleads that, despite the odds, he was motivated by the hope of victory, he does not remove the stain of guilt. He merely shows that . . . *he does not know the difference between true hope and false hope.*[68]

If we applied this to climate change, the implication would be that activists and policymakers do not have false hope in continuing to strive for mitigation even if the chances of *complete* success are slim: *as long as the cause is worth fighting for*, perseverance in the face of even desperate odds may yet be warranted. If this is right, then climate writers do not need to overstate the chance of success in order to make 'the case for hope'—indeed, they *should* not. For one thing, as Aquinas explained to us, true hope does not have to be grounded on *probability*, merely on *rationality*—which we may define here as possibility in combination with a just cause.[69] For another, there is a different danger that clings to any overestimation of success—and this is the risk that if hope is seen to hinge on probability, and this probability is overstated, then any negative information to the contrary will all too easily puncture the case for hope.[70]

What you get, then, are the voices of those who proclaim loudly, and almost proudly, that 'we're doomed', because the odds are worse than they first perceived them to be.[71] This kind of despair Aquinas might have tempered by explaining calmly that bad odds do not mean a cause is lost, and that hope need not hinge on probability: some battles may make sense to wage even if full-on victory seems unlikely. To which we may add that, in the case of the climate crisis, the matter is more complicated still, because even if *some* level of catastrophe cannot be avoided, it can be postponed and attenuated; and any measure of attenuation means a decrease in death and suffering on the short term and the long.[72]

While critics are right to warn that the case for hope can be and has been overstated, they are wrong to draw from this the conclusion that the 'war' therefore is 'lost',[73] and in dismissing *all* hope as false hope show merely that they do not know 'the difference between true hope and false hope.' Such misunderstandings are what happen when we don't understand hope correctly, when we fail to separate hope from certainty and optimism, and good hope from bad. And this seems crucial: we need to have an appropriate attitude to false and deficient hope in order to know what good hope means.

Rethinking Hope

These 'shadows' of hope are each in different ways cases of *bad hope*. (We have to add epithets like 'bad' or 'false' to hope because we assume it to be good, just as ancient writers had to add 'good' to hope because they assumed it to be neutral or even bad.) Such cases of bad hope are presumably *not* what is meant by the many books and articles making the case for hope today. What hope's advocates are (or should be) arguing for is *good hope*, that is: hope for a *genuine good* (1) that is closely linked with *action* (2) and aims at something that is *possible* though not *certain*, (3) thus shedding each of the three shadows mentioned above.

If they aren't always successful in avoiding these dangers, this is in part because the concept of hope is subject to many confusions. Take, for instance, this conversation between Douglas Abrams and Jane Goodall in *The Book of Hope*:

> 'So what actually is hope—an emotion?'
>   'No, it's not an emotion.'
>   'So what is it?'
>   'It's an aspect of our survival.'
>   'Is it a survival skill?'
>   'It's not a skill. It's something more innate, more profound. It's almost a gift. Come on, think of another word.'
>   '"Tool"? "Resource"? "Power"? . . . A survival mechanism?'
>   'Better, but less mechanical. A survival . . .' Jane paused, trying to come up with the right word.
>   'Impulse? Instinct?' I offered.
>   'Actually, it's a survival trait,' she finally concluded. That's what it is. It is a human survival trait and without it we perish.'[74]

There's something interesting about this confusion: after all, we wouldn't be as hard put to define anger or fear (or perhaps even love). And this hesitation towards defining it is somehow appropriate, because 'hope' is a feathery concept, used in lots of different ways and contexts, both culturally and (as we have seen) historically inflected.[75]

For instance, despite what Goodall says, we do very often use hope in a subjective sense, to designate an emotion or a passion. In philosophy, the 'standard account' or 'orthodox definition' of hope defines it as having to do crucially with *desire* and some level of *probability*: if we hope for something we *desire* it, and we assume the thing or event we desire is *possible*, but not *certain*. 'On this definition, to hope is to desire an outcome we deem neither certain nor impossible,' in the words of hope scholar Béatrice Han-Pile.[76] (If we said we 'hoped' to get a promotion we were already certain of, we would be either speaking disingenuously or misapplying the word 'hope'.)[77] But hope can also be used in a different, 'objective' sense, to designate a state of affairs. Sometimes 'there is hope' is simply shorthand for 'there is a chance' (for success, survival, improvement, etc.). Where this is the case, the question 'Is there hope?' can be quite neutral—it is just a question about whether we think there is still an objective chance of success, however slim.

The vagueness between the subjective and objective uses of hope leads to serious confusions, with the result that for a person to say they are not hopeful is often considered the same as saying that *nothing can be done, we're doomed, we may as well give up*. 'What happens if we don't have hope?' as Goodall told the *Guardian*. 'We give up. If you don't think what you do is going to make any difference, why bother to do it?'[78] But the one does not follow from the other. A person may feel *subjectively* hopeless (or be without the positive emotion of hope) and yet believe that, in another sense, 'there is still hope' (i.e., *there is still a chance*). And vice versa: a person may be subjectively hopeful while believing all is lost. Thus, when Goodall says: 'You won't be active unless you hope that your action is going to do some good. So you need hope to get you going, but then by taking action, you generate more hope,' she is actually using 'hope' in two different senses.[79] By hoping in sense 1 (subjectively), we create a situation in which there is more hope in sense 2 (objectively: i.e., there is a greater chance of success). And realising there is more objective hope in sense 2 will in turn enforce the subjective hope in sense 1.

But it is in fact unclear whether this is necessarily the case. Considering what we have seen of pessimistic resistance, there may be grounds for action based purely on the recognition that there is *some* possibility of success, or that the cause is worth fighting for, without feeling any of the emotions usually associated with hope. If so, then this sense of hope may be *entirely compatible* with a subjective sense of despair.[80]

To make things more complicated: hope is also used as a disposition or character trait, or even as a 'skill' (as in Goodall's 'survival skill'). Some would go further and designate hope as a virtue, or at least as a trait adjacent to virtue: this, we have seen, is part and parcel of the Christian tradition, but it is unclear whether it works outside this tradition. Can hope still be deemed a virtue in a secular age?

We know what Schopenhauer and Nietzsche would have answered. But some philosophers disagree. Recently Béatrice Han-Pile and Robert Stern have argued that hope (considered not as an emotion but as a disposition that can be cultivated and actualised in the right circumstances) does indeed meet all the criteria of a (secular) virtue. For instance: hope is good for the hoper; hope stands as a mean or midpoint between two vices (despair and 'unwarranted optimism'); and hope can be cultivated by the hoper. On this view one can indeed learn to be more hopeful or even train oneself to hope, though this is not like flicking a switch, and certainly not like the trend of 'positive thinking' that suggests we learn to maintain a feeling of subjective hopefulness in all circumstances. This, according to the authors, would be more 'like optimism than hope', and would involve a measure of irrationality that means 'it could not offer a long-term strategy for a virtuous agent.'[81]

This is important, as some of the hope literature seems to suggest that subjective hopefulness—which is often used as a synonym for optimism—is always a good thing. But as Terry Eagleton has argued, 'If hope were simply a feeling, it would not count as a virtue. . . . It is because hope can be cultivated by practice and self-discipline that it is a question of merit.'[82] Mere optimism or 'temperamental cheerfulness' would not suffice: for hope to be worth its while, it must be fallible, and it must be cultivated.[83] Therefore, while the case for hope as a secular virtue can (and I believe convincingly) be made, this can only be done *under strict conditions*.

And even if hope is recognised to be a virtue, there are still circumstances under which it would be wrong or inappropriate to hope: in some cases it might be better to refrain from hope altogether. Crucially, to be a skilled hoper means also knowing *when to give up hope*. As Han-Pile and Stern write, 'there is no one-size-fits-all answer to the question of whether it is right or not to hope in specific circumstances,' and cultivating the virtue of hope involves precisely learning to recognise this. Knowing 'when to stop hoping and to adopt another attitude is precisely part of the virtue of hope.'[84] This is important, and all too often forgotten by narratives that frame any hopefulness as strength and any loss or laying-down of hope as weakness. There are circumstances under which abandoning hope is exactly what is required of the virtuous: this is not a flaw or failure but a difficult and important skill, which may even (as Han-Pile and Stern argue) require courage. Consider, for instance, a person suffering from unrequited love. If they perpetually continued to hope against hope, this might make for good romantic fiction, but it would be terrible as a rule of life. Sometimes we need to know when to graciously resign our hopes and opt for a different strategy, such as resignation.[85]

This is a truth vaguely intuited by some in the climate debate but put to ill use and fraught with misunderstandings. Not only is resignation not a path to be chosen lightly, but we may not even be entitled to making such a choice, when its consequences affect all humans as well as other species living now and for centuries to come. Part of the virtue of hope is to know when to give it up—but the greatest vice is to give it up unduly.[86]

At the very least, the ambiguous history of hope should remind us that to declare one's hope is not *by default* a good thing. The value of hope depends at least on three things: on whether the thing hoped for is *worth* hoping for; on whether hope is appropriately linked to action; and on whether true hope is correctly distinguished from false hope. Even if, as some have argued, hope is a virtue, that does not mean all hope is virtuous. If anything, hope is a concept that needs to be handled with infinite caution, as false hope can devastate like few things can, and disappointed hope lead to bitterness. 'What price hopelessness, indeed?' as China Miéville asks. 'But what price hope?'[87]

5

Radical Hope Revisited

For you perhaps, if as I hope and wish you will live long after me, there will follow a better age. When the darkness is dispelled, our descendants will be able to walk back into the pure radiance of the past.

—PETRARCH, *AFRICA IX*
(IN MANTEL, *THE MIRROR AND THE LIGHT*)

FIGURE 5. Josiah Wedgwood, Sydney Cove clay medallion,
1789. © State Library of New South Wales.

IN 1789 the English potter Josiah Wedgwood created a medallion made of clay from Sydney Cove in Australia to celebrate the establishment of a colony in New South Wales. The medallion features Hope (with an anchor) 'encouraging Art and Labour under the influence of Peace, to pursue the employment necessary to give security and happiness to an infant settlement.'[1] But hope *for whom*? For the colonists, certainly, but not for the native inhabitants, who might well have responded, paraphrasing Kafka, 'There is hope, but not for us.'[2] As Brigid von Preussen remarks: 'The fact that other people had a prior claim to the land, and to the local clay, had no place in his picture.'[3]

The medallion may thus serve to remind us not to endorse hope blindly, without knowing what it is that we are hoping for. In the words of Greta Thunberg: 'Right now, many of us are in need of hope. But what is hope? And hope for whom? Hope for those of us who have created the problem, or for those who are already suffering its consequences?'[4]

In the context of colonial invasions, we see that the case for hope is not as clear-cut as we might think. From the perspective of the invaders, who believed they were bringing civilisation to promised lands, the hope was for a successful completion of their mission, and for prosperity to come. But what if we flipped the coin and looked at the matter from the perspective of the original inhabitants of ancestral and sacred soil—in what way should *they* be hopeful? What could hope even mean in the face of cultural collapse?

This is the question asked by Jonathan Lear in his book *Radical Hope: Ethics in the Face of Cultural Devastation* (2006). The work is centred on the case of the Crow, one of the native Plains tribes of North America who in the 1880s were pressured by the white colonisers to move into reservations—and especially on their leader, Plenty Coups, 'the last great chief of the Crow nation.'[5] Lear opens with a staggering quote from Plenty Coups, who at the end of his life said that after the Crow's transition into reservations there were no more happenings: 'when the buffalo went away the hearts of my people fell to the ground, and they could not lift them up again. *After this nothing happened.'* Similar statements were made by women who lived through this transition, such as Pretty Shield: 'I am trying to live a life that *I do not understand*'; and Two Leggings: 'Nothing happened after that. *We just lived.'*[6]

Taking his cue from the historical case of the Crow, who survived the white man's encroachment at the cost of their traditional way of life, Lear asks: 'What is it about a form of life's coming to an end that makes it such that for the inhabitants of that life things *cease to happen?*' The cultural devastation that the Crow lived through, Lear argues, was different in kind from what it would have been for them to suffer total defeat at the hands of their traditional enemies, the Sioux or Cheyenne. Such a defeat, however catastrophic, would still have been something they had 'the conceptual resources to understand.' But the move into the reservation was not simply a disastrous occurrence; it was, Lear argues, 'a breakdown of the field in which occurrences occur,' as actions crucial to Crow culture and Crow virtues (such as planting the coup-stick in battle, thus marking a line that the enemy shall not pass) ceased to make sense.[7]

The cultural devastation Lear is addressing, therefore, is one that encroaches upon concepts and virtues as well as concrete modes of living: part of what the Crow lost was the ability to make sense of what their lives were about—as acts that used to be meaningful ceased to be intelligible in the new situation. This was what it meant for things to *cease to happen.*

Of course the Crow's predicament was rooted in very specific historical circumstances—and yet Lear believes that what happened to them (or rather: the breakdown of things happening) is meaningful for all of us: 'What I am concerned with is an *ontological vulnerability* that affects us all insofar as we are human.' The question he asks is not only what it would be for a culture to 'face the prospect of utter devastation' but also what it would be to do so virtuously—with moral excellence.[8] 'This is a problem for moral psychology,' Lear suggests. 'If, roughly speaking, we believe *ought* implies *can*: if we think that in these challenging times people ought to find new ways—not just of surviving—but of living *well*, we need to give an account of how it might be psychologically possible to do so.'[9]

From underneath this question, others emerge. What would it mean to hope in the absence of anything conceivable to hope for? What would it mean to be virtuous when old concepts of virtue are no longer available? Lear focuses on the virtue of courage, which was crucial to the Crow's understanding of the good life. Courage, for the Crow as for the Sioux and Cheyenne, 'was understood in terms of the *thick* concepts of Crow culture': for these warrior cultures, courage meant bravery in battle. But how could Crow men, and in particular the Crow chief Plenty Coups, still manifest the virtue of courage when the way of life that allowed for courageous deeds (such as the planting of coup-sticks) collapsed entirely? 'When the Crow were confined to the reservation they were confronted with a stark choice: either they had to give up the idea that there was any longer a courageous way to live, or they had to alter their conception of what courage was.' Such a conceptual change would have to 'begin with a culture's thick understanding of courage' and 'find ways to *thin it out.*' According to Lear, 'Plenty Coups did make just this sort of transformation.'[10]

The great challenge for the Crow, Lear argues, was not just that the tribe had to face the external threat of hostile forces, a situation endemic to their way of life, but that they had to 'struggle with the intelligibility of events that lay at the horizon of their ability to understand.' This created a 'communal sense of anxiety,' as the Crow lacked the conceptual resources to make sense of what was happening: 'A way of life was anxious about its ability to go forward into an unfathomable future.'[11]

The Crow were not equipped to navigate this radical uncertainty, any more than *any* culture is, for the simple reason that, as Lear puts it, 'a culture does not tend to train the young to endure its own breakdown.'[12] They were, however, able to draw on certain imaginative resources that their culture amply provided: by seeking guidance of the cosmic forces by way of dream-visions. And in fact it had been Plenty Coups himself who, as a boy, was sent into the wilderness in search of a vision, and the dream he brought back to the elders would one day help him guide his tribe into an unknown future.[13]

Guided by the dreams that were given him in his youth, the mature Plenty Coups decides to hope *radically*—that is: to hope for something that he cannot yet have any conception of, as it lies beyond the boundary of the known. This is a peculiar form of hopefulness, 'a commitment to a goodness that transcends his understanding,' a hope that 'something good will emerge,' while leaving open what that is: 'The hope is held in the face of the recognition that, given the abyss, one cannot really know what survival means.'[14] What makes this hope *radical* is 'that it is directed toward a future goodness that transcends the current ability to understand what it is. Radical hope anticipates a good for which those who have the hope as yet lack the appropriate concepts with which to understand it.' And Lear asks: 'What would it be for such hope to be justified?'[15]

One way to justify radical hope would be on the basis of historical vindication: Lear could argue that Plenty Coups's radical hope was justified because history proved him right. And there are times where Lear comes close to saying exactly this. Empowered by radical hope as well as by the cosmic visions of youth, Plenty Coups (on Lear's account) does perform the kind of imaginative transformation that allows him to exercise courage in previously unimagined ways. To be courageous, in this catastrophic time and for this particular leader, was to be open to collaboration with the dreaded occupiers, even to ally his cause to theirs, and thereby to preserve what he could of his people's ancestral lands—an effort in which Plenty Coups was to some extent successful.[16] While the cultural collapse *was* devastating—to the extent that Plenty Coups himself said that *things stopped happening* after the event—by working with the colonising forces the Crow were able to keep their lands and preserve *something* amidst the great loss. Radical hope, then, is not a bid for complete victory so much as for '*revival*: for coming back to life in a form that is not yet intelligible.'[17]

But to let the argument hinge purely on this historical case (which in any event is open to multiple interpretations) would make the argument too vulnerable to a variety of counterarguments: for instance, that the Crow perhaps lost more than they gained; or that other responses were equally justified, such as courageous resistance in the face of brutal colonial injustice. Recognising this, Lear remarks that 'the point is not to establish the historical claim that Plenty Coups actually did manifest such radical hope,' nor 'is the aim to defend Plenty Coups'; rather: 'The aim is to establish what *we* might legitimately hope at a time when the sense of purpose and meaning that has been bequeathed to us by our culture has collapsed.'[18]

This deeper justification of radical hope—as exhibited by Plenty Coups but not limited to his case—is a challenge, because Lear does not want to simply state (as many accounts of hope do) that *there is always hope* or that *we have to keep hoping for salvation even against all odds.* Such statements may be emotionally appealing, but they are not rooted in reality—and in fact Lear is at pains to distinguish hope from 'mere optimism' (as manifested by those who kept resisting the occupying forces in the belief that they could stem this tide).[19] Instead Lear seeks to vindicate radical hope by showing how it is related to courage—which is the kind of virtue that can be 'thinned out' in times of radical change, when previous 'thick' concepts of courage (planting coup-sticks) are no longer available. A thinned-out conception of courage, Lear argues, would reframe it more broadly as 'the ability to live well with the risks that inevitably attend human existence.' In times of cultural devastation such risks 'include not only malnutrition, starvation, disease, defeat, and confinement; they include *loss of concepts*'—so that 'courage would have to include the ability to live well with the risk of conceptual loss.'[20]

It is this kind of courage that Plenty Coups manifested, and that was crucially informed by the radical hope he drew from the dreams of his youth: dreams that brought him face-to-face with a dark vision of the future while enacting a trust that a way forward might be found even in this radical uncertainty; that the Crow might yet survive. 'Thus the message of the dream, while pessimistic, also holds out hope.'[21] In such a context, 'radical hope might be not only *compatible* with courage' but even function as 'a *necessary* constituent.'[22] If it is possible to live a virtuous life in times of cultural collapse—for instance to continue to exercise courage even as old concepts of courage are disintegrating— then some kind of hope may be a necessary part of any such virtue. But this hope cannot be founded on any determinate vision of the good—as that is precisely what is being eroded. It has to be a hope beyond our usual modes of hope—a hope that is truly *radical*. And so, to the extent that we can show that 'radical hope is an important ingredient of such courage, we have thereby provided a legitimation of such hope.'[23]

Radical Hope and Climate Change

First published in 2006, Lear's *Radical Hope* predates the irruption of climate change into our collective consciousness,[24] but it is impossible to read, in current times, without this crisis in mind. For instance, when Lear says that the Crow experienced 'a communal sense of anxiety'; that a 'way of life was anxious about its ability to go forward into an unfathomable future'; that 'a culture does not tend to train the young to endure its own breakdown'; and that this 'inability to conceive of its own devastation will tend to be the blind spot of any culture'[25]—he seems to be describing word for word the anxiety, the sense of *losing the future*, experienced by many people in response to climate change. Indeed, as we have seen, young people especially frame the existential challenge of our times in exactly such terms. *What may we hope for in the age of climate crisis? Which projects still make sense to pursue? How can I live a good and meaningful life when all the things that constituted meaning are becoming increasingly uncertain?*

And so, when Lear proposes to establish 'what *we* might legitimately hope at a time when the sense of purpose and meaning that has been bequeathed to us by our culture has collapsed,'[26] and proposes radical hope as, if not quite a solution, then at least a fully *courageous* response to such circumstances—this seems to speak directly to those who are seeking a way forward at a time when the future itself seems to be slipping away. Consider a passage such as the following, about one of Plenty Coups's dream-visions:

The dream was a manifestation of radical hope . . . in that it enabled them to go forward hopefully into a future that they would be able to grasp only retrospectively, when they could reemerge with concepts with which to understand themselves and their experiences. If we can make the case that this stance was a manifestation of courage, we could presumably come to see how radical hope can be not just psychologically advantageous but a legitimate response even to a world catastrophe.[27]

For a book not about climate change, such passages capture the predicament of this age more effectively than many climate books do—almost as if, like the dreams of the Crow, the book is itself a dreamlike imaginative exercise, channelling the hopes and anxieties of an entire culture without knowing that that is what it's doing.

It is then not surprising that soon after the book's appearance, articles appeared arguing that this is what we need in current times: that in response to the 'increasingly dire warnings about the severity of climate change'[28] we should adopt *radical hope*. For instance, Allen Thompson defines radical hope as 'a novel form of courage appropriate to a culture in crisis' and proposes it can play a role in our times to reconfigure environmental virtues, as traditional 'conceptions of environmental goods are endangered by the emerging climate crisis.' According to Thompson: 'Radical hope, as courage manifest in environmental virtues of transition, is primarily against despair and hopelessness, which the apparently intractable problem of climate change can supply in spades.' This might mean, for instance, having the radical hope 'that good human lives do not require the material conditions and amount of energy required to support contemporary standards of living.'[29] Similarly, Byron

Williston argues that, while hope is warranted as a response to scientific warnings about climate catastrophe, this hope must take the form of *radical hope* if it is to avoid the extremes of wishful thinking on the one hand and desperate resignation on the other. As we should indeed understand climate breakdown as 'a threat to human flourishing,' Williston proposes that 'our foundational hope now ought to be that humanity can come through the climate crisis in a way that allows us to flourish as the sorts of beings we constitutively are.'[30]

In both cases, radical hope is proposed as a response or alternative to despair and resignation. This, according to philosopher Simon Hope, is a mistake, as it overlooks 'the *conceptual* nature of the loss Lear is concerned with.' Both authors seem to assume that the 'normative disorientation' experienced by the Crow 'is something ultimately demoralising'—but this 'gets things backwards: for Lear, despair isn't the cause of loss of ends, loss of ends is the cause of despair.'[31] The solution offered by both Williston and Thompson to normative disorientation is to 'propose a new virtue, a reinterpretation of courage in the face of climate catastrophe.' But, Hope argues, once we're at the stage where normative disorientation has set in and we have lost our grip 'on virtue concepts as concepts to live by,' then we are far beyond the stage where a specific virtue can fill the gap, precisely because there is no well-defined gap to fill—and so 'the solution to our plight cannot be to add another virtue to the list.'[32]

Hope points to another problem, having to do with the important role played by courage in Lear's account—a role that is easily misunderstood. Importantly, Lear does not define radical hope as a *kind* of courage but explores its potential as an 'ingredient' or 'necessary constituent' of courage (that is: *thinned-out courage*) in times of cultural collapse.[33] (To the extent that such thinned-out courage is justified, radical hope is justified too.)

And in order to make his point that courage can be salvaged even when our old conceptions of courage cease to make sense, Lear employs a firmly Aristotelian account of the virtue as a mean between two extremes (cowardice on the one hand; 'rash boldness' on the other).[34] According to Hope, Lear invokes this Aristotelian conception of courage 'because he wants to exploit an unusual feature of Aristotle's account'—namely, that on Aristotle's view 'courage is an unusually "executive" virtue.'[35]

Unlike a virtue such as justice, which has a distinctive end of its own (the 'just person refrains from unfairly taking more *because that is unfair*'), courage is oriented not on its own end but on the good. 'What does the courageous person do? Face danger because it is danger? Only an idiot does that. The courageous person faces danger *for the sake of the good*.' This is important because Lear's argument would not have worked had he focused on a different kind of virtue: 'precisely because courage doesn't have a distinctive end of its own, it is possible to substitute *for the sake of the good* with *for the sake of some future possibility of the good* and retain the structure of the virtue.' But Hope also notes that the version of courage we are left with is at some remove from where we started: 'as Lear insists, this can only be a "thinned out" understanding of courage—it has not survived unscathed.'[36]

I think these criticisms are correct—and they seem to get at a tension that emerges when radical hope is picked out as a solution to a specific problem, as a useful virtue to guide us through a difficult time. When authors commend radical hope as an excellent response to some crisis (climate change, but also international war or pandemic), what they seem to describe is really just *indeterminate hope*: a hope that is somehow vague or unusual, but still far removed from the normative disorientation experienced by the Crow. To hope for greater ecological responsibility or for a just world where the interests of future generations are taken into account is admirable, even necessary—but is this radical hope, or simply *hope*? There is something paradoxical about even trying to describe what radical hope might look like in our times, let alone to sketch what it may lead to. Almost by definition, this is not *radical* hope.

It is true that Lear argues that if radical hope is possible and justified in the specific context of Plenty Coups and the Crow, it may also be possible and justified in other circumstances of cultural devastation. But this does not mean we could cut Plenty Coups's strategy from this context and paste it onto the climate crisis—as if some sort of evident moral could be drawn from the story.[37] It is not at all clear that radical hope is the kind of thing we can and should bravely recommend to each other: indeed, from Lear's account it sometimes sounds as if such hope stands in a close relation to what we would commonly call despair.

It is worth pointing out, for instance, that the radical hope Lear attributes to Plenty Coups comes on the heels of a devastating resignation, as the chief comes to understand and accept the futility of further resistance to Western colonisation—radical hope is a response to the conviction that *this is a fight we cannot win*. And the reason he knew this with not just a measure of probability but with a deep unsettling certainty was precisely because he had access to a source of knowledge that the Crow trusted beyond 'mere' rational prognoses: it was through prophetic dreams that the Crow not just believed but *knew* that a terrible change was to come, and that this tide could not be stemmed. I emphasise this point not only because it highlights the particular nature of the Crow's predicament but also because it is this mixture of confidence and resignation that makes radical hope really *radical*: it is justified only insofar as it

comes on the ruins of ordinary hopes. This is not at all a message to make us sleep more safely at night: it is truly a hope of
the abyss, and we should think twice before recommending it
even in times of crisis. As one reviewer aptly put it: 'Radical
hope is *terrifying*.'[38]

Recall that the practical result of this radical hope was collaboration with an enemy who disrespected the Crow's culture
and traditions—a fate that some would have said was worse
than death, and worse than being defeated by a traditional
enemy such as the Sioux. In vindicating the Crow strategy,
Radical Hope thus accepts a specific reading of historical
events—which has important consequences for how we understand the resistance and rebellions of the time.

Lear frames Plenty Coups's radical hope as the golden mean
between two extremes: on the one hand, the deficiency of 'a
craven capitulation to the dominant culture'; on the other, the
excess of a 'rash and ineffectual rebellion.'[39] As an example of
the latter, Lear points to Wraps His Tail, a young Crow who in
1887 led a group of young warriors to take horses from the rival
Blackfeet tribe, after they had stolen horses from the Crow—
and later, in an act of provocation, stuck a gun into the belly of
a hated agent before firing it into the air. Things escalated and
the young warriors were arrested as horse thieves, leading Wraps
His Tail to declare his indignation: 'They, the palefaces, who
make treaties only to break them, who have stolen our buffalo
and our land, they call us "thieves."' A potential Indian uprising
was quickly squashed by the U.S. authorities; the Crow rebels
surrendered and Wraps His Tail was shot by a member of the
Crow Agency after having tried to escape.[40] Lear reads this rebellion as not just 'futile' but a 'nostalgic evasion.' While Wraps
His Tail's action would have been courageous in an earlier
time, his provocation (which before would have counted as the

planting of a coup-stick) could lead to nothing, and so 'has ceased to be an intelligible act.' Wraps His Tail attempted to take up the position of a Crow warrior, but the world in which such a position made sense was itself 'collapsing around him. Wraps His Tail tried to hold onto this position in spite of the fact that it became unintelligible.'[41]

A similar indictment is reserved for Sitting Bull, the last great chief of the Lakota Sioux and principal challenger of Plenty Coups's response to the white man's invasion. In sharp contrast to Plenty Coups's decision to work with the U.S. authorities (and fight against other tribes), Sitting Bull united rival tribes in a major revolt against the occupying forces, a rebellion that culminated in the Battle of the Little Bighorn, where Lakota and Cheyenne warriors defeated the U.S. forces led by Custer before being eventually crushed. It is important to remember that, like Plenty Coups, Sitting Bull drew from visions to guide the way forward: both his rebellion *and* his cooperation with rival tribes were inspired by divine guidance. It was while camping with leaders from other tribes and performing the traditional Sun Dance that Sitting Bull began to understand what was being asked of him: 'The Great Spirit has given our enemies to us. We are to destroy them. We do not know who they are. They may be soldiers.'[42]

While Lear explicitly states that 'both these leaders command our respect; and our aim is not to sit in judgment of either of them,' he does proceed to act as 'a straightforward advocate for Plenty Coups's vision in opposition to Sitting Bull's.'[43] Lear interprets Sitting Bull's vision as a kind of wishful thinking, in particular because the Lakota chief was drawn to the messianic Ghost Dance movement that spread across the Sioux reservation in the late 1880s, according to which the buffalo would be restored in an apocalyptic end of the white domination in 1891. 'It is a hallmark of the wishful that the world will be magically transformed—into conformity with how one would like it to be—without having to take any realistic practical steps to bring it about.' And so, at least 'from Plenty Coups's perspective, Sitting Bull deployed religious imagination in the wrong sort of way.'[44]

While Lear is careful to emphasise that both chiefs 'were men of extraordinary dignity and ability' and 'both deserve our respect,' still one might wonder if the vindication of Plenty Coups is not too much at the expense of Sitting Bull.[45] For instance, we should be cautious in applying the wisdom of hindsight to a situation where the outcome was not yet known: we may now agree with Plenty Coups that the eventual victory of U.S. forces was inevitable, but this was not a certainty at the time—except insofar as Plenty Coups was able to trust his visions (and then, recall that Sitting Bull had visions of his own). More importantly, it seems crucial to any rebellion that it is not purely or primarily motivated by the confidence in a triumphant victory—that there are other reasons for resistance, having to do rather with the defence of what a culture holds most dear. This seems to have been the case for Sitting Bull, as the historian Frederick Hoxie writes in a passage quoted by Lear: 'Sitting Bull insisted that authentic tribal leaders would never cooperate with the American government. To do so would be to surrender one's personal authority and sacrifice one's followers to the whims of petty officials.'[46]

If this is right, then alternative readings are possible of either Wraps His Tails's momentary insurrection or Sitting Bull's extensive uprising, not as futile or pointless but as deeply meaningful for other reasons than their practical outcome. As Slavoj Žižek writes of the doomed rebellion of Spartacus: 'their act of rebellion itself, whatever the outcome, already counts as a success.'[47] To make such a statement is to claim that there can be value in resistance even against all odds, *because it is the right thing to do*. The resistance of the 1880s can indeed be read as futile acts of wishful thinking, but it can also be read differently: as a radical act in the name of what is held most precious in the world—in the awareness that whatever one does in this life is being watched by the spirits and ancestors, and extends a line in which one would be proud to stand.

We might go further still and argue that, on Lear's own conception, desperate resistance can itself be a manifestation of radical hope. To see how this might work, let's take another look at the book *Revolutionary Yiddishland*, which we have seen cited by Andreas Malm to make the case for committed climate action *even if* success is perceived to be unlikely.[48] According to the authors (Brossat and Klingberg), 'The combativeness of Jewish Resistance fighters was based on a paradoxical and dramatic combination of historical optimism and absolute despair.' On the one hand, their 'historical optimism' (hope would be a better word) 'rested on the conviction that at the end of the day barbarism would be conquered and Nazism defeated, that the Jewish people would rise again, that *a better world would be born on the ashes of the barbaric empire*.' But there was also another, more desperate side to their resistance:

> On the other hand, however, there was the *absolute despair* of those witnessing a crime that as yet still had no name, that human consciousness and their Jewish consciousness were incapable of conceiving, who witnessed the disappearance of their world. In this dead of night they often had the impression of fighting against phantoms, in an absolute disproportion of forces; what could bullets do against a barbarism that the highest reason and historical understanding could

not even name, *no more than they could conceive the future beyond this catastrophe?*[49]

They quote a passage from the novel *Qu'une larme dans l'océan* (*Like a Tear in the Ocean*, 1949–55) by the Jewish author and psychologist Manès Sperber:

> He felt free from everything, the gratification of a useless freedom. The freedom to commit destructive acts, to shoot one of these gaping bystanders, to set fire to a cinema filled to bursting, to kill a German officer on the public road, to kill themselves with a bullet to the heart. *But there was no freedom to dream of a future, to imagine a different tomorrow. He was not free to escape his helpless being.*[50]

Such expressions begin to approach the conceptual confusion experienced by the Crow: they could not 'conceive the future beyond this catastrophe'; 'there was no freedom to dream of a future, to imagine a different tomorrow.' If there was a belief 'that a better world would be born on the ashes of the barbaric empire,' this vision seemed less motivated by optimism than by a kind of radical hope, as Lear portrays it in a more recent book: 'The hope acknowledges that we cannot be all that determinate about what we are hoping for.'[51]

More specifically, during the Warsaw ghetto uprising defeat was almost certain—the rebels knew this, and yet decided it was worth rebelling: 'It would not be said that the Nazis managed to liquidate the entire Jewish community of Poland in the crematoria of Treblinka without resistance. . . . This affirmation of life by way of a sacrifice and combat with no prospect of victory is *a tragic paradox that can only be understood as an act of faith in history,* in the capacity of humanity to rise again beyond barbarism.'[52] Such resistance can only tortuously be read as a mode of optimism: more likely it is an affirmation that there are causes worth dying for; that certain rebellions are justified by their orientation on the good and the just more than by their 'tangible result'. As the authors themselves put it: 'We have seen, in the revolts of the ghettos and extermination camps (in Sobibor, Treblinka, Auschwitz), rebels whose motivation was above all else the desire to testify for the future, *the moral and historical meaning of the action being more important than its tangible result.*'[53]

Such 'moral and historical meaning' can be oriented on the future, in the hope that a culture's descendants will see the deeds for what they were and look back in gratitude and wonder under the opened horizon of a clearer day.[54] But it can equally be oriented on the past. 'Not only our experiences,' wrote Viktor Frankl, 'but all we have done, whatever great thoughts we may have had, and all we have suffered, all this is not lost, though it is past; we have brought it into being. Having been is also a kind of being, and perhaps the surest kind.'[55] Or, in the words of Terry Eagleton:

> It is not dreams of liberated grandchildren that spur men and women to revolt, but memories of oppressed ancestors. It is the past that furnishes us with the resources of hope, not just the speculative possibility of a rather more gratifying future. . . . In some obscure sense, then, we are responsible for the past as well as for the present and future. The dead cannot be resurrected; but there is a tragic form of hope whereby they can be invested with new meaning . . . their struggles for emancipation can be incorporated into our own.'[56]

Either way, this widening of perspective to include the deep past as well as an unknown future allows for a different view of hope than one oriented primarily on this-worldly consequences—a view on which the desperate resistance of Wraps His Tail and Sitting Bull may yet be acts of courage, without denying that the road of compromise sought so painstakingly by Plenty Coups was also.

This is all the more important in the context of the cosmic animism of the Plains tribes, where the human world is so closely interrelated with the spirit world and meanings of actions are not bound to the here and now. Even if those who resisted lost the fight, this does not mean their resistance was not justified or their visions were less true: to obey the message of a dream, even a prophetic dream, does not guarantee one will be saved from catastrophe. Sitting Bull's legacy, like that of Plenty Coups, is remembered by his descendants, his presence still felt over the ancestral grounds.[57] From the perspective of those living today his actions may seem tragic—but from the perspective of his ancestors and his descendants yet to come, let alone from the spirit world he felt so near, who knows what their meaning is? And so perhaps there is a sense in which both Plenty Coups and Sitting Bull were justified.

Climate Hope

I have paused at length at these features of radical hope as recounted through the Crow in order to get a clearer picture not only of radical hope but of hope itself—and what hope we should be cultivating in the climate crisis. My aim in reconsidering Sitting Bull is not to criticise Lear's account of radical hope or even to vindicate one chief against another but to forestall a potential misapplication of radical hope—for instance by singling out an historical agent (be it Plenty Coups or Sitting Bull) and applying their actions to modern times. It should be remembered that what applies to the specific crisis faced by the

Plains tribes of North America does not straightforwardly apply to other circumstances. The attitude of Plenty Coups is an example of courage and 'imaginative excellence'—but that does not mean his actions are a blueprint for radical hope, any more than Sitting Bull's are a blueprint for uncompromising resistance.[58]

As Charles Taylor pointed out in his review of *Radical Hope*, our situation in a globalised secular age is very different from that of the Crow, who experienced what he calls a 'culture death': 'We find it hard to grasp the full, devastating impact of this kind of culture death because of the differentiated and loosely articulated way of life that seems normal to us.' For instance, if you're a computer designer or violinist and suddenly the world of computer design or classical music collapses entirely, you would no longer 'be able to do what really matters to you'—but this blow would be practically but not conceptually devastating: 'there would still remain many things you could meaningfully do.' For the Crow, it's very different: 'There are no alternative careers waiting for an ex-warrior; he probably has a wife and children, but what does it mean to be a father if you can't hand on the skills of a warrior? If a relatively limited range of significant actions becomes impossible, how can a person find a meaningful life?'[59]

Lear himself is very cautious not to straightforwardly apply Plenty Coups's radical hope to current times: in his later book, *Imagining the End*, which discusses our attitudes towards current crises, the term 'radical hope' does not appear once, except in a footnote reference to the earlier book.[60] This silence possibly reflects some discomfort with the earlier concept—but it is also a missed opportunity, as one crucial question is left unanswered: whether radical hope is 'for' exceptional circumstances only or is available more generally.

In *Radical Hope*, Lear seems to take the first road; in *Imagining the End*, it sounds at times as if he is taking the second, suggesting that it is possible more generally to hope without exactly knowing what we're hoping *for*.[61] For instance, Lear considers Freud's essay 'On Transience', which discusses the world situation and deep anxiety experienced at the time of World War I; here Freud, says Lear, was 'grappling with how to live with the radical uncertainty of the immediate future.'[62] What Freud is hoping for, on Lear's reading, is transience '*of the bad and evil,*' coupled with a return of the good:

> The return is itself an expression of hope. We may not be able to say what we are hoping for, but in the broadest and most indeterminate sense, hope hopes for the good. So, what we have here is a *return of hope, which is itself a hope for a return of the good.*

It is in this context that Lear states that 'the hope acknowledges that we cannot be all that determinate about what we are hoping for' and in a footnote refers, without comment, to *Radical Hope*.[63] In a different essay, discussing the legacy of Gettysburg, Lear mentions the founding ideals of the U.S. Declaration of Independence—'liberty and equality'—and closes with an intriguing passage:

> It is internal to the concepts *freedom* and *equality* that there is an open-endedness that stretches out beyond the horizons of our imagination. If things go well, we should hope future generations will understand freedom and equality better than we do precisely because they are living in ways that so much better instantiate them. So, in dedicating ourselves now to this 'unfinished work,' we need to acknowledge that part of what is unfinished are the very ideals to which we are

dedicating ourselves. This imposes a constraint on the structure of our hopes. In so dedicating ourselves, we can sincerely say that we hope for the unfolding of freedom and equality, but we need to recognize *that we do not and cannot yet know all that well what we are hoping for.*[64]

These are terms very reminiscent of how Lear described radical hope in his earlier work, but the context is not one of cultural devastation or normative disorientation: Lear is here describing a relationship to the future that recognises that our projects and ideals will transform themselves in ways we cannot yet understand. If this is indeed an instantiation of radical hope, then it would seem to deflate its 'radical' nature and allow it to be more readily available in modern times.

But perhaps the most striking feature of such passages is that Lear does *not* call such hopes 'radical': he refrains to apply (at least explicitly) the concept of radical hope to contemporary circumstances (such as the ecological crisis or the pandemic); instead he says only that it is possible, and sometimes necessary, to hope without knowing exactly 'what we are hoping for.' This, I think, is not quite the same as *radical hope*, which Lear himself linked to the extreme case of cultural collapse experienced by the Crow, and to the 'abysmal reasoning' that such times demanded. It is rather a hope based on openness, more along the lines of what other philosophers have called 'absolute hope' (Gabriel Marcel), or simply 'hope'; as Terry Eagleton has pointed out, 'Ernst Bloch holds likewise that what we hope for is ultimately unknown to us.'[65] This is a significantly more modest proposal, and if my reading is right then the later Lear is after all not willing for radical hope to be made available outside truly 'abysmal' circumstances—at most suggesting a more gradual difference between hope and radical hope.

For my part, I believe it is worth preserving a considerable distance between radical hope and other hopes—and to reserve the former for situations that involve the kind of extreme normative disorientation and cultural collapse experienced by the Crow. Again, as Charles Taylor has pointed out, it is not at all clear whether this is an experience available to us in the modern globalised world, where the majority of people don't have as narrow a conception of the good as was available to a warrior culture. It is true that, as several authors have recently argued, the ongoing development of the climate crisis may involve a level of disorientation and conceptual loss, precisely because this crisis has the potential of engendering a future so vastly different as to make the lives of our descendants ungraspable to us—and, perhaps, to them. But even if it were possible to predict such eventual disorientation, it does not follow that radical hope would be the right response for us *now*. In fact, we could easily imagine radical hope as being the *wrong* response entirely. For instance, there are those who believe, with great subjective conviction, that the fight against climate catastrophe has already been lost, and instead of continuing the struggle we should 'accept that disaster is coming, and begin to rethink what it means to have hope'; that 'we're doomed' and should 'learn to die in the Anthropocene.'[66]

If a case might (tenuously) be made that such gestures of radical resignation are also manifestations of radical hope—to the extent that they see the crisis as insurmountable and seek different outlets for virtuous action[67]—a case can also be made that such responses are deeply misguided. This is, first and foremost, because they misunderstand the nature of the problem posed by climate change. Unlike one-off disasters like meteors falling on earth—which is the incredibly unhelpful but stubbornly persistent metaphor for the climate crisis—the latter is not the kind of catastrophe that is immediate or total. Barring complete extinction, the fight against climate change 'will *never be lost*,' to repeat the words of David Wallace-Wells—'because however warm the planet gets, it will always be the case that the decade that follows could contain more suffering or less.'[68]

This is the great but wholly unappreciated risk of 'now or never' narratives, repeated across the board by the staunchest advocates of climate action, who fail to realise that while the 'now' of the slogan is justified, the 'never' is not. While it is crucially important to emphasise the importance of acting *now*— because actions taken in this decade have a greater ability to prevent catastrophic suffering than actions in later ones—this does not mean that if we do not act *now*, we can rest by acting *never*. Even if climate targets come and go, even if deadlines are missed and political promises broken, even after points of no return are passed, we will still have reason to continue to do what we can, because the disaster is not one that is ever complete and it is our duty to prevent what suffering we can. To opt for resignation in this context is to opt for other people suffering for decades, even centuries to come—which is not a decision that can be made undemocratically, if it can be made at all.[69]

'And no matter how dark things may become, giving up will never be an option,' Thunberg reminds us. 'Because every fraction of a degree and every tonne of carbon dioxide will always matter. It will never be too late for us to save as much as we can possibly save.'[70] If anything, then, the slogan for climate activism should not be 'now or never' but 'now—and *forever*.'

In discussing the possibility of thinned-out versions of courage, Lear is quick to warn that 'there might be false simulacra of courage: cases in which an insistent and unresponsive "optimism" is at work, rather than an appropriate manifestation of hope.' This is exactly right—and it means steering clear of shallow optimism as well as false despair. As Lear also reminds us: 'To be a manifestation of courage, radical hope must be well deployed.'[71]

What makes such good deployment of radical hope a more remote possibility for us is that, unlike the Crow, we have no objective guarantor that our hopes are justified and rightly oriented on the good. Recall that Plenty Coups's hope was grounded in a supernatural source of knowledge about the future—a cosmic forecasting of imminent doom *combined* with a trust that, if they followed the 'divine guidance' offered in the dream-visions, 'they would survive.'[72] The trust of the entire community was rooted in these visions, which were collectively interpreted as a message of the spirit world.[73] These are not sources we can *collectively* draw on in a pluralistic global context, and so another of the questions that *Radical Hope* leaves open is precisely this: What would radical hope be like *without* being anchored in cosmic trust—that is, in *faith*? Charles Taylor is not sure this is even possible:

> Is this kind of radical hope really possible? Certainly, if one means a hope that we shall survive, or come through, or 'overcome,' even though one can't say in advance exactly what this will amount to. All religious hope, as well as much of our basic confidence in life, is of this form. But can this be sustained without some kind of formulated faith in something, whether religious or secular—faith in God, or in History, or in our own resources, or in human resilience? Of this I am less certain.[74]

In reconstructing Plenty Coups's reasons for radical hope, Lear explicitly includes the premise that 'God—*Ah-badt-dadt-deah*—is good.' It is on the basis of this commitment to 'God's transcendence and goodness' that Plenty Coups is committed 'to the idea that something good will emerge even if it outstrips my present limited capacity for understanding what that good is.' This is why the Crow could be confident that '*We shall get the good back*, though at the moment we can have no more than a glimmer of what that might mean.'[75] Their radical hope, therefore, was rooted in a robust conception of the good and fuelled by divine trust, directly revealed through dream-visions. It is unclear, in the absence of such collectively and objectively empowering faith, what such hope might look like. This is of course precisely the point—we don't know what radical hope will look like—and until we know this, we had better be cautious about recommending it as a practical moral stance.

This does not mean that radical hope will have no role to play in times to come. If it is indeed true that the future will be so unimaginably different that our conceptions of the good life cease to make sense to us—or to those who come after us—it may well be that committing ourselves to 'the bare idea *that something good will emerge*' remains the only possible avenue for warding off, perhaps not all despair, but the wrong kind of despair: the kind that paves the way for premature resignation and forestalls the possibility of a 'return to life.'[76] But *in this day and age*, radical hope, or even just indeterminate hope, should not be invoked too quickly to guide our moral and practical responses to a disaster that is still very much underway.

Because, at this point in time, we know exactly what to hope for. And we know what we have to do.

6

Blue Hope

In the difficult times we face, what more can I hope for than the power to exclude nothing and to learn to weave from strands of black and white one rope tautened to the breaking point?

—ALBERT CAMUS

IN THESE troubled times, these decades of ecological depletion and devastation, this age of floods and fires and heat ceilings that no one had thought possible, the popularity of hope is without parallel. You find it everywhere, in political slogans and film trailers as well as on the covers of books and magazines. 'Even in our own disenchanted days,' Terry Eagleton has noted, 'writers of dust-jacket copy regularly try to discern glimmers of hope in the darkest of fictions, presumably on the assumption that readers are likely to find excessive despondency too dispir-iting.'[1] And it is no different in the climate debate. For all the outcry about 'doomism', it is in fact hard to find any article or book about climate change that doesn't start or end with some reference to hope or optimism, or even these words in the title (for instance: *Hope Matters, Hope in Hell, The Book of Hope*, etc.).[2]

The phrase 'we must not despair', meanwhile, is repeated so many times that one wonders if there is not something of despair in this: as if the more loudly we clamour forth 'the voice of hope', the more our desperation shows.

The concerns are twofold. On the side of media producers, the worry seems to be that if climate change reporting is too gloomy or depressing, readers will stop reading and viewers stop viewing, as weariness sets in. On the side of writers and campaigners, there is a common fear (and sometimes an accusation) that if we are confronted with too much 'doom and gloom' we will be deflated, we will 'just give up'. 'Please believe that, against all odds, we can win out,' Jane Goodall writes, 'because if you don't believe that, you will lose hope, sink into apathy and despair—and do nothing.'[3]

Such fears are not entirely unfounded: the spectre of fatalism or apathy does sometimes take very real forms, and when it does we are right to be concerned. But these are shadows that haunt the steps of optimism as well as those of pessimism, and sometimes in more pernicious forms.

As I have argued, the view that pessimism is the same as giving up is simply mistaken: in fact pessimism and activism are perfectly compatible, and sometimes they are an especially powerful combination. And I have suggested that in countering the perceived threat of fatalism one can bend too far to the other side, not only rejecting any kind of pessimism but endorsing a narrative of hope that is almost indistinguishable from optimism. This move is not only ill founded but potentially irresponsible: in (over)stressing the case for hope we risk overburdening activists by adding to the heavy load of battling the climate crisis the additional burden of proclaiming their hopefulness at all costs.

Now, I will argue that the orientation on hope is not altogether mistaken—much of this book is a defence of one kind of hope against another—but there is a danger in the way many have come to use hope as a stopgap, as a glossy finish, to make their views more palatable to the public. Take, for instance, the discovery of hope's appeal by politicians. This use of hope as 'a politically useful stimulant' has a long lineage: in the Augustan age the Roman emperors did not hesitate to employ hope or *spes* for ideological and political reasons.[4] But the most famous recent use of hope was during the Obama presidential campaign, which featured posters with the one-word slogan of 'Hope' (or, alternatively, 'Progress' or 'Change'), and was later followed by Obama's book *The Audacity of Hope* (a phrase he borrowed from Jeremiah Wright, who was in turn inspired by Watts's painting).[5]

As a result, hope is usually associated with liberal or progressive politics: thus literary scholar Adam Potkay traces the political use of hope back to the French Revolution and its optimistic aspirations for a remade world.[6] But on further scrutiny, this connection is not so clear, as conservatives have equally made use of hope. As Ronald Reagan said in his acceptance speech for the Republican presidential candidacy in 1980: 'For those who have abandoned hope, we'll restore hope and we'll welcome them into a great national crusade to make America great again.'[7] Similarly Eagleton has commented that 'optimism is a typical component of ruling-class ideologies' and quotes an American historian who remarked that '"presidential inaugural speeches are always optimistic whatever the times."'[8]

Those in the UK may remember Boris Johnson's triumphant first speech as prime minister, when he set himself up as a heroic visionary against the 'pessimists' who dared to question the wisdom of Brexit: 'the doubters, the doomsters, the gloomsters— they are going to get it wrong again.'[9] What some have called the 'hope bug' was picked up by his successors.[10] After the astounding turmoil in UK politics of autumn 2022, which ended in the resignation of Liz Truss and succession by Rishi Sunak, *both speeches* on the handover day of 25 October made sure to end on a hopeful note. Moments after Truss's resignation speech ended with her saying 'I know that brighter days lie ahead,'[11] Rishi Sunak closed *his* first speech as follows: 'We will create a future worthy of the sacrifices so many have made and fill tomorrow, and everyday thereafter with hope.'[12] A few weeks later, against the backdrop of a cost-of-living crisis and 'government forecasters predict[ing] the biggest drop in living standards since records began,' the new chancellor Jeremy Hunt in an interview about the bleak new budget twice spoke of giving 'hope' to families across the UK. 'I'm not pretending these aren't going to be difficult times,' he admitted to BBC's Chris Mason, 'but there's a plan, there's hope—and if we follow this plan, if we stick with it, we can get through to the other side.'[13]

These are just a few examples from recent political history, but they serve to show what the Romans knew long ago: that hope *sells* in politics—on both sides of the divide—and we should be suspicious of it as a piece of political rhetoric. Or if not suspicious, at least *cautious*. When confronted with hope in politics, we might do well to employ the kind of reservation with which Cornel West, who supported Barack Obama's presidential candidacy in 2008, gently but firmly cautioned him: 'It's unclear whether we're going to make it. I'm not an optimist at all. Brother Barack Obama says he has the audacity to hope. I say, "Well, what price are you willing to pay?"'[14] Obama's candidacy was indeed 'a source of hope,' West wrote. 'Yet hope is no guarantee. Real hope is grounded in a particularly messy struggle, and it can be betrayed by naïve projections of a better future that ignore the necessity of doing the real work.'[15] Similarly to Salvage's hesitation after the Corbyn leadership success, West warned against the temptation of optimism, or of unfettered hope: 'My deepest fear is that, we the people, now faced with the hard work required to advance societal transformation, could easily fall into a despair given the shattering of our high expectations of the Obama victory.'[16] Real, 'costly' hope is not a pleasant feeling or a simple state of mind: 'blood-stained and tear-soaked,' it proves itself only by its deeds.[17] *Hope must stand the test.*

But not all hopes do. That is to say: not all hopes are tested, and those that are don't always stand the test. This is as true in political debates as it is in the ongoing discussion on the psychology of the climate crisis. Here, too, it has become a staple of the discourse to end with a message of hope or optimism (recall that the two are not necessarily the same but are often used as if they were), and interviews with writers, scientists, and activists typically end with some variety of the question: *Are you still hopeful/optimistic?*

'Do you feel hopeful?' a *Guardian* reporter asked Naomi Klein.[18] 'How do you balance optimism and pessimism?' the *New Statesman* asked Björk and Greta Thunberg.[19] Sometimes, on the part of the interviewee, a hint of exasperation sets in. 'I have complicated feelings about the hope question,' Klein prefaced her response. And Thunberg: 'It feels like people are obsessed today with asking "Is there hope?"—because they feel that without it, they cannot act. In fact, it's the exact opposite: when they act, they create hope.'[20] 'As a climate scientist, I am often asked to talk about hope,' writes Kate Marvel. 'Particularly in the current political climate, audiences want to be told that everything will be all right in the end. And, unfortunately,

I have a deep-seated need to be liked and a natural tendency to optimism that leads me to accept more speaking invitations than is good for me. Climate change is bleak, the organizers always say. Tell us a happy story. Give us hope. The problem is, I don't have any.'[21]

They are right to be reluctant. As Thunberg especially keeps reminding us, the overuse of hope risks its trivialisation—precisely because it costs us so little. Constantly declaring or demanding hope is a little like overusing the word 'love' for things about which we feel lukewarm, at best. Inflation inevitably occurs. If we say 'love' or 'like' to everything, are we saying it to anything?

A case could be made that we've become far too used to pushing the hope button in our social, political, and ecological debates. This is why some politicians have come to treat hope as something they *may as well* use, as it comes cheap, and will package their message nicely—with the result that hope has become a mere piece of political rhetoric, rather than as the principle of sustained action that hope's advocates rightly think it could be. Ever perceptive, Thunberg has expressed concerns precisely about the way hope is used as a nice way to veneer noncommittal policies in lieu of acting:

'We can still do this,' the powerful voices of the Global North say in their tremendous struggle to maintain a system that has been proved flawed, incapable and doomed in more ways than we can possibly imagine. 'We pledge to be climate neutral by 2050,' they say, sending everyone back to sleep. If they were honest about hope being something we need, then they would immediately reduce their emissions for the benefit of the billions of people who are already being affected, and for their own children. But they are not being honest. *Instead they use hope as a powerful weapon to delay all necessary changes and prolong their business as usual.*[22]

We might call this *hopewashing*—a process whereby hope is used to package unpopular policies, to disguise inaction, or simply for some people to feel better about themselves. As Thunberg reminds us, 'hope is not about pretending that everything will be fine. It is not about sticking your head in the sand or listening to fairy tales about non-existent technological solutions. It's not about loopholes or clever accounting'—lest 'our desire to deliver this hope get in the way of taking action and therefore risk doing more harm than good.'[23]

This is not to say we should do away with hope altogether but that we should save it for when it matters: when we really need it, and when we know what it means to use it, what it commits us to. To counsel caution here is not to attack hope but to protect it. It is to remind ourselves that a truly, *deeply* hopeful message does not need to constantly declare itself as such, but that hope, like humility, is something that must proclaim itself by our actions, not by our statements about those actions. Above all, it is to distinguish hope as a pleasant feeling or emotion (one that is amenable to rhetorical sleights of hand) from hope as a hard-won virtue, carefully cultivated and appropriately linked to action.[24] 'Hope, to be enduring and well-founded, needs to be dearly bought,' as Terry Eagleton says in his discussion of Ernst Bloch's massive work on hope, 'whereas one problem with Bloch's universe is that the place is awash with the stuff.'[25] We might say the same of the oversaturation of our public discourse today, drenched as it is in pleas for hope and hopefulness, which threaten to drown out what hope there truly is.

For hope to be of lasting use to us, we need to save it from itself.

The Two Hopes: *Amdir* and *Estel*

In *The Book of Hope*, when Jane Goodall is asked to give an example of a truly hopeful story, she mentions J.R.R. Tolkien's trilogy *The Lord of the Rings*. 'What makes it such an appropriate story for the hopeless?' Douglas Abrams asks her. 'Because the might the heroes were up against seemed utterly invincible—the might of Mordor, the orcs, and the Black Riders on horses and then on those huge flying beasts,' Goodall replies, adding that this might provide us 'with a blueprint of how we survive and turn around climate change and loss of biodiversity, poverty, racism, discrimination, greed, and corruption.'[26] She is not the only one to draw inspiration from the novels in this way. In our cultural imaginaries, *The Lord of the Rings* is perhaps the prime example of a story encapsulating hope in the even darkest circumstances—to such an extent that it has become the paradigm for 'a literary and artistic movement that celebrates the pursuit of positive aims in the face of adversity': *hopepunk*.[27]

The latter term was coined in 2017 by fantasy writer Alexandra Rowland in response to the 'grimdark' of, for instance, George R. R. Martin's *Song of Ice and Fire* and *Game of Thrones* series. As Rowland stated on Tumblr: 'The opposite of grimdark is hopepunk. Pass it on.' In further posts she added that, to grimdark's view that 'the glass is half-empty' hopepunk replies that 'the glass is half full.'[28] 'Hopepunk says that kindness and softness doesn't equal weakness, and that in this world of brutal cynicism and nihilism, being kind is a political act. An act of rebellion.'[29] As a characteristic example she referred to the famous exchange between Sam and Frodo in the film version of *The Two Towers*, where Sam says that 'in the end, it's only a passing thing, this shadow. Even darkness must pass. A new day will come. And when the sun shines it will shine out the clearer. . . .

[T]here's some good in this world, Mr. Frodo. And it's worth fighting for.'[30] Though Rowland later modified her overly optimistic descriptions of hopepunk (especially the 'glass half full' metaphor), others still tend to associate the movement with 'radical optimism' or even (without reference to Lear) 'radical hope' and point to *The Lord of the Rings* as a typical example.[31]

This association of *The Lord of the Rings* with hopeful optimism is understandable: what tale could be more hopeful than that of 'two little hobbits, traveling into the heart of danger on their own'?[32] But what is little recognised is that hope, in the mythological universe underlying *The Lord of the Rings*, is itself a two-winged creature—and recognising this may well be crucial to understanding the story as a whole. This, at least, is the theory of classicist and Tolkien scholar Giuseppe Pezzini, who argues that the plot of *The Lord of the Rings* is centred on 'a clash of different hopes'—what the Elves call *Amdir* and *Estel*.[33]

Amdir (literally, 'looking up') is what is commonly called hope by Men: 'An expectation of good, which though uncertain has some foundation in what is known' (a definition not far from how philosophers such as Cicero and Aquinas described hope).[34] This is the kind of hope that rises when we point out rational grounds for hope, for instance on the basis of previous experiences or other types of evidence. There is a level of uncertainty involved in *Amdir* (or otherwise it wouldn't be hope), but there is also a level of probability, 'some foundation in what is known.' It is this hope, Pezzini argues, that the Fellowship of the Ring harbour at the start of the quest, when Gandalf is still alive: the errand is dangerous and difficult, but there is a reasonable chance of success. And when Gandalf is torn down by the Balrog of Moria—*it is this hope that dies*.[35]

Thus, when the Company leaves Moria after the catastrophe, Tolkien writes that 'they came *beyond hope* under the sky and felt the wind on their faces.'[36] Aragorn then cries in despair: 'Farewell Gandalf! . . . What hope have we without you?' And, turning to the Company: 'We must do without hope.'[37] If the Fellowship still continues, this is not because they still have the same hope they had before: there is a sense in which the quest is now truly hopeless. Instead, they must do 'without hope' and continue for other reasons: because there are some things that must be done or at least attempted, regardless of the consequences. As Aragorn later says in response to Gimli's comment that Gandalf's 'foresight failed him': 'The counsel of Gandalf was not founded on foreknowledge of safety, for himself or for others. . . . *There are some things that it is better to begin than to refuse, even though the end may be dark*.'[38] And as Frodo says to Sam in Mordor: 'I am tired, weary, I haven't a hope left. But I have to go on trying to get to the Mountain, as long as I can move.' And later, upon seeing the unsheltered lands that lie between them and Mount Doom: 'It's no worse than I expected. I never hoped to get across. I can't see any hope of it now. *But I've still got to do the best I can*.'[39] If Frodo and Sam were told to be hopeful, let alone optimistic, this would be to miss the point entirely: they, and the others, are to go on *without hope*.

At least, without hope of the usual kind: without what we humans would normally call hope—that is, *Amdir*. The perceptive reader or watcher will recall that, when the Fellowship reaches Lothlórien, some hope is rekindled through the Elven lady Galadriel, who tells them that 'even now there is hope left'; that 'hope remains while all the Company is true.'[40] But the question is whether this 'hope' is the same as the hope that died in Moria. For the Elves also speak of a different kind of hope, which goes by the name of *Estel*.

This hope (*Estel*; literally, 'trust') is 'founded deeper' than *Amdir* and is grounded in belief in Eru, the Creator. 'It is not defeated by the ways of the world, for it does not come from experience, but from our nature and first being,' as the Elven Finrod explains to the Wise-woman Andreth in their dialogue on death.[41] In Tolkien's own words, *Estel* is 'the trust in Eru, that whatever He designed beyond the End would be recognized by each *fëa* [soul or spirit] as wholly satisfying (at the least).'[42] It is a hope based on spiritual trust—that the One 'will not suffer Himself to be deprived of His own, not by any Enemy, not even by ourselves,' in Finrod's words. 'This is the last foundation of *Estel*, which we keep even when we contemplate the End: of all His designs the issue must be for His Children's joy.'[43]

Estel, then, is 'hope beyond hope': unlike *Amdir*, it is based not on expectation of outcome or on rational evidence but on trust in some higher power. Aragorn (whose Elven name is *Estel*) seems to recognise this when he accepts Frodo's decision to continue on his own: 'I do not think that it is our part to drive him one way or the other. Nor do I think that we should succeed, if we tried. *There are other powers at work far stronger.*'[44] And when Gandalf does return, Aragorn exclaims: '*Beyond all hope* you return to us in our need!'[45] According to Pezzini, the distinction between the two hopes is central to the plot of *The Lord of the Rings*, which hinges on a 'contrast of hopes': the loss of hope as commonly understood at Gandalf's fall (*Amdir*) followed by the fulfilment of 'hope beyond hope' by Gandalf's death and return (*Estel*).[46]

If this is right, then it would be a mistake to read *The Lord of the Rings* as *straightforwardly* a 'hopeful' story—insofar as our 'hope' typically designates *Amdir*, not *Estel*—let alone an exemplification of the worn-out cliché that the glass is 'half full'. There is an awareness throughout *The Lord of the Rings* that 'hope oft deceives'; and that worldly hopes may quickly falter ('hope died in his heart').[47] Frodo, at the end of the story, harbours no illusions: 'it's like things are in the world. Hopes fail. An end comes. We have only a little time to wait now. We are lost in ruin and downfall, and there is no escape.'[48] If he is eventually saved in one sense, he is not in another: 'I tried to save the Shire, and it has been saved, but not for me. It must often be so, Sam, when things are in danger: some one has to give them up, lose them, so that others may keep them.'[49] This is not at all a straightforward happy ending; the quest is completed, but the shadow remains.[50]

But what of Sam and Frodo's courageous journey into Mordor—is this not an exemplification of what sheer hope can do? Well, yes, but it depends, again, on what we mean by hope. As we have seen, Frodo is explicit about his commitment to continuing long after his hopes have failed: 'I've still got to do the best I can.' And there is a sense in which Frodo himself is 'doomed to failure,' as Tolkien himself put it: there is no way in which he could have completed the task by his own forces, and Frodo shows that he knows this.[51] His reason for continuing, again, is not hope in the usual way. It might not even be *Estel*. As Tolkien later explained to a reader, Frodo's errand was not to succeed in his task but simply to do what he can: 'His real contract was only to do what he could, to try to find a way, and to go as far on the road as his strength of mind and body allowed. He did that.'[52] It is not clear that this is even *Estel*, or rather a pure sense of duty: a sense, as the film version puts it, 'that there are things worth fighting for.' This is perhaps why, at the burial of Théoden, Gandalf renames Frodo not 'hope' or even 'hope beyond hope' but *Bronwe athan Harthad*: 'Endurance *beyond* hope.'[53]

As for Sam, the matter is more ambiguous still. Gandalf renames him *Harthad Uluithiad*, 'Hope unquenchable'—but Sam doesn't believe the new name suits, as there were times his 'hope [ran] low.'[54] By his own accounts, Sam is temperamentally inclined to *Amdir*,[55] but he finds this hope tested in Mordor—tested, and transformed. The famous exchange between Frodo and Sam in the film version of *The Two Towers* (considered paradigmatic for hopepunk) is based loosely on several passages in the novels, such as this one, in the darkness of Mordor:

> There, peeping among the cloud-wrack above a dark tor high up in the mountains, Sam saw a white star twinkle for a while. The beauty of it smote his heart, as he looked up out of the forsaken land, and hope returned to him. For like a shaft, clear and cold, the thought pierced him that in the end the Shadow was only a small and passing thing: *there was light and high beauty for ever beyond its reach.* His song in the Tower had been defiance rather than hope; for then he was thinking of himself. *Now, for a moment, his own fate, and even his master's ceased to trouble him.*[56]

This is hope, but no ordinary hope: Sam's heart is swept up by contemplation of a high goodness that is untouchable by the forces of darkness, and it overpowers the concerns he has for his and Frodo's fate. Without knowing anything about the higher powers glimpsed beyond the shadows, Sam is here letting go of *Amdir* and giving himself over to *Estel*.

To be precise, then, *The Lord of the Rings* is an *estel-ful* but not an *amdir-ful* story: an account not of plain hope conquering over fear and despair but of 'how *hope beyond hope* was fulfilled.'[57] This is closer to religious hope or even to Lear's radical hope than anything we would commonly recognise as hope—and, like radical hope, there is something unsettling about it. *Estel* is what Tolkien called a 'Hope without guarantees':[58] to trust in it is not to be confident of a good outcome but to sacrifice one's own will to higher powers—in the knowledge that what they decide may be very far from what mortal souls desire. And the question then arises whether this is the kind of hope we should be looking to in this crisis, this secular age.

Or perhaps we could take a somewhat different approach. Instead of choosing either *Amdir* or *Estel* (perhaps in a secularised version) as a model for hope, we could consider what it would be like for our hopes to be dual in the same way. Would it be possible to hold on to *Amdir* while supplementing it with something else, something along the lines of *Estel* though not (or not necessarily) religiously motivated—a hope that might sustain us even when our worldly hopes have failed? Might we speak, not of *Amdir* and *Estel*, but of green hope, and blue?

Green Hope

'Blue is the colour of hope,' said one of the first critics to comment on Watts's painting *Hope*—but he might have said the same of green.[59] Both colours have been historically associated with hope—and in the Christian tradition, it was green that had the upper hand. When the theological virtue of Hope dances with her sisters Faith and Love in Dante's *Purgatorio* she is distinguished by her green garb. If upon entering the gates of Hell *all hope must be abandoned*, it is not so in Purgatory, where no one is entirely lost beyond salvation 'as long as hope maintains a thread of green.'[60] Blue, from the twelfth century onwards, was similarly associated with hope, courage, and consolation—but also with grief and mourning, especially through its association with the Virgin Mary.[61] Of course we cannot draw conclusions from such historical connotations; after all, green has also been associated with envy, and blue with deep sadness ('the blues'). But it can perhaps be said that when Watts painted *Hope* for a second time, changing the colours from mostly green to mostly blue, the meaning of the painted changed as well. In giving us two perspectives of the same scene, it is almost as if he were showing us two faces, two modes of hope (see plate 1 for the first, 'green' version and the book cover for the second, 'blue' version).

These two modes can also be sensed in the way hope is invoked today. It will be clear by now that most calls for hope are carried out in a specific register. The common strategy is to demand we focus on positive accounts (which are described as 'hope-giving', 'hopeful'), success stories, small victories, achievable goals and solutions, and maintain throughout a positive and upbeat tone—while rejecting the 'doom and gloom' of 'overly' negative information, which supposedly pave the way for despair and defeatism.[62]

Let's call this *green hope*. Such hope is characterised by its focus on rational 'grounds for hope', for instance in recent success stories and concrete reasons to expect change, and by its expectation of positive outcomes. As such it is strongly reminiscent of what Tolkien called *Amdir*: 'An expectation of good, which though uncertain has some foundation in what is known.' It is hope based on evidence, hope as expectancy. While green hope usually distances itself from optimism (with some exceptions),[63] in fact it is continuous with it—both are mostly carried out in the same register of cheerful confidence and tend to share the same assumptions about the importance of positive thinking. The difference between green hope and optimism, then, is really just a difference of degree: they are not the same, but they tend to operate on the same spectrum.

Now, let's get one thing absolutely clear: there is nothing wrong in principle with expressing or advocating such hope—as long as the hoper stops at this and doesn't make it a moral failing if others are unable to express hope in this way. But many advocates of such hope go further still. Instead of simply making the case for green hope, they constantly declaim the warning that exposing oneself to negative information and 'doomism' will lead to despair, depression, and deflation. The discourse has become *highly moralistic*, as if it is a moral failing not to espouse or express green hope, even if a person might feel there is little ground for it. Again, to some extent this tendency of green hope to overstate its case is understandable—especially considering the fact there are those among us who say it is 'too late' and we may as well give up the fight, which anyhow has 'already been lost'. But it is also deeply problematic, as it adds an emotional burden of responsibility to those already weighed by down the awareness of an unprecedented crisis. Beyond this, there is a real risk attached to the green hope narrative. After all, if such hopes are defeated again and again—if one day we run out of positive stories or if the negative information given not just by anyone but by *climate scientists* becomes impossible to balance with good news—what conclusion is then to be drawn?

On the logic of many (though not all) green hope advocates, the necessary consequence would be to give up the fight, since a narrative that bets everything on positive forecasts leaves no basis for action other than the evidence-based confidence in success. But that logic is itself just a hypothesis: it's not a law of nature. It may even get things the wrong way round. If the loss of hope results in despair, does that tell us we must always be hopeful—or that there is a risk in raising our hopes too high?

This is a question touched on by the Jewish Austrian psychotherapist Viktor Frankl (1905–97) in his astounding book *Man's Search for Meaning*, a work often cited as making the case for maintaining hope even in the darkest of times. Frankl was imprisoned in Auschwitz during World War II, made it out alive (though losing most of his family), and later drew from his experiences to formulate the psychological theory of logotherapy, which places not pleasure or power but *meaning* at the centre of human existence and psychotherapy. His book *Man's Search for Meaning* recounts his experiences in the camps and tries to show that even in these most terrible conditions 'it was possible for spiritual life to deepen.'[64]

Frankl also discusses the danger of utter hopelessness—the losing of the will to live—which gave rise to suicides and other deaths. 'The prisoner who had lost faith in the future—his future—was doomed,' Frankl writes. 'With his loss of belief in the future, he also lost his spiritual hold; he let himself decline and became subject to mental and physical decay.'[65] As an example he describes his fellow prisoner 'F', who had a dream in February 1945 that the camp would be liberated on 30 March 1945. Frankl says that when F told him the dream 'he was still full of hope and convinced that the voice of his dream would be right.' But as the promised date drew closer, it seemed increasingly less likely that the dream would come true. On 29 March F fell ill, and by 31 March he was dead, supposedly from typhus, but in reality (says Frankl) from 'the sudden loss of hope and courage,' which affected F's bodily resilience. 'The ultimate cause of my friend's death was that the expected liberation did not come and he was severely disappointed.' Frankl believes this was also the reason for higher death rates at the end of the year, as 'the majority of the prisoners had lived in the naïve hope that they would be home again by Christmas. As the time drew near and there was no encouraging news, the prisoners lost courage and disappointment overcame them.'[66]

Now, on a first reading of such passages, their message may seem clear: hope must be maintained at all costs, lest we give in to despair and defeat. But on a closer look, the matter is much less straightforward. On Frankl's account, what drove his fellow prisoners to despair was not the absence of hope—but the sudden *disappointment* that followed from having set their hopes too high. While it is certainly true that Frankl warns against the danger of losing hope, he equally warns against the danger of 'harboring false illusions and entertaining artificial optimism.' As he elsewhere puts it, there were some who 'lost all hope, but it was the incorrigible optimists who were the most irritating companions.'[67] It is not clear, on this account, which is the greater danger: having too high hopes, or having no hope at all.

A similar confusion haunts the proponents of green hope. We hear a lot about the dangers of burnout and disillusionment, but the question raised by Frankl remains undiscussed. Are such burnouts an effect of having too little hope—or of having had one's hopes raised *too high*?[68]

Again, there is nothing wrong in principle with drawing inspiration from previous victories—but green advocates should not suggest that these are the *only* grounds for hope, or that sustained action is impossible without them. They should, moreover, be aware of the risk involved of overstating the case for hope and making hope hinge purely on empirical success. After all, if such evidence-based hope wears thin—if the darker side of things becomes impossible to ignore—how then should we respond? One common strategy is to say: we must then find *more* evidence for hope, as the only alternative is giving up. This is why some journalists now argue that the media should report more positive news, not in order to give both sides of the story or because it is objectively relevant but in order 'to give people hope'; not as a mode of faithful reporting but as 'a defiant way of being in the world.'[69]

But a different response is possible. Namely, that to hope in this way is not the point, or not the only point: that we have reasons to continue the struggle not because there is hope of success *but because it is the right thing to do*.

What might such hope look like?

Blue Hope

In 1985, just four years before becoming the last president of Czechoslovakia (and after that, the first president of the newly founded Czech Republic), the Czech playwright and activist Václav Havel was asked whether he saw 'a grain of hope anywhere in the 1980s.' The question gave him pause. At the time, Czechoslovakia was still locked in a repressive regime, and Havel himself had only recently been released from a four-year imprisonment for his political activism (1979–83). But the reason for his hesitation was not that he thought the situation hopeless: rather, he wanted to be clear on what hope really means. And so, before answering the absent journalist's question (absent because Karel Hvížďala was living in West Germany, Havel in Prague, and they could not visit each other),[70] Havel first offered a distinction between two kinds of hope: hope as 'a state of the world,' or oriented on consequences in the world; and hope as 'a state of mind,' grounded in a deep inner experience, having to do rather with 'the certainty that something makes sense, regardless of how it turns out.' The latter is what Havel regards as hope. 'Hope is not prognostication. It is an orientation of the spirit, an orientation of the heart; it transcends the world that is immediately experienced, and is anchored somewhere beyond its horizons.' Such hope should not at all depend on 'some favorable signs in the world' but has 'its deepest roots' elsewhere, in what Havel calls 'the transcendental.' He continues:

> Hope, in this deep and powerful sense, is not the same as joy that things are going well, or willingness to invest in enterprises that are obviously headed for early success, but, rather, *an ability to work for something because it is good, not just because*

it stands a chance to succeed. The more unpropitious the situation in which we demonstrate hope, the deeper that hope is. Hope is definitely not the same thing as optimism. It is not the conviction that something will turn out well, but *the certainty that something makes sense, regardless of how it turns out.*[71]

Having explained his own conception of hope, he does, then, answer Hvížďala's question about the state of the world—but as a question entirely separate from that of hope, 'this deep, inner hope that is not dependent on prognoses.'[72]

What Havel describes is clearly hope. But it could hardly be further removed from the green hope that does depend on 'prognoses about possible outcome[s].'[73] This is a hope that sounds much more like Tolkien's *Estel* than *Amdir*—and indeed in his earlier *Letters to Olga*, written from prison, he speaks of 'faith and hope' as if they are the same.[74]

Both faith and hope are to be sharply distinguished from optimism, or 'the belief that "everything will turn out well"'—which Havel thinks is 'a dangerous illusion': 'I don't know how "everything" will turn out and therefore I have to admit the possibility that everything—or at least most things—will turn out badly.' But such expectations are beside the point, as faith (or hope) 'does not depend on prognoses about possible outcome[s].' In contrast to optimism, genuine faith 'does not draw its energy from some particular reality or assumption, on whose existence it is utterly dependent and with whose loss it would collapse like a pricked balloon.' Instead it is 'an intrinsic "state of the spirit," a profound "existential dimension," an inner direction that you either have or don't have, and which—if you have it—raises your entire existence onto a kind of higher level of Being.'[75]

Such language, and the mention of hope and faith side by side, sounds religiously oriented—and yet Havel is adamant that this hope is not dependent on religious belief: 'The most convinced materialist and atheist may have more of this genuine, transcendentally rooted inner hope ... than ten metaphysicians together.'[76] What characterises it, instead of a narrow focus on 'prognoses' of outcomes or success, is that it acknowledges the uncertainty of any future and shifts our attention instead on meaning and value. As such it is closely aligned with the vision offered by Viktor Frankl, who likewise rejects 'artificial optimism', arguing instead that the point is not to believe at all costs that everything will be all right in the end but to have *a reason for living*:

> What was really needed was a fundamental change in our attitude toward life. We had to learn ourselves and, furthermore, we had to teach the despairing men, that *it did not really matter what we expected from life, but rather what life expected from us.* We needed to stop asking about the meaning of life, and instead to think of ourselves as those who were being questioned by life—daily and hourly. Our answer must consist, not in talk and meditation, but *in right action and in right conduct.* Life ultimately means taking the responsibility to find the right answer to its problems and to fulfil the tasks which it constantly sets for each individual.[77]

And it is allied to Cornel West's articulation of 'blues hope' or tragicomic hope, which is again sharply distinguished from optimism but also from inadequate forms of hope—that is, from hopes that *have not stood the test.* 'When you talk about hope, you have to be a long distance runner,' West tells us. 'This is again so very difficult in our culture, because the quick fix, the overnight solution militate against being a long distance runner in the moral sense—the sense of fighting *because it is right, because it is moral, because it is just.*' Activism for global and racial justice must be aimed at justice rather than victory: 'You do the right thing regardless of the consequence—because you want to be a decent and compassionate person before you die!'[78]

These are all examples, from very different contexts, of what I will call *blue hope*: a hope that is not oriented on outcomes in the way that green hope is but finds its value in commitment regardless of effect. As even these examples show, articulations of such blue hope can differ greatly—just as there can be many different shades and tones of blue, some warmer than others, some darker, some deeper—and yet they have enough in common to let us recognise them for what they are.

The first of such 'family resemblances' has to do with a recognition of openness, or uncertainty. While green hope seeks to instil a sense of confidence in the future, based on evidential 'grounds for hope', blue hope draws its strength rather from the fact that the future is uncertain. This is the point made even by that often-cited 'optimist' Karl Popper, who in fact was adamant that 'I am *not* an optimist regarding the future.' According to Popper, future-oriented optimism ignores the fact that '*the future is open*. There is no historical law of progress. We do not know what tomorrow will be like. There are billions of possibilities, good and bad, that no one can foresee.' Popper rejects not only future-oriented optimism but *any* prognoses about the future based on past experiences: 'We should not try at all to derive trends and directions from the past in order to make predictions about the future. *For the future is open. Anything can happen.*'[79] And this uncertainty should free us to focus not on what is likely to happen but on what is right to do.

Thus, whereas green hope (*Amdir*) draws its strength from what we know, blue hope draws its strength precisely from what we *don't* know: from the sheer fact that, as George Perkins Marsh once put it, 'The future is more uncertain than the past.'[80]

This is an attitude that can be infused with religious or spiritual faith, as it was in *Estel*, but it need not be filled with anything at all: mere openness is enough. As Rebecca Solnit puts it, in one of her 'bluer' modes: 'We don't know what is going to happen, or how, or when, and that very uncertainty is the space of hope.'[81] She cites Virginia Woolf, who wrote in 1915: 'The future is dark, which is on the whole, the best thing the future can be, I think.'[82] This perspective, says Solnit, produces 'an entirely different sort of hope: that you possess the power to change the world to some degree or just that the world is going to change again, and uncertainty and instability thereby become grounds for hope.'[83] So too Terry Eagleton has noted: 'There is hope as long as history lacks closure. If the past was different from the present, so may the future be.'[84]

This attitude, based on openness and uncertainty rather than evidence and probability, is also the hope expressed by the pessimists of old. As Julien Offray de La Mettrie put it in the eighteenth century, 'everything is always changing, all things are subject to vicissitude; the happiest are not always in their pleasure, the miserable not always in calamity.' Even on the loveliest day, a cloud may rob us of the sun; even on the darkest night, a star reappear to rekindle joy in our hearts. And this very changefulness, *for better and for worse*, this itself is hope.[85] Or as Schopenhauer wrote, imagining an earth-spirit descending among us to show us all the rise and fall of history: 'In this world of the phenomenon, true loss is as little possible as is true gain.' For reality is never exhausted of possibilities, and 'undiminished infinity is still always open for the return of any event or work that was nipped in the bud.'[86] If the idea of invincible progress is ridiculous, so too is the idea of inevitable decline.

Such uncertainty may be the despair of optimism, but it is the hope of pessimism. And yet there is a double side to it. Accepting

radical uncertainty is as much a cause for fear as it is for hope—
and any blue hope worth its while fully recognises this. If, as Schopenhauer noted, 'true loss is as little possible as is true gain,' that
equally means that true gain is as little possible as true loss: everything may change for the better, but also, at any time, everything
may change for the worse. 'The truth that the custodians of cheerfulness cannot stomach is that as long as there is contingency,
there is the possibility of permanent failure,' writes Eagleton, adding immediately: 'And, to be sure, the possibility of mind-shaking
advances as well.'[87] As even Popper noted, 'The possibilities lying
within the future, *both good and bad*, are boundless.'[88]

Thus, while it is true that 'the context for hope is radical uncertainty,'[89] this is not a space in which one can ever be at ease.
This is why blue hope is a restless hope—a hope that can and
often does go hand in hand with despair. As Cornel West wrote
in the context of the ongoing fight against racism and injustice:

Those who have never despaired have neither lived nor loved.
Hope is inseparable from despair. Those of us who truly hope
make despair a constant companion whom we outwrestle
every day owing to *our commitment to justice, love, and hope.* It
is impossible to look honestly at our catastrophic conditions
and not have some despair—it is a healthy sign of how deeply
we care. It is also a mark of maturity—a rejection of cheap
American optimism.[90]

There is, then, something unsettling about this hope that is so
unlike the upward-looking and cheerful guise of either leaf-green
hope or gilded optimism. What West calls 'a costly hope, an
earned hope, a blues-inflected hope that grapples with despair' is
a hope that knows it can always be defeated, but as it does not
depend on outcomes it won't disintegrate on this. This is close to
what the existentialist philosopher Gabriel Marcel called 'abso-

lute hope', insisting that 'hope (one cannot repeat too often) can only take root where perdition is a possibility.'[91] As Eagleton comments: 'Such hope acknowledges the realities of failure and defeat, but refuses to capitulate in the face of them and preserves an unspecified, nonpurposive openness to the future.'[92]

Blue hope, then, is fundamentally based not on probability or evidence but on openness and uncertainty—on the fact that, as Eagleton quotes Epicurus, 'the future is neither wholly ours nor wholly not ours.'[93] Such hope may not seem very useful in specific situations such as the climate crisis, where we do clearly have a lot of information and prognoses about the future, many of them dire, so that the natural question is how we should respond to such negative information. But the point is that, while it is crucially important to recognise the expectations and prognoses that scientists present to us, our response does not have to be framed in the same terms. We don't have to offset dark scenarios with positive stories or 'reasons for hope', as if some things are worth doing only when we're confident of their success. No: some things are worth doing because we recognise our duty to our fellow humans, fellow creatures, future generations, and ourselves. All we need to reject is fatalism: all we need is the 'radical uncertainty' that is the space for hope.[94]

'It had to be done'

This brings us to a second characteristic of blue hope: its orientation, not on whether the matter is likely to succeed but *on whether it's worth doing*. Such hope, as Havel told us, is 'not the conviction that something will turn out well, but the certainty that something makes sense, regardless of how it turns out.'[95] When Viktor Frankl gave hope to his fellow prisoners in Auschwitz, it was not by telling them to hope for rescue against all odds but by a shift in perspective: 'They must not lose hope but should keep their courage in the certainty that the hopelessness of our struggle did not detract from its dignity and its meaning.'[96] And Cornel West seeks to inspire full-hearted activism not by optimistic rallies but a 'turning of the soul', a shift of attention 'toward truth, justice, compassion, and service.'[97]

This is a tendency we have encountered several times before, for instance in the desperate resistance of the Warsaw ghetto insurgents, which was founded not on the concrete hope of success but on the value beyond reckoning of *the cause itself*. If one thing is clear from such accounts it is that there is something in matters of great importance that *compels the will*—something that cuts through all consideration of outcome or effect. What still matters, even at the zero point of the most desperate resistance, is not whether 'we can' do this but that *we must do this*. This is what Brossat and Klingberg write of Jewish Resistance fighters, who 'committed themselves to the Resistance without hesitation, in a movement that was quite natural, "*because it had to be done*", and they acted anonymously, rarely with any glamour, and with their existence constantly in peril.' They cite Janine Sochachewska, one of the leaders of the Jewish resistance in Lyon during the Nazi occupation in World War II: 'I was young, I was strong, *I had a moral strength as never before.*' And they cite a Jewish man from eastern Europe, who said shortly before his arrest in 1943: 'I only did *what had to be done*; if more people in this country had done as much, the situation would have been quite different.'[98]

I had to do it; it had to be done. These are words that occur throughout history, and across different contexts, from political resistance in the face of oppression to environmental activism. Thus, when Jane Goodall describes her activism on behalf of chimpanzees who were being cruelly treated in laboratories, she frames her decision not in terms of hopefulness or confidence but of sheer duty, in spite of the odds: 'Probably if I'd really thought it through I would never have tried. But having seen those videos of the chimps in the labs—well, I was so upset and angry that *I just knew I had to try*. For the sake of the chimps.' Several times she repeats this phrase: 'I knew *I had to try* . . . I just knew *I had to do something*. I didn't know what or how— only that just doing nothing was not an option. . . . I felt *I had to go*.'⁹⁹ So too Vanessa Nakate writes of her choice to become a climate activist almost as if it wasn't a choice at all: 'I began to feel like I *had* to become a climate activist.'¹⁰⁰

This is not green hope, fuelled by confidence that success is possible: it is a blue hope powered instead by a sense of justice; a deep certainty that *it had to be done*. When such a conviction, such 'moral strength' compels the will, it is no longer relevant to what extent the matter is achievable: all that matters is that we know where our duty lies. As Frodo said in Mordor: 'I never hoped to get across. I can't see any hope of it now. But I've still got to do the best I can.'

It is this blue hope that lies behind Greta Thunberg's refusal to offer us 'hopeful' stories, insisting instead that we see the 'climate and sustainability crisis' as 'the ultimate moral test'; 'if we fail that moral test, then we will fail all else too.' What is crucial for meeting this challenge is not that we be subjectively hopeful or optimistic about our chances but that we hold to the values of 'honesty, solidarity, integrity and climate justice.'¹⁰¹ This is also the point made by writer Amitav Ghosh, who acknowledges that the 'picture is grim' but insists that 'action shouldn't be framed around hope and despair, but around duty. *It is our duty to do what we can for the future*.'¹⁰² Such responses seem to rec-ognise that to bolster action even in the face of sustained defeat, a different hope is needed: a restless, hard-won hope that is focused less on outcomes or prognoses and rather on questions of value—on what is *right* and *good* to strive for. This is the point made by writer and activist John Jordan in an email to Rebecca Solnit:

> If all is uncertain, if uncertainty is the only certainty, then the uprooted, the fragile, those that crave something to give them meaning in their lives, simply get washed away by the flood and flux of an unsure universe. For them, hope is often found in certainty. Not necessarily certainty rooted in a predictable future, but *certainty that they are doing the right thing with their lives*.[103]

In blue hope we find the recognition of fundamental uncertainty coupled with a deep and different kind of certainty: the certainty of having done the right thing.

None of this means that activists—by which I mean *all who wish to act for a certain cause*—should not care about outcomes or results.[104] Not only would this be callous and silly, but it would be inconsistent: to care about a cause necessitates a wish for one's efforts to be fruitful, and that means to choose one's actions wisely, precisely because the cause demands it. But the point of blue hope is that the drive for action doesn't hinge on results or expectations—its orientation is elsewhere, on justice and duty, and the rightness of the cause.

What this means is that this is not the kind of hope that is easily disappointed—because action founded on value and commitment can create the kind of endurance needed in order to be 'a long distance runner in the moral sense'—out of a sense that some things are worth fighting for.[105] And ironically, precisely because it is not dependent on outcomes in the short run, such hope may lead to better outcomes in the long run. As the former Archbishop of Canterbury Rowan Williams has said to young environmental activists:

> You may not succeed in averting climate disaster. What you can do is live more truthfully and honestly today. And the catch is, if you live more truthfully and honestly today, then probably you have a better contribution to make to averting climate disaster. In other words, if you see it simply as a problem-solving exercise, you may well be overcome by frustration, disillusion, even despair. If you see it as something which ought to flow naturally from your own attempt to live more truthfully, more in the light of reality—well then who knows what might be possible?[106]

Hope without Expectancy

No hope is certain about the future, or it would not be hope. But green hope is confident, expectant; its message is that *we can do it*.[107] Blue hope is confident, too, but not about the future: its message is that *we have to try*, regardless of our chances. If green hope is future-oriented, blue hope is value-oriented: it is focused on goods such as justice and duty rather than an expectation of results.[108] That does not mean, however, that blue hope is, like radical hope, indeterminate: we can still know exactly what we are hoping for while being oriented on value instead of outcome.[109] And both hopes, if rightly founded, will have as their beating core a readiness for action. In China Miéville's words: 'We must learn to hope with teeth.'[110] Hope without commitment is a hope not worth having; whether blue or green, it has to stand the test.

The distinctions between these hopes are not sharp but fluid, gradual, just like green flows into blue. As a result, it may sometimes be unclear if we're looking at one hope or the other—and that is fine. Your blue may not be my blue, but most of the time we still know what we mean with blue or green. There can be degrees of either, and combinations of both. Thunberg's hope, like that of Havel and West and many activists in the global south, is a deep, deep blue. Goodall's hope is mostly green, but sometimes the blue shines through—for instance when she writes about the 'indomitable human spirit,' which 'makes us tackle what seems impossible and never give up. Despite the odds, despite the scorn or mocking of others, despite possible failure.'[111] *Hopepunk* blushed green before flushing blue: 'It's not about glory or noble deeds; it's not about an end result because *there is no end*.'[112] Solnit alternates between the two. When she writes that hope is based on uncertainty, 'an embrace of the essential unknowability of the world, of the breaks with the present, the surprises,' her hope is blue. But when she grounds hope on positive stories or pits hope against 'gloom' and 'the teddy bear of despair,' her hope is green.[113]

I want to repeat that to open up a space for blue hope does not mean this hope is better than the green. There is nothing wrong with expressing green hope or drawing inspiration from hopeful stories about past successes, as long as we then put that hope to work: 'hope should shove you out the door.'[114] But in darkening times, when the evidential grounds for hope run thin—when green hope's reasons fail us—we have to be able to fall back on a different and more sustainable kind of hope: a hope that is oriented not on positive prognoses but on the moral conviction of the just; a hope strangely close to hopelessness.

In *The Lord of the Rings*, when Sam realises he and Frodo will not make it back alive from Mount Doom, he loses hope, and in the losing unlocks a different kind of strength:

But even as hope died in Sam, or seemed to die, it was turned
to a new strength. Sam's plain hobbit-face grew stern, almost
grim, as the will hardened in him, and he felt through all his
limbs a thrill, as if he was turning into some creature of stone
and steel that neither despair nor weariness nor endless bar-
ren miles could subdue.[115]

This is not *Amdir*, perhaps not even *Estel*: it is a sort of hardened
will, a strength of sheer resolve that has shed all resemblance of
green hope; if it is still hope, then it is dark, dark blue.

Was this the blue Watts had in mind when he repainted *Hope*
in darker tones? 'I do not think I am pessimistic,' he said in reply
to a question about the meaning of *Hope*, which some thought
seemed closer to despair. 'Hope need not mean expectancy. It
suggests here rather the music which can come from the remaining chord.'[116] The hope of the painting, then, is a *hope without expectancy*. It is a blue register of hope, one that remains
open even in extreme uncertainty and at the final desolation—a
hope compatible with grief, pain, fear, and all the sorrows of a
darkened age.

PART III

Our Ladies of Sorrow

7

Our Lady of Tears

ON GRIEF

But your heart was deeper than the Danube; and, as was your love, so was your grief.

—THOMAS DE QUINCEY

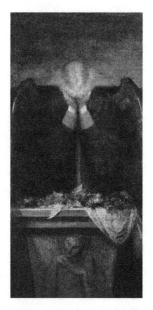

FIGURE 6. G. F. Watts, *A Dedication* (*To all those who love the beautiful and mourn over the senseless and cruel destruction of bird life and beauty*), 1898–99; see plate 2. © Watts Gallery Trust.

IN HIS essay collection *Suspiria de Profundis* of 1845, the English writer Thomas De Quincey looks back at his life and at the sorrows he has known—from his childhood grief at the death of his sister to his later trials of addiction and despair. He recalls that, as a student in Oxford, he often saw Levana, the Roman goddess of childbirth, in his dreams. This he understands: for any gods who watched over a child at birth would continue to watch as it grows and is besieged 'by passion, by strife, by temptation, by the energies of resistance'—and by grief. For while some may think that children are not liable to deep grief, De Quincey knows it is not so: many sorrows of life may fade, but not 'the deep deep tragedies of infancy.'[1] This is why he used to see Levana conversing with her 'ministers', who like the Graces and the Furies are three: three mythological sisters who govern the realm of sadness and despair. 'These are the Sorrows, all three of whom I know.' Together, the sisters stand as guardians and witnesses over our human trials, but also as the bearers of unexpected gifts and consolation.

But what to call them? 'I want a term expressing the mighty abstractions that incarnate themselves in all individual sufferings of man's heart; and I wish to have these abstractions presented as impersonations, that is, as clothed with human attributes of life, and with functions pointing to flesh.' He suggests that we call them 'Our Ladies of Sorrow'—'I know them thoroughly, and have walked in all their kingdoms.'[2] Well-acquainted with the Three, De Quincey knows that the Ladies do not speak themselves—'eternal silence reigns in *their* kingdoms'—but they may speak through humans, and through the signs they leave in nature. Having read their symbols, De Quincey lets them speak through him, hoping thereby to give words to an experience that is otherwise ineffable.[3]

De Quincey did not know what it meant to mourn our fellow species; to mourn the future; to mourn the world. But he knew what it was to grieve, to suffer, to despair. He would have understood that to live in the age of climate breakdown is to live in an age of sorrow. And that to acknowledge this is not the same as giving up or accepting defeat: it is to recognise that there is so much to grieve for—so much 'that we are losing and have lost.'⁴

In this final part of the book, I suggest we take inspiration from De Quincey and from the voices he brings to us—Our Lady of Tears, Our Lady of Sighs, Our Lady of Darkness—and cautiously, tenderly, imagine what it might be for us to welcome the darker feelings born of this time as hope's shadow-sisters: as companions on the road ahead.⁵

Grief and Mourning

The eldest of the Three is '*Mater Lachrymarum*, Our Lady of Tears.' She is the lady of grief and sadness; 'She it is that night and day raves and moans, calling for vanished faces.' She stands with parents at the loss of a child; she stood in Bethlehem 'on the night when Herod's sword swept its nurseries of Innocents.' 'Her eyes are sweet and subtle, wild and sleepy by turns; oftentimes rising to the clouds; oftentimes challenging the heavens.' She carries keys that 'open every cottage and every palace,' as no one is secure from grief and loss. 'By the power of her keys it is that Our Lady of Tears glides a ghostly intruder into the chambers of sleepless men, sleepless women, sleepless children, from Ganges to the Nile, from Nile to Mississippi.' But grief can burn with anger, and she is often 'stormy and frantic; raging in the highest against heaven; and demanding back her darlings.' Her reign is universal, stretching across all times and all nations; first and foremost of the Three, we might call her the 'Madonna.'[6]

As De Quincey reminds us, every age is an age of grief—but there are differences in how we grieve, and why. Half a century after De Quincey whispered into being Our Lady of Tears, G. F. Watts was approached by Etta Lemon and Eliza Phillips (cofounders of the Royal Society for the Protection of Birds) to produce an artwork in support of their campaign against the annual killing of millions of birds for 'trimmings and decorations alone.'[7] Watts poured the grief of many into a painting of an angel weeping over a tomb of blue feathers—birds that had been sacrificed to the vanity of the ladies of society, who wore their plumage in their hats and coats. He dedicated his 'Shuddering Angel' 'to all those who love the beautiful and mourn over the senseless and cruel destruction of bird life and beauty.'[8]

The painting was thus an expression of grief as well as activism, reminding us not only that some sorrows transcend the bounds of the human but that some acts of mourning are meant to do more than mourn. Just as Aldo Leopold's famous comment that 'for one species to mourn the death of another is a new thing under the sun' was not just a lamentation but a cry to action, so too Watts's shuddering angel called upon the viewer's conscience with a direct moral appeal.[9] *Look at this!* it called; *look at what we are doing!*

It is perhaps hard for modern viewers to reclaim this experience: the age of killing birds for fashion long behind us, we are not asked to give anything up in coming eye to eye with Watts's sorrowing angel. But there are other reasons for participating in the angel's grief—reasons that call upon our love, but most of all upon our conscience, our willingness to act.

What if these feathers and broken wings were the ruins of all the deaths and suffering caused by fossil fuel and global warming, as well as the pollution and entrenched global injustice to which some parts of the world keenly sacrifice their neighbours? What if the thing the angel shuddered over was the wreckage of this climate age?

Scholars have defined ecological grief as 'the grief felt in relation to experienced or anticipated ecological losses, including the loss of species, ecosystems and meaningful landscapes due to acute or chronic environmental change.'[10] This is the grief expressed by Aldo Leopold when he spoke of interspecies mourning, and when he said that 'one of the penalties of an ecological education is that one lives alone in a world of wounds.'[11] When it comes to climate change, the grief is a little different still. It may incapsulate all the aspects of ecological grief, but also, it may extend to the experience of losing the future itself. As Clive Hamilton wrote in 2010, in climate grief 'the "death" that is mourned is the loss of the future'; it is the loss of 'an expectation that the world will unfold in a certain way, as an enhanced version of the world we have now'; it is the realisation that 'our conception of the future and the hopes that are built on it are illusory.'[12] Writing in a time when climate denial was rife, Hamilton noted that 'the early mourners feel lonely and isolated, sometimes keeping their thoughts to themselves for fear of alienating those around them with their anxieties and pessimism. It is as if the doctors had declared there is no hope of recovery for a sick child, yet all around friends and family are saying, "Don't worry, she will be fine."'[13] This feeling of grief in isolation, of living 'alone in a world of wounds,' is still experienced by those who are cut off, by having looked into this darkness, from those who have not. It is the experience of activists convicted of 'hysteria' and exaggeration by online forums; it is what we saw in Greta Thunberg's tears at Davos, when surrounded by the rich and powerful she showed a grief infused with anger, or an anger infused with grief.

But if the grief is still present, some of the loneliness, perhaps, has been dispelled—as protests and marches allow activists and protestors to engage in what Freud called 'the work of mourning' (*Trauerarbeit*). At one Extinction Rebellion rally a young woman speaks slowly while others stand silent in the street: 'There are days when I pretend that nothing is wrong. Days also when I'm afraid that it's already too late. Days when I know that that's not certain. That the future is before us. *Hopeful.*' As she continues, one young man starts to cry. 'All over the world people are losing their family, house, job. They raise the alarm: the climate will not wait. There's no Plan B. What happens far away affects us too.'[14] This is not simply a protest: it is a public and collective act of mourning. Such acts, according to Naomi Klein, are among Extinction Rebellion's major achievements: 'One thing they have done so well is break us out of this classic campaign model we have been in for a long time, where you tell someone something scary, you ask them to click on something to do something about it, you skip out the whole phase where we need to grieve together and feel together and process what it is that we just saw.' Climate grief is not simply an emotional by-product or something that stands in the way of action; it is a crucial part of the process: 'We need to be struggling with our climate grief together and our climate fears together.'[15]

Such grief is not exclusive to the young: it is experienced, too, by older people who know they will leave the world worse than they found it, and very concretely, by the elders of indigenous communities facing the loss of their way of life. The Labrador Inuit have always been known as 'people of the sea ice'—but every year the ice is later in coming and earlier in melting, isolating communities that depend on it for transport, hunting, and wood gathering. Underlying these losses is the loss of cultural identity: as one of the elders asks, 'if there's no sea ice, how can we be people of the sea ice?'[16] Such expressions recall Glenn Albrecht's concept of *solastalgia*, which he describes as 'the lived experience of negative environmental change'—the 'homesickness you have when you are still at home.' And indeed Albrecht has suggested 'that "the age of solastalgia" is likely to emerge during this period of massive change.'[17]

But there are important differences between various modes of grief. Sometimes grief is helpless, responding to a loss that we were powerless to prevent. This is the grief of those who have lost a person dear to them—such as writer C. S. Lewis, who wrote in wide-eyed bafflement: 'No one ever told me that grief felt so like fear. I am not afraid, but the sensation is like being afraid. The same fluttering in the stomach, the same restlessness, the yawning. I keep on swallowing.'[18]

It is also the grief tied in with extinction. When all that remains of the mountain mist frog, the white-handed gibbon, and the Irriwaddy dolphin (all declared extinct in 2022)[19] is the echo of their memory, there is nothing to be done but to stand and mourn, as Frodo stood in the circle of trees at Cerin Amroth, 'hearing far off great seas upon beaches that had long ago been washed away, and sea-birds crying whose race had perished from the earth.'[20] This is the grief expressed by Plenty Coups when, in a dream, he witnessed the destruction of a forest by a terrible storm: 'Pity was hot in my heart for the beautiful trees. I felt pity for all things that lived in the forest, but was powerless to stand with them against the Four Winds that together were making war. I shielded my own face with my arm when they charged!'[21] Plenty Coups knows that he is powerless to stand against these destructive forces—and such powerlessness can be a central part of grief. When this is the case, the only possible response, perhaps the only right response, is to bear witness to the suffering and mourn what has been lost.

But not all grief is like this. Sometimes grief is coupled with the knowledge that there is more loss yet to be prevented—or with a commitment to action that must be taken even if there is loss that cannot be undone. When in 2014 the Marshallese poet Kathy Jetñil-Kijiner addressed the UN Climate Summit with a poem for her baby daughter, 'Dear Matafele Peinem', she mingled sorrow with defiance, righteous anger with lament. Recognising that some losses, some injustices cannot be made right—*'to the Carteret islanders of Papua New Guinea / and to the Taro islanders of the Solomon Islands'*—she called upon the conscience of all to continue the struggle at all costs, as there is so much suffering yet to be prevented—*'I take this moment / to apologize to you / <u>we are drawing the line here</u>.'*[22]

It may then be possible to grieve without springing into action—but it is perhaps not possible to access this sort of *passionate* commitment without an element of grief. 'Sooner or later we must respond,' wrote Clive Hamilton in 2010, 'and that means allowing ourselves to enter a phase of desolation and hopelessness, in short, to grieve.'[23]

Mourning and Melancholia

One writer who has argued for the importance of mourning as part of the ethical life is Jonathan Lear. As I have mentioned, *Radical Hope* was written at a time when the climate crisis was not yet at the forefront of our collective consciousness, though in subsequent years many have read it with this in mind. Lear's most recent book, *Imagining the End*, is, however, set against the backdrop of various contemporary crises, among them 'climate change and ecological catastrophe, threats to the democratic political order, [and] the menace of pandemic.'[24] In times of crises such as these, Lear believes it is natural that 'our imaginations should come alive'—but they can do so in different ways:

> In health, we imagine alternative possibilities. Our imaginations open up the future, recreate the past, and enliven the present. These are virtues, or excellences, of imagination. But we also know that imagination can get in our way, distort our vision, and insist that falsehoods are true. When it comes to imagination, there is such a thing as ill health. So, what I am concerned with are real threats to the imagination as we face real threats coming from the world.[25]

Making a play on the double meaning of the word 'end' in English, Lear argues 'that our concerns with the *end* of the world in the sense of catastrophe [have] interfered with our sense of the *end* of the world in the sense of the ideals and values that in healthy times inform human life and [give] us a sense of what life is all about.'[26] What he means by this is that there are healthy and less healthy ways of exercising our imagination in response to the threat of catastrophe: 'even if the threats of world catastrophe are real, and even if our imaginations are stimulated by those very real threats, that does not in itself make our imaginings healthy.'[27]

It is not entirely clear what Lear is targeting here—climate 'doomism', dystopian fiction? Lear gives only one concrete and anecdotal example: the comment of a young academic at the end of a lecture on climate change: 'We will *not* be missed!' The 'joke' is then analysed as the wrong kind of response—as 'an expression of despair' but also 'an active *refusal to mourn*.'[28] This, for Lear, is representative of a wider cultural tendency 'to express a desire to get the whole thing over with,' a 'refusal to mourn' that sustains despair and suggests not only that we are to blame for the current crisis but that it's too late to do anything about it

now; all we can do is 'recognize our guilt and suffer.'[29] To argue
that such an attitude, however implicit, is deeply problematic,
Lear employs the Aristotelian concept of the *kalon*. A Greek
term sometimes translated as *noble, beautiful,* or *fine,* but not
quite captured by any of these, the *kalon* gestures towards the
excellence of the moral life—for instance, 'a generous person
living generously.'[30] The practice of mourning, Lear argues, is
itself *kalon*: something of great value whose loss, if ever it oc-
curred, should itself be mourned. 'Part of what it is to mourn
the *kalon*—in the sense of mournfully anticipating the *kalon*
going out of existence—is to acknowledge that the universe will
be impoverished in the sense that something good will have
gone out of existence.'[31] Mourning thus reminds us of what we
value and what we stand to lose if value itself should be lost. If
mourning itself went out of existence, Lear reminds us, this
would not just be one loss among others, it would be the 'loss of
loss'. And therefore, 'It cannot be funny that the *kalon* recognized
as such should go out of existence.'[32]

The academic's comment is perhaps not the best-chosen example for the point Lear is trying to make. The 'joke', if it is a
joke, can be interpreted differently, not as misanthropic but as
a warning (*If we go on this way, look at what we stand to lose!*), or
as a reminder that humans are not the *only* things that have
value in the universe. Not having been in the room, it is hard to
tell whether the comment was indeed meant as a joke or rather
as a call to action, an expression of justified despair. But Lear's
point is clear: it is that certain modes of 'imagining the end' are
unhealthy or at least unhelpful as we navigate this crisis. And he
unpacks this further through rereading two of Freud's essays:
'On Transience' and 'Mourning and Melancholia'.

The first of these, written against the backdrop of World War I,
finds Freud 'grappling with how to live with the radical uncer-

tainty of the immediate future.'[33] Reading Freud through a Kier-
kegaardian lens, Lear thinks we can see a 'positive conception of
repetition in the writings of Freud.' The world may overwhelm or
destroy us—'But *if it does not*, then it is characteristic of us that
we respond to loss with pain and suffering but then tend in the
direction of returning to life.' Such a return is itself already an
'expression of hope': 'We may not be able to say what we are hoping for, but in the broadest and most indeterminate sense, hope
hopes for the good. So, what we have here is a *return of hope,
which is itself a hope for a return of the good.*'[34] Mourning, then, is
a way of responding positively to the actual or potential loss of
things we love—a response that does not cut us off from life but
opens the way for a return to life and a return of the good.

Such 'good' mourning is pitted against the opposite, negative
response—which Lear, after Freud, calls melancholia. Both
'Mourning and Melancholia' are responses to loss; they are 'two
modes of living in a world that is not entirely up to us.' But
whereas mourning 'tends in the direction of a return to life' and
lets our imaginations 'come alive,' melancholia 'is an angry attack on the possibility of repetition'—a foreclosure of the possible return to life.[35] Lear recognises that there is not a simple
choice to be made between the two: 'It is not a matter of just
deciding or exercising our will.' But, he adds, 'that does not
mean we cannot become active with respect to shaping our
own lives and manners of being, that we cannot work in the
direction of repetition' and 'take seriously the healthy use of our
imaginations.'[36]

It is, again, not entirely clear what Lear is targeting here—or
what it means exactly 'to work in the direction of repetition.'
One possible reading is that this is the moralistic point so often
made by advocates of green hope: that we must reject 'doomism'
and instead focus our minds on the positive, such as success

stories which provide 'reasons for hope'. But this would seem to ring false, considering not only Freud's deep awareness of the suffering of his age but Lear's own rejection of 'mere optimism' in his earlier work.

Another possibility is that mourning is a clearly delineated exercise that can successfully be completed—whereas the 'unhealthy' use of our imaginations obstructs this completion. This would be more along the lines of Freud, who suggests in 'Mourning and Melancholia' that 'when the work of mourning is completed the ego becomes free and uninhibited again.'[37] But as Judith Butler has noted, we may well wonder whether 'the work of mourning' can ever be successfully 'completed': 'I am not sure I know when mourning is successful, or when one has fully mourned another human being.'[38] The question becomes more poignant when we consider the ambiguity of the German word *Trauer*, which can mean either *grief* (the 'psychological phenomenon' in response to loss) or *mourning* (the 'more public and often ritualistic' exercise of grief).[39] It is, for instance, common to speak of a period of mourning, whereas grief can last a lifetime—we may not ever want or need it to go away.[40]

This points to a more general problem in using the term 'grief' or 'mourning' to designate not concrete interpersonal bereavement but the kind of 'ambiguous loss' inherent in ecological devastation—a 'loss that goes on without answers or closure and leads to feelings of being frozen, halted, or stuck in the grief process, living with both the presence and the absence of what was lost.'[41] Freud describes mourning as a reaction to an unambiguous and final loss: 'the loss of a loved person' or alternatively, 'the loss of some abstraction . . . such as one's country, liberty, an ideal, and so on.' And he notes that, once the work of mourning has begun, we 'rely on its being overcome after a certain lapse of time.'[42] However, when it comes to climate grief and ecological grief more generally, the person who grieves is not straightforwardly in a grieving relationship. Except when we mourn concrete losses, such as a species that has gone extinct, a forest that has been burned down, or a community that has been displaced, the object of climate grief is often diffuse, ambiguous, even obscure: one might mourn not just the Irrawaddy dolphin but the many species that have gone extinct even before they are discovered (a phenomenon known as 'dark extinction'); one might mourn the loss of a way of life, a set of values, or even 'an expectation that the world will unfold in a certain way.'[43] Not only is the object obscure, but the loss is protracted, stretching out into a vague and distant future and blocking our view of what is truly lost and what can still be salvaged. Such grief is not clearly delineated—and it is not at all clear what it would mean for the associated work of mourning to come to 'completion.'[44]

What complicates things further is that the context for climate or ecological grief is not *purely* or *simply* a situation of loss or bereavement—insofar as there is much loss that can still be prevented. There is a risk involved in using the language of mourning in such a case, as mourning typically involves a level of acceptance, if not resignation: it involves *coming to terms* with the dead being dead, the lost being lost. Mourning, says Freud, 'impels the ego to give up the object by declaring the object to be dead and offering the ego the inducement of continuing to live'—what Lear calls the 'return to life.'[45] But surely this would not be the right response if the thing whose loss we fear and rue is not yet dead—if the loss is still ongoing. Consider again Poe's story 'The Masque of the Red Death'—where the rich and wealthy withdraw in their castle to dance and feast, drowning out the cries of the suffering with wine and music. Would it have made a big difference to the moral of the story if instead of withdrawing to party they were withdrawing to mourn? Either way, they are turning their back to the living and suffering outside their gates; either way, theirs is a failure to act. The same is true for those who claim it's time to 'learn to die in the Anthropocene,' to mourn what is not quite dead instead of saving what can still be saved—in which case mourning, too, forestalls the return to life.

Mourning, then, may after all not be the right word for what is needed—at least, not on its own. We should indeed mourn species that are extinct; we should mourn the nature we have lost; we should mourn the dead and the displaced. *But we should not mourn that which is not yet dead.* Where the loss is not yet final, the tragedy still underway, a better response may be to cry out our despair to any who will hear it—which is perhaps precisely what the young academic was doing when she stood up and said, jokingly or grievingly, *We will not be missed.* Maybe this attitude does indeed represent what Freud called 'the open wound' of melancholia—but then again, maybe sometimes the wound has to stay open for healing to occur.

None of this is to say that we cannot speak of grief and mourning in this age of sorrows: emphatically, we can and should. But it has to be the kind of grief that commits its love to the living while mourning only what is truly dead—as Lear says, the kind that beckons a return to life. There is a third way of reading Lear's reprisal of the Freudian distinction between mourning and melancholia, one that places the contrast not in the positive *vs.* the negative but in the active *vs.* the passive. If mourning is the grief-infused recognition of what we love and stand to lose, coupled with a commitment to prevent whatever loss and suffering we can, then mourning can itself be a basis for climate action, a manifestation of blue hope. By contrast, melancholia would then be marked by inactivity and resignation—a simulacrum of mourning that turns its back on life and, like Denethor in *The Lord of the Rings*, builds the funeral pyre for that which is not yet dead.

This, to my mind, is the most productive reading of Lear's work in the context of the climate crisis: one that acknowledges that mourning must retain an active component and work in the direction of a 'return to life'—not by forgetting or replacing what is lost but by strengthening our commitment to prevent further suffering, further erosion of the good. But there is no reason why this sort of mourning cannot go hand in hand with the kind of melancholia or despair expressed by those on the front line of climate and environmental activism, or with the exercise of our imaginations in the direction of disaster. In the words of Daniel Sherrell: 'I no longer believe that grief and resistance are mutually exclusive: I think the former is *necessary* to the latter, that honest sorrow is perhaps *the only thing* that makes a real fight even possible.'[46] Some imaginary activities are painful because they confront us with the possibility of loss—but in awakening our grief, they awaken our love as well, our readiness to act, precisely by wrapping our attention around the open and unsettling wound of melancholia.

This is what Watts's painting did to those who saw it, inviting them to mourn while demanding that their conscience come alive. *Look at this*, the angel whispered to them; *look at what we're doing, what we've done.* And so I wonder only if the earnest darkness that grips the hearts of activists today is indeed an unhealthy use of the imagination, or if it is the piercing cry of conscience that cuts through all subterfuge and commands the obedience of all that will hear it—a manifestation of grief, despair, and darkness, yes—but a manifestation, too, of love.

The Gift of Climate Grief

There is another reason why the language of grief, of mourning, is so important. As Freud pointed out, we tend to see melancholia or depression as pathological conditions, but not grief or mourning, terms which suggest a natural and even healthy response to real loss, and which Lear even counts among the *kalon*.[47] We would not usually refer grieving persons to seek medical help unless in exceptional cases—and even then it would only be to shift the manifestation of grief into a manageable form. But our common discourse for climate sorrows—drenched in terms such as *eco-anxiety, climate depression, environmental melancholia*—often suggests precisely the pathological.

In an episode of *The Simpsons*, Lisa is diagnosed with 'environment-related despair' after giving a school presentation about global warming and the bleak future awaiting them. As the principal tells her, 'Lisa, your outburst is either a sign of deep emotional imbalance or a passionate response to a sobering truth. Luckily the treatment for both is intensive therapy.' She is prescribed a new drug, 'Ignorital', a happy pill that masks anything negative but also dissociates her from reality, until Marge takes her off the meds. Clearly, to frame climate despair as a pathological condition and respond by symptom management alone is not the right response—because Lisa is not under any illusions; she perceives that there is something in reality that calls on us to change it: *'Face things as they really are.'*[48]

The value of speaking of climate grief or mourning instead of depression or melancholia is that the language of grief recognises that the attitude is *veridical* or *justified*: it is a response to a real loss that has been or is still taking place.[49] The challenge for anyone writing or speaking about the psychology of climate change is, first, to help reconceptualise the sorrow involved as *grief* (that is:

as a natural response to a real loss, rather than a pathological problem); and then to unlock the potential of this grief as a basis for action—thus transforming the passive language of depression and anxiety into the active language of grief and mourning. Not only may activism well be the best psychological response to the deep sorrows that spring from facing up to a darkening world, but to use the language of grief is itself to unlock the transformative potential of loss. As Judith Butler suggests, there is something to be gained 'from tarrying with grief,' which returns us to 'a sense of human vulnerability, to our collective responsibility for the physical lives of one another'—and perhaps, one might add, to the lives of the nonhuman. Against the idea that grief renders us powerless or passive, Butler writes: 'To grieve, and to make grief itself into a resource for politics, is not to be resigned to inaction, but it may be understood as the slow process by which we develop a point of identification with suffering itself.' Grief may halt us in our steps, but it may also propel them, though we do not always know beforehand what direction they may take. 'Perhaps mourning has to do with agreeing to undergo a transformation (perhaps one should say *submitting* to a transformation) the full result of which one cannot know in advance. There is losing, as we know, but there is also the transformative effect of loss, and this latter cannot be charted or planned.'[50]

And how could we *not* grieve? How, knowing (as Thunberg knows, as Kathy Jetñil-Kijiner knows) that people are suffering, not in some distant future, not just in the near future, but *now*—that species are dropping away every moment, islands sinking, dry lands becoming drier, wet lands becoming wetter? Knowing that there is so much that is already lost, so much we still stand to lose, the question should be not *Why do we grieve?* but *How can we not grieve?* How, unless we have no place upon this earth, among these people?

To embrace the language of grief (if rightly grounded) is not to evade, to deflate, or to sedate: it is to give confidence and consolation to those who stand face-to-face with the climate crisis and grieve for what is being lost, even while fighting to preserve it. It is to reassure those experiencing anxiety, grief, and sadness that this experience is not one to be ashamed of or to be avoided: on the contrary, that it can be a moral source, a spring of ethical activity and motivation. That grief, like pity for the Crow, is 'an emotion appropriate to the gods.'[51]

This is the gift of Our Lady of Tears.

8

Our Lady of Sighs: On Despair

Neither hope nor joy are my pilots—restless despair and fierce desire of change lead me on.

—MARY SHELLEY

THE SECOND sister is '*Mater Suspiriorum*, Our Lady of Sighs.' Of her De Quincey writes that 'her eyes, if they were ever seen, would be neither sweet nor subtle; no man could read their story; they would be found filled with perishing dreams, and with wrecks of forgotten delirium.' But her eyes are not seen: her head 'droops for ever; for ever fastens on the dust.' Whereas the first sister rages against the heavens, 'Our Lady of Sighs never clamours, never defies, dreams not of rebellious aspirations.' If she murmurs, it is in her sleep; if she whispers, 'it is to herself in the twilight.' 'She weeps not. She groans not. But she sighs inaudibly at intervals.' She is the companion of the downcast and enslaved, the oppressed and the disgraced, of 'all that are betrayed, and all that are rejected': 'all these walk with "Our Lady of Sighs."'[1]

The 'Sorrow' this lady expresses seems to be that of utter hopelessness, or despair. And for this reason alone, we are unlikely to look at her, or listen. De Quincey paints an unflattering picture of her, as passive and submissive, as *defeated*: 'She is humble to abjectness. Hers is the meekness that belongs to the hopeless.'[2] And this, indeed, is how we often think of despair.

For all our reimaginings of hope and pessimism, it may seem that one dichotomy is left standing: that which pits *hope* or *optimism* or even *hopeful pessimism* over and against *despair*. I've criticised several authors for equating pessimism with despair and defeatism—but what about the latter equation? Is despair indeed the same as 'giving up'?

Most writers on the topic seem to think so. Jane Goodall worries that it is because people are 'overwhelmed by the magnitude of our folly' that they feel helpless and then 'sink into apathy and despair, lose hope, and so do nothing.'[3] Rebecca Solnit contrasts hope with 'despair, defeatism, cynicism, and pessimism', calling these the 'enemies of hope.'[4] Theorists and activists making the case for climate justice have written articles and chapters 'against despair', while environmentalists have suggested that rewilding 'could be our best defence against despair.'[5] Even Greta Thunberg, so critical of the casual use of hope, is adamant on this point: 'But we cannot despair'; 'there is no time for despair.'[6] This, at least, seems one thing that all are agreed on: despair is a road that leads to nowhere.

But are we so sure of that? If someone came up to us and said, *I am desperate*—what are they telling us? Are they saying, *it's no use, I've given up, it's no point trying*—or are they saying, *the situation is urgent; I desperately need your help*? Far from being a sign of giving up, could despair also be a cry for help?

This may be difficult to conceive, as despair is a state that is hard to imagine from the outside, but for those of us who hope, we should be able to imagine what it would be like for that hope to be imperilled. As Viktor Frankl wrote, paraphrasing Lessing,

'There are things which must cause you to lose your reason or you have none to lose.'[7] So too might we say: there are things which must cause you to lose your hope or you have none to lose. And I suggest it is also possible to imagine situations where we might be in a state of despair *without* being in the state of giving up. This can be an irrational stance but also a rational one, stemming from the recognition that some causes are not ours to concede; that giving up is just not an option, no matter how 'hopeless' the odds.

If this is right, then despair is after all not *necessarily* the same as defeatism, as giving up. As there are different conceptions of hope, there are also different conceptions of despair, and if we trace them closely we may find that the two are not so incompatible as we might think: on the contrary, that they can exist alongside each other, two primal forces clenching each other like hands above an abyss, knowing that if either releases, both will fall.

The Other Side of Despair

This is not as strange as it may seem. On the 'standard account' of hope in philosophy, we hope for something when we desire some state of affairs and think it's *in some degree* probable for it to come about: the degree of probability must lie somewhere between 0 (impossible) and 1 (certain).[8] But as some philosophers have argued, this would make hope almost indistinguishable from despair, as similar expectations of probability can lead to drastically different attitudes.

The paradigmatic example in this debate is drawn from *The Shawshank Redemption*, the 1994 film based on a novella by Stephen King, in which two inmates of a prison, Andy and Red, are serving a life sentence for murder but respond to this situation in fundamentally different ways. As philosopher Ariel Meirav points out, the two men are 'in many ways similar': on the one hand, they both understand the workings of the prison and the 'very small chances of escaping'; on the other, 'neither of them has lost the desire to be free again'—and yet 'Andy lives in the hope of escaping, whereas Red despairs of this.' Meirav emphasises that the difference does not seem to lie in the probability they assign to escape: it's very possible that both men would agree that 'the chances are one in a thousand.' And yet their responses come sharply apart. 'Red will say, "I grant you it is *possible*, but the chance is only one in a thousand!" whereas Andy will say, "I grant you the chance is only one in a thousand, but it is *possible!*"'[9]

Such examples are usually taken as a reason to redefine hope, so as to make it more distinct from despair.[10] But it might, on second thought, not at all be a weakness for any account of hope that it stands in close relation to despair: there might even be something *right* in the assumption of this closeness. Hope and despair are not necessarily diametrically opposed or mutually exclusive—at least not in the way that other concepts (*hot/cold, full/empty*) are. Adapting a famous dictum from Paul Tillich, we might say that the opposite of hope is not despair but *certainty*. We cannot hope for something that we are certain will (or will not) occur—but when the thing hoped for is perceived to be especially unlikely, or difficult, or *nearly* impossible, hope may survive precisely as despair.[11] That is to say: *despair is the shape hope takes in dire straits.*

At least, it can be. Everything depends on how we define despair—as the absence of hope, as resignation, or as an especially anxious kind of hope. There are different conceptions of despair just as there are of hope, though there isn't a neat symmetry between them. We use despair to cover a range of emotional and cognitive responses, some of which are incompatible with hope, while others are not.[12] This is as true in the climate change debate as it is elsewhere.

For instance, when authors in the climate debate militate 'against despair', what they have (or should have) in mind is despair of the 'debilitating' or fatalist variety; it is the belief that we are powerless to make a difference and therefore may as well give up. This is what Michael E. Mann means by '*despair*-mongering': 'if they can convince us it's too late to act, it potentially leads us down the same path of disengagement as outright denial.'[13] 'Not acting is a luxury those in immediate danger do not have, and despair something they cannot afford,' writes Rebecca Solnit. 'But *despair is all around us*, telling us the problems are insoluble, that we are not strong enough, our efforts are in vain, no one really cares, and human nature is fundamentally corrupt.'[14] And Catriona McKinnon: 'Does the frightening future that climate change promises, and our bleak prospects of avoiding it, justify despair? Given the parlous state of climate change and its lamentable politics, ought we to despair *and give up*?'[15]

What these authors are (rightly) objecting to is not so much an affective response but a sort of defeatist logic, which has many different versions but can be summarised as follows:

1. It's already too late to stop climate catastrophe.
2. If it's too late, there's no point in acting.
3. *Therefore* we should just give up.[16]

This kind of despair (understood as the logic of defeatism) can be straightforwardly refuted by three philosophical points. Against (1)—*It's already too late to stop climate catastrophe*—the crucial thing to note is that there is an important ambiguity in the notion of 'catastrophe' or 'disaster', which is not an all-or-nothing state of affairs. As activists keep reminding us, 'the Problem isn't binary like nuclear war; it's not like we either press the button or we don't. Even if it's ongoing and inevitable, there's still a world of difference between two degrees Celsius and six degrees Celsius in terms of human suffering and general chaos, and so every marginal bit of good we do in the present allays some of that pain in the future.'[17]

Defenders of defeatism like to refer to science to bolster their claim that 'it's too late', but in fact climate scientists are perfectly clear that there is a huge difference between, for instance, 2 and 3 degrees Celsius of global warming. 'For every increment of global warming, changes in extremes become larger,' in the words of one climate scientist, and the IPCC equally stresses that risks increase wildly with every increment of warming, as it is unclear when exactly fatal tipping points are reached.[18] Even a difference between 2°C and 2.2°C means a dramatic difference in the percentage of world territory that becomes inhabitable due to heat or flooding; even minor shifts can have huge impacts in the intensity of suffering inflicted on hundreds of millions of people in vulnerable areas—whether by death, drought, displacement, or the many other climate evils.[19] Considering the extreme instability of the atmosphere and the uncertainty of tipping points, some have argued that we should not be casual about individual luxury emissions, as the effect of even a single carbon splurge may be the death of a child by cholera.[20] The point is that even if *some* level of catastrophe is unavoidable, this is not the same as saying *we're doomed* altogether: there is always more suffering to be prevented, and therefore there is *always* a reason to keep on with the struggle.[21]

Against (2)—*If it's too late, there's no point in acting*—it is enough to note, with Popper, that 'the future is open'; there is no empirical ground for fatalism. This is not optimism: as I've said before, it was precisely the pessimists who were most adamant in stressing the intrinsic uncertainty of existence.[22] It should be noted, furthermore, that even the erratic author of the book *We're Doomed. Now What?* hedges this doom by a margin of uncertainty: 'it's *probably* already too late to stop it'; the next decades are '*likely* going to be grim, brutish, and bloody'; 'we're *almost certainly* already over the cliff.'[23] As his critics have rightly pointed out, this uncertainty is all that is needed to defeat defeatism itself: 'No more is required to maintain a minimum of hope: success is neither certain nor probable, but *possible*'; as 'the context for hope is radical uncertainty.'[24]

Finally, against (3)—*Therefore we should just give up*—the point to make is simply a democratic one: it is not up to us (any of us) to decide unilaterally that it's not worth continuing the fight. Climate change is a global problem, whose harms are borne disproportionately by the most disenfranchised: millions are already suffering its effects, and many more stand to lose their homes and lives in the years to come. The more and the faster we act, the greater the future harm that can be prevented; the sooner we give up, the more devastating the death and grief to come. No one, least of all those who stand furthest from the front lines of disaster, is entitled to decide on behalf of those most vulnerable that their suffering is not worth fighting for.

It is just this sort of despair—the logic of defeatism, or the 'loss of belief that the struggle is worthwhile'[25]—that needs to be refuted for climate action to retain its urgency and legitimacy. But some authors criticising despair don't stop there. Instead of simply attacking the defeatist logic (which is easily done), some go further and attack two other things as well: the representation of negative information in general, and the subjective experience of despair.

With regard to the first, it has become a staple of climate commentators to condemn the 'doom-and-gloom' representation of the crisis, on the basis that too much negative information will necessarily lead to defeatism. Hence the dismissal of 'alarmist narratives' and 'bad-news bringers [who] seem in love with defeat.'[26] But the underlying assumption that being confronted with negative information will *necessarily* lead to apathy and defeat is itself a form of fatalism. Against it, Greta Thunberg insists that media coverage, far from being too negative, is still much too positive to do justice to the scale and urgency of the problem—and that this positivity is much more likely to forestall action as it downplays the extent of political inaction: 'since the media long for positive news as part of their policy of both-side reporting—It can't be all doom and gloom!—the overall message that is conveyed, if any, is that action is being taken.'[27] In response to psychologists telling her that her strategy (focusing on fear and urgency) was ill-advised, she points out that she and Fridays for Future were able to mobilise millions of people not by offering hope or inspiration but by serving up the stark and scary facts undiluted. She compares it to the Covid-19 pandemic, suggesting that society's shift in thinking and willingness to act was triggered by the media:

> And they did it simply by objectively telling the reality as it was. It turns out they did not have to offer any *inspiration* for people to change their behaviour—contrary to what all the communication experts have been saying for years and years. Nor was it hopeful stories about ninety-five-year-olds who miraculously survived the disease that got us moving. The media just told us the facts, and we reacted to them. We did not become paralysed. We did not give in to apathy. We simply reacted to the information and changed our norms and our behaviour—as you do in a crisis.[28]

Whether or not this is exactly true of the pandemic, there is an important point here. Activists and scientists are told again and again that if they paint a too gloomy picture of affairs, it will disincentivise. But although this is a possible consequence in individual cases, it is not a necessary and perhaps not even a very likely one. After all, few have done more to trigger wide-spread individual and collective action as the desperate voices of Thunberg and others, harnessing not just despair but also fear, anger, grief, and all the sorrows of this age.

This brings us to the second point often made by the critics of despair, when they attack not only the logic of defeatism but the subjective experience of despair—despair as an emotion. By this I don't mean to say that despair, considered as an emotive response, is somehow irrational: like hope, despair too can be rationally grounded, as when one feels desperate in response to a desperate situation. But, and this is crucial, to despair in this sense is not the same as giving up. As Rebecca Solnit rightly points out, despair can be understood as either an emotion or an analysis:

> The desperate themselves are sometimes embittered and ex-hausted, but often stubbornly hopeful. Even if they would say they don't hope, their perseverance is itself a kind of hope, a refusal to surrender. *Despair can be true as an emotion, but false as an analysis.*[29]

This is helpful, as it counters the assumption that anyone who feels authentically desperate is thereby automatically on the side of the resigned. But the ambiguity of 'despair' is such that this clarity proves hard to maintain, as Solnit elsewhere does seem to criticise the emotion as well—for instance, by dismiss-ing expressions of 'gloom' and by speaking of despair in highly emotive terms: 'a dank little foxhole of curled-up despair.'[30] Such statements miss the point of what subjective despair is trying to express. As I've said before, when someone says, *I am desperate*, that does not place them at the point of giving up: it places them in front of an abyss. The response to this need not be passivity—it may be precisely at the threshold of despair that we experience that dark epiphany which spurs us into action, or to call for help.[31]

And so I would like to suggest that even the last dichotomy (*hope vs. despair*) should be reconsidered. To be *in despair*, to be truly *desperate*, is to be confronted with a terrible reality that is about to breach upon us and exposes our vulnerability; it is to stand face-to-face with the acute possibility of losing something we value more than ourselves. This sort of despair (as emotion) can indeed go together with the fatalistic kind (analysis) and lead to giving up—but the two can also come sharply apart.

Whereas *resignation* suggests the surrender of an attachment (such as a hope, an aspiration) and thereby restores a sense of calm, there is nothing calm about despair itself. When one despairs, in the subjective sense, one remains with the attachment, the desire.[32] The hoped-for reality is seen as *almost impossible*—but the possibility remains, and one cannot give up the desire entirely. In some cases this may be a vice; in others, a virtue, as there may be reasons to stay with the struggle regardless of expectations: 'Even when [despair] is realistic as an analysis, many still stand up and resist on principle.'[33]

What this means is that in *some* cases (but not all), despair can be a manifestation of the most urgent, most anxious, and most ardent hope. This is perhaps what authors of the past were getting at when they said that fear and hope march together; that 'there is no hope unmingled with fear, and no fear unmingled with hope.'[34] The desperate suitor in Jane Austen's *Persuasion* gets it right when he tells the one he loves, 'You pierce my soul. I am half agony, half hope.'[35] Hope can express itself as agony, and when it does, it is not so easily distinguished from despair:

indeed, in such cases the opposition between hope and despair seems less clear than the opposition between despair and resignation. Compare the calm resignation of Scranton and other proponents of 'climate stoicism', who seek to get away from suffering, to the turbulent agony of desperate activists, who choose to remain with the suffering, push through it, even draw power from it. Despair can indeed take the form of resignation (and there are times when it should),[36] but it may also take the form of desperate resistance.

Desperate Resistance

I have spoken of 'desperate resistance' before, to describe the anguished uprising of the Warsaw ghetto and other historical examples.[37] But I draw this term from a different rebellion, which shook the streets of Amsterdam in the late 1960s.

Its name was 'Provo'. Originating in curious dada-esque 'happenings' around a small statue in the inner city, Provo went on to articulate itself as a deliberate collective of *provocation* against the authoritarian structures of the time. In the years 1965 to 1967, Provo rebelled against the monarchy, against police brutality, against the encroachment of profit-minded capitalism on social structures and the lulling-to-sleep of human creativity by capitalist consumerism. It was anarchistic but in an idiosyncratic way, as it would successfully stand for city council in Amsterdam and elsewhere, and one of its founding members would go on to have a lifelong career in local politics. It rebelled against the 'terror' of motorised traffic on the crowded streets of Amsterdam and launched a system for free bicycles, later adding a plan for communally shared electric cars. It advocated the rights of women and proposed plans for free contraception and sex education before marriage. It also launched an anti-smoking movement, calling into question the power of the tobacco and advertising industries. It opposed pipelines and oil refineries, and asserted a human right for clean air.[38]

And it did all of this out of an explicitly pessimistic starting point. As is stated in Provo's first manifesto, dated 12 July 1965:

> PROVO believes we are given a choice: *Desperate resistance or passive downfall.*
> PROVO calls for resistance where it is possible.
> PROVO recognises it will be the eventual loser, but does not want to miss this final chance to wholeheartedly provoke society.[39]

In contrast to most other movements of the time, Provo refused to appeal to either hope or optimism, clinging instead to what they called 'the power of despair':

> There is no place for heroism or hopeful expectations. . . . Why do we provoke? You do it because you think: I am that I am and I will resist all those who try to estrange me from myself by death or by brainwashing. Even if I resist with no other weapon than with *the power of despair*, for it is in resistance that I am myself.[40]

This is not to say that Provo did not care about results: its creative strategies and 'ludic actions' were designed precisely to have maximal societal impact, and often they were successful in this. But Provo's commitment did not hinge on these results. On the contrary: 'We are deeply aware of the eventual pointlessness of our days, we gladly believe that neither Johnson nor Kosigyn will listen to us, *and that is precisely why we are free to do what we do.*'[41] Provo found something liberating in being stripped from expectations, and from this stance grew a stark and energetic activism that outlasted the movement itself (which in its chaotic structure was inevitably short-lived).

There is something very powerful in this stance, as manifested today by the many *desperate* activists taking to the streets. 'I am hopeless', climate activists write on banners; 'I am in despair.' They say this not to announce they have given up but to plead for change. This is also what Greta Thunberg famously told her audience at Davos in 2019: 'I don't want you to be hopeful. I want you to panic. I want you to feel the fear I feel every day. And then I want you to act.'[42] The point bears repeating: if activists tell us, *I am in despair*, this does not mean they have given up the fight: it means that their hope has condensed itself into something else, something harder and fiercer, like a balled fist. To proclaim that one is in despair is to make more than a statement: it is to set a boundary—*here and no further*.

This does not mean that despair is not terrible; that it does not 'plunge the soul into a sense of suffering.'[43] It is, and it does. But it may also be the case that despair, as Kierkegaard wrote, is 'the sickness concerning which it is the greatest misfortune never to have had it.'[44] Like anger, like grief, despair comes to teach us something—something that may resist our vision in the light of day.[45]

This is why some have suggested that despair should not be shunned entirely but cautiously acknowledged for what it is, what it can be: a harbinger of danger but also a custodian of truth. As Cornel West reminds us, 'Those of us who truly hope make despair *a constant companion* whom we outwrestle every day owing to our commitment to justice, love, and hope.'[46] So too China Miéville has suggested that for hope 'to be real, and barbed, and tempered into a weapon, we cannot just default to it. We have to test it, subject it to the strain of *appropriate near-despair*.' To the question 'Is it better to hope or to despair?' we might answer, simply, 'Yes.'[47] This is not simply to play with words: activists and scientists commonly attest how they oscillate between hope and motivation on the one hand, 'sheer panic, raw terror, complete conviction that we are doomed' on the other.[48] But far from a dissonance to be resolved, this may be a tension we are required to sustain: to walk with despair as a companion, at least as much as to walk with hope. 'If you don't feel despair, in times like these, you are not fully alive,' Paul Kingsnorth has written. 'But there has to be something beyond despair too; or rather, something that accompanies it, like a companion on the road.'[49] The statement can be inverted to caution those who emphasise only the need for 'hope' and optimism and positive thinking, forgetting all the ways in which these, too, can lead us astray.

This is why despair should be considered not hope's antithesis but one of hope's shadow-sisters, while never forgetting the depth of suffering it carries in its folds. There remains something deeply problematic about the all-too-common dismissal of the experience of despair, as if it were a choice, and as if it were 'easy' or comforting ('the teddy bear of despair').[50] This is perhaps true for certain postmodern postures, which prioritise the personal relief of resignation over justice and compassion, but not for the truly desperate, whose only crime may be that they have grasped something that the rest of us are struggling to comprehend. As Terry Eagleton has noted, 'Optimism does not take despair seriously enough.'[51] What it keeps forgetting is that to denounce the *genuine* experience of despair is to further burden those who are already carrying a heavy load; and that despair, too, can be a moral source.

And so Our Lady of Sighs is misunderstood even by her interpreter. If she hangs her head sometimes, this does not mean she is defeated. If we could see her eyes, we would see them

filled not just 'with perishing dreams, and with wrecks of forgotten delirium' but also with the clear-sighted knowledge of
what needs to be done. If she seems silent, it just means that
we're not listening. Were we to listen, we would finally be
reminded that despair, far from being a weakness of the will,
may simply be an appropriate response to a desperate situation.
That despair, like anxiety, 'means you're paying attention.'[52]
That despair, like hope, can serve to 'shove you out the door.'[53]

This is the gift of Our Lady of Sighs.

9

Our Lady of Darkness

For there's no place that does not see you.
You must change your life.

—RAINER MARIA RILKE

FINALLY DE QUINCEY brings us to 'the third sister, who is also the youngest,' and places a finger on his lips: 'Hush! whisper, whilst we talk of *her*!' Whereas the first sister walks with 'uncertain steps, fast or slow, but still with tragic grace,' and the second 'creeps timidly and stealthily'—the third 'moves with incalculable motions, bounding, and with a tiger's leaps.' Unlike the others, she has no key, 'for, though coming rarely amongst men, she storms all doors at which she is permitted to enter at all.' She holds her head high—so high that it 'rises almost beyond the reach of sight.' And yet her eyes 'cannot be hidden; through the treble veil of crape which she wears, the fierce light of a blazing misery, that rests not for matins or for vespers, for noon of day or noon of night—for ebbing or for flowing tide—may be read from the very ground.'[1]

Her name is '*Mater Tenebrarum*, Our Lady of Darkness.' What could *her* gift be? De Quincey believes she is not just 'the defier of God' but also 'the mother of lunacies, and the suggestress of suicides'—but in this he is mistaken, just as he was mistaken about the silence of despair. Our Lady of Darkness comes not to foster illusions but to force us to see what we do not want to see; she comes not to tempt us from this world but to bind us to it. She does this in all ages, but most of all, in times of trial, when we need to be reminded of what we are in danger of losing, and what we have already lost. This is why she is the youngest of the sisters: she comes to bring something *to our age*.

But the truth she brings can only be seen in darkness. 'Deep lie the roots of her power; but narrow is the nation that she rules,' De Quincey tells us. 'For she can approach only those in whom a profound nature has been upheaved by central convulsions; in whom the heart trembles and the brain rocks under conspiracies of tempest from without and tempest from within.' Only at the hands of darkness shall they 'see the things that ought *not* to be seen—sights that are abominable, and secrets that are unutterable'; only by darkness shall they 'read elder truths, sad truths, grand truths, fearful truths.'[2] Only through darkness comes vision.

The hour is late. Our Lady of Darkness arrives at dusk, because it is at dusk that we most need her. She invites us not to flinch or look away from the gathering shadows but to look into the darkness—for it is in darkness that new virtues are found.

Dark Epiphanies

In recent years some philosophers have suggested that thinking about *virtues* might be an especially useful and meaningful way to shape our actions and attitudes in response to climate change.[3] For instance, using the language of virtues and vices seems to capture an important part of our moral experience: it is natural to describe callous polluters or emitters as, for instance, 'selfish, inconsiderate, disrespectful,' while praising as 'careful, considerate, conscientious' someone who does their best to reduce their (luxury) emissions.[4] Aside from this, it has been suggested that virtue ethics presents a better response than most other moral theories to the problem of *inconsequentialism*: the problem that our individual actions seem to have little or no meaningful effect, and so it's unclear why we should blame or praise individuals for their negative or positive contributions.[5] Considering that climate change is a collective problem exacerbated by entrenched systemic injustices, some bite the bullet and suggest climate action should not at all be framed in terms of individual responsibility, while others argue that even small additions or reductions in greenhouse gases are effective (or even that one can 'help, without making a difference').[6]

A virtue-oriented approach sidesteps these issues by suggesting we focus not on the measurable consequences of our actions but on the kinds of vices and virtues they manifest.[7] On such a view, it does not matter that we be certain about the exact efficacy of our actions, as long as we know 'that characteristic ways of living can produce climate harms'.[8] A person who joins a climate protest or forgoes a distant carbon-costly holiday can thus be said to exercise the virtues of justice and beneficence, while a systematic luxury emitter who does nothing to change their ways manifests the vice of callousness. On this view action ought not be premised on consequences or 'tangible results' but on what it means to live a virtuous life in a darkening age.[9]

The problem is that cultivating virtues typically takes a long time—even a *lifetime*—and so a virtue-oriented ethics seems ill-equipped to tackle an acute crisis such as climate change. As philosopher Sophie Grace Chappell has noted, 'virtue ethics is not primarily about what-should-we-do-right-now questions, it is primarily about *the dispositions that will make us into the kind of people who will give the right answers to* what-should-we-do-now questions.' When Plato and Aristotle wrote the foundational texts of virtue ethics, they were not trying to establish an 'emergency ethics' but a society-wide 'moral education' spanning several generations. And so it seems that 'for virtue ethics, in a sense, it is *always too late* for emergency ethics', as in order to respond in the right way to an emergency, 'you need *already* to have developed the right dispositions.' Even if the virtues may help us in the long run, they don't seem to be able to help us *now*.[10]

To this Chappell responds that the dilemma is overstated: 'In real life, no one is either completely virtuous or completely lacking in virtue'; we're not trying to summon virtue out of the blue:

> Hence adjuring people to do the virtuous thing is not like addressing them in a language that they don't speak at all; it is more like improving their grasp of a language that they already speak a bit, by practising it with them and getting them to repeat and imitate the sounds. . . . It is more like an invitation to see things a certain way, and to respond in a certain way, that is open and possible to them right now: a way that may not be *full* virtue, but is at least an approach to it, and an improvement on anything else that they would be at all likely to do instead.[11]

Even if this remains a difficult feat, Chappell suggests that the person new on this road might begin to exercise unfamiliar virtues precisely by imitating the *phronimos*, the moral exemplar who has already cultivated them.[12] And this is one way in which activists, in the broadest sense of the word, have an exceptional role to play—not just by their actions themselves but by showing what it means to place one's life in service of a greater cause.

Another way is by *epiphany*—a 'peak experience' that breaks into us from outside and has the power to change, radically and disruptively, our understanding of the world, each other, and ourselves.[13] 'In general, people do not choose or change their ways of life, or their individual actions, by reference to any deductive or quasi-deductive system of reasoning about values,' Chappell writes in her book on the subject. 'But people *do* choose their ways of life and their individual actions, and change them too, in response to epiphanies.'[14] In the case of animal rights, for instance, 'it seems to be not just frequent but usual that what changes views is not philosophical argument, but direct experience or perception, or at the least a fresh appreciation, of the sufferings of animals. Such experiences, harrowing as they often are, can be epiphanic too.'[15] As an example, she mentions a Facebook post by *Guardian* journalist Owen Jones:

> Someone told me of a clip in which a van is taking pigs on their last journey to be slaughtered, and one of them sticks their snout out the side to enjoy the sensation of wind on their face. I'm never eating pork again.[16]

Chappell calls this a 'small epiphany', and notes: 'The insight evokes empathy and moral concern, not by falling under some theoretical criterion, but simply by its vividness and directness.'[17] But epiphanies can also take life-altering proportions. Consider what Jane Goodall describes as her 'Damascus moment':

> It was after that conference in 1986, the one where I saw the secretly filmed footage of chimps in labs. I didn't see how I could help them, but, as I told you, I knew I had to try. And at the same conference we had a session on conservation—and it was shocking. Images from across Africa of forests

destroyed, horror stories of chimps shot for bushmeat and infants snatched from their dead mothers to sell, and evidence of a drastic decline in numbers of chimpanzees wherever they were being studied. Again, I just knew I had to do something. I didn't know what or how—only that just doing nothing was not an option.[18]

Such 'epiphanies', both on the small scale and the large, are widespread in the age of climate crisis, as each new IPCC report evokes fresh experiences of dismay, terror, anger, and despair. Not everyone reacts as the young Goodall did: often the response is rejection or evasion (what Camus called *l'esquive*), or the quick lash-out of denial. But there are many who hear the call, and answer.

Vanessa Nakate was finishing her business degree in Kampala in 2018 when news stories began to break of 'massive floods devastating whole swathes of East Africa', while arid regions in the northeast suffered new extremes of drought. Her own country, Uganda, also suffered flood and landslides, as it had done before. 'But something was different about the extreme events marking 2018,' Nakate recalls. 'They seemed to be happening more frequently, occurring all over the country, lasting longer, and displaying greater ferocity.' Nakate had learned about global warming in high school but had only been taught that this was a problem for the future, and for other parts of the world. 'Could it be, I asked myself, that climate change wasn't in the future and elsewhere, but here and now: in Africa, in Uganda, in Kampala?' She began to look for information about 'the world's response to climate change,' learned about the Paris agreement of 2015, learned also that emissions were still rising in spite of that agreement, and 'that the planet was on course for potentially a 3°C (5.4°F) temperature increase by 2050 and

7°C (12.6°F) by 2100—a civilization-ending scenario.' She recalls
her response: 'I was stunned. Worry. Sadness. Fear. Anger. Be-
wilderment. Frustration.' Seeing the example of Greta Thunberg
striking for climate, 'I felt the pull to strike too. I began to feel
like I *had* to become a climate activist. . . . If I didn't, would I
ever forgive myself?'[19]

Listening to the stories of activists, scientists, journalists, and
anyone concerned with these matters, it is common to hear an
epiphanic story of this kind—a moment when a sudden 'encounter with value' brings us face-to-face with something we
had not known about the world, or had not known *fully*. There
doesn't have to be any new information revealed in an epiphany:
in some cases everything is already in place, but the epiphany
plugs it in. Daniel Sherrell was in possession of all the relevant
information about climate change ('the Problem') when he sat
down to watch the film *Melancholia* with his mother (a film that
is not about climate change):

> When the movie ended, we watched the credits scroll across
> the screen, neither of us making a move to break the spell. I
> could feel the heat from the bottom of the laptop, the belea-
> guered whir of its little fan. Then all of a sudden I was sob-
> bing, really sobbing, like the sobs were gripping my arms and
> shaking me hard enough to dislodge tears. It was so sudden
> that at first I didn't know what was happening, and so
> couldn't explain to my mother that the movie had finally in-
> duced the kind of feeling I'd always assumed was latent in my
> understanding of the Problem: this fathomless realization
> that the world I knew could end, might end, was perhaps in
> the process of ending.[20]

Nor do epiphanies need to be sudden: as Chappell notes, some
epiphanies are 'the culmination of a story-line, "the moment of

truth", the arrival at last of something long awaited.'[21] It can be like encountering a new reality, but also like seeing the same reality with new eyes—'like waking up from a dream.'[22]

The point is that there must be a place for such experiences— *dark epiphanies* we might call them, where it is not beauty but terror or grief or outrage that shocks us into knowing. We tend to reserve the term 'epiphany' for rare life-changing moments, but if Chappell is right, they are much more common and diverse than we think, driving our personal choices but also, crucially, our moral ones: according to Chappell it is these 'crucial foundational experiences of value that are generally the real roots of our ethical convictions.'[23]

This is all the more important to note because in the early years of climate reporting the sickening campaign of denialism tried to keep these sorts of epiphanies at bay, and so too did all those who pressured journalists and scientists to tone down the message. The mistake was tragic, and perhaps catastrophic. It is, furthermore, a mistake that persists, as writers and activists are still advised to end on a 'hopeful' note, to keep 'despair' at bay. But this is to forget that, as Chappell reminds us, 'horrible suffering can reveal value just as much as beauty can—maybe even more so.'[24] This is why it is not just permissible but imperative that the facts are reported in an undiluted way, since 'it is precisely knowing the facts that makes the decisive motivational difference. And the more factual detail, the stronger the motivational effect.'[25]

This is not to say that the climate movement should be focused exclusively on fostering awareness. As Jacob Blumenfeld has argued, awareness can be a strategy of evasion just as much as denialism, perhaps even more nefariously so.[26] This is the great risk of climate barbarism, where awareness leads not to the dismantling of structural injustices but to privileged countries 'adapting to an unjust world.'[27] Awareness, in other words, can be just another method of looking away. As Chappell has noted, this too is a reality that clings to the epiphanic: *betrayal of vision*—the experience 'that we haven't responded as we should.' This is why we shouldn't rely solely on epiphanies but also need to practice *constancy*: the sheer hard work that must follow upon answering the call.[28] And this is another reason why we need other people, not just to bring the vision into reality but to be called out when it is in danger of being betrayed. That means committing to collective action and engagement, even on a small or local scale. But it also means keeping with the darkness, instead of opting for the kind of optimism that tells us the solution is simple, or the case is closed.[29]

This, more than anything, is what Our Lady of Darkness brings to our remembrance. She arrives at this late hour to re-mind us of the quick unquiet intuition that something can be gathered in the black vision; that our eyes may be opened in ways they were not before; that we may see in the darkness.[30] It is why hopeful pessimism may not be a contradiction but a manifestation of the wild power that is harnessed only when life's darkest forces are gathered into the strange alchemy of hope.

The Virtue of Pessimism

Throughout this book I have suggested that concepts such as optimism and pessimism, hope and despair, are often misun-derstood; that pessimism need not stand in the way of activism, on the contrary, that it can be an especially powerful moral source; whereas optimism and even hope carry dangers of their own. Most of all, I have suggested that pessimism can have value. But could we go further? Could it be, in fact, a *virtue*?

To some, the very notion of a *virtue of pessimism* may seem absurd. For instance, we may subscribe to Hume's notion that the mark of any virtue is that it is *useful and agreeable*, either to the person who possesses it or to others.[31] But surely pessimism is neither useful nor agreeable. It is not *useful*, the argument goes, because it renders us passive, depresses not only ourselves but 'our sense of the possible,' as Marilynne Robinson has said of cultural pessimism in particular.[32] And it is not *agreeable*, since it intensifies our suffering, making us focus on the bad side of life rather than the good (or so arch-optimists such as Leibniz and Rousseau would have it). It is not surprising, then, that certain studies of supposed 'moral exemplars' identified positivity, hopefulness, and optimism among the characteristics that such exemplars had in common.[33]

But then, think of Greta Thunberg. If there is such a thing as a 'climate virtue', she would seem to exemplify it—considering the hard personal choices that she has made, the steadfastness of her vision, and the courage with which she holds world leaders to account and takes them to task for their half-heartedness, their unwillingness to commit fully to the cause. If this is not an exercise of virtues, then I don't know what is—and yet there is nothing positive or optimistic about Thunberg. If there is hope, it's a dark, bleak hope, full of rage and grief and pain for what is being lost—but infused also with insistence, perdurance, determination. It is clear that this activist, at least, will continue to strive *even if* her efforts are doomed to fail. This is not optimism: if anything, it is a hopeful pessimism, and I believe it has every right to be called a virtue in our age.

It is a virtue, furthermore, that many are already cultivating. Thunberg's example is striking precisely because it personifies the stance and experience of many. As Andreas Malm has written of the rise of the climate movement in 2019: 'there was also a darker undertone to the events: a simmering anger. Greta Thunberg personified it. Her silhouette hovered above millions of young people, as a sign of the intergenerational injustice at the heart of climate breakdown.'[34] It is no coincidence that her example has had such an incisive appeal for the imagination of a generation, even if, as one psychologist told her, in a way the school strikers 'did everything wrong.'[35] What many activists prove by their actions and attitudes is that it is possible to be deeply pessimistic about the state of affairs in the world without being fatalistic; that it is possible to be desperately and adamantly activistic without any certainty of success. In this they are aligned with activists of the past, among them Albert Camus, who showed that pessimism can indeed be the drive of sustained action and commitment: that perceiving a bleak reality can be the first step to changing it. 'So I decided then to speak and act clearly,' as one of Camus's heroes told us, 'to put myself on the right path.'[36]

This also suggests that what I have called *hopeful pessimism* is not a new virtue after all—it has risen again and again in times of death and darkness. As writer Mary Annaïse Heglar has pointed out in her open letter to the climate movement, climate change is not the first existential threat to have irrupted upon a population, and activists would do well to take a lesson from the civil rights movement and its desperate, unbending struggle against racism, slavery, and genocide:

> You don't fight something like that because you think you will win. You fight it because you have to. Because surrendering dooms so much more than yourself, but everything that comes after you. Acquiescence, in this case, is what James Baldwin called 'the sickness unto death.'
>
> Can you understand what Fannie Lou Hamer meant when she said, 'What was the point of being scared? The only thing

they could do was kill me, and it kinda seemed like they'd been trying to do that a little bit at a time since I could remember.'

What, now, do you have to lose? What else can you be but brave?[37]

Considering the long history of desperate resistance, it should not be considered strange to imagine pessimism (hopeful, activistic pessimism) as a virtue, and optimism (crude, self-confident optimism) as a vice. Defying the suspicions of fatalism and passivity that have always haunted it, pessimism may even turn out to be one of the oldest virtues in the book; it just has not dared to announce itself that way. It is a virtue, furthermore, that is especially well adapted to emergency, as unlike other virtues, pessimism is committed to confronting acute as well as slumbering dangers, and so carries a sense of urgency within itself. This is why it can be allied with hope, but also with certain tenses of despair.[38]

And so I would argue that hopeful pessimism is neither invention nor innovation: *there are already a lot of hopeful pessimists in the climate movement.*[39] The problem lies not with activists or with their attitudes: the problem rises only when they are told to be boldly optimistic and express hopeful confidence even when they don't feel it—when their experience dwells rather with the shadows of our age; with what De Quincey called the Sorrows. This is why hopeful pessimism, as a concept, can be useful, to give confidence and consolation to those who stand face-to-face with climate change and grieve for what is being lost, even while fighting to preserve it. While new terms are no solution, sometimes they can serve as tools to help us understand ourselves and our experience, and to pry open old concepts that have become too stilted or rusted: that have closed us off from the strange and new. Hopeful pessimism, I argue, can be such a tool, wielded to reassure those experiencing anger, grief, and sadness that this experience is not one to be ashamed of or to be avoided: on the contrary, that it can be a moral source, a spring of ethical activity and motivation.[40]

Hopeful pessimism breaks through the rusted dichotomy of *optimism* vs. *pessimism*. It is this perspective that is exemplified in Thunberg and other figures who by their example give an affirmative answer to the question once posed by Paul Kingsnorth: 'Is it possible to see the future as dark and darkening further; to reject false hope and desperate pseudo-optimism without collapsing into despair?'[41] The thing to avoid, I have argued, is not so much pessimism but fatalism or self-serving resignation. Even despair need not be completely avoided, since it too can energise and encourage us to strive for change, but we should avoid the kind of despair that causes us to collapse. These things are not the same as pessimism, which is simply the assumption of a dark view of the present as well as the future and does *not* imply the loss of courage or insistence to strive for better: on the contrary, often these are the very gifts that pessimism can bestow. Nor are these truths confined to the context of climate change. As Mariana Alessandri has pointed out in her book *Night Vision*, 'Dark moods struggle for sympathy in a world that would like to see them corrected, cured, or converted.'[42]

I envision hopeful pessimism as the answer to a question we struggle even to ask ourselves. A way of breaking through a false dichotomy that anchors us to old habits of thinking and being in the world. A way of holding both sides of reality in one vision; a way of residing within that tension. A way of proving to ourselves and others that we have matured in our awareness as well as our convictions: in our ability to look into that darkness and with clear eyes enter into an uncertain future. A way of persevering without expectancy, in the knowledge that each effort for the cause is one worth making—as countless activists have known before. 'You've got to be in trouble to be transformed,' as Cornel West has said. 'If you do not have the courage to be where the crisis is, where the catastrophe is, you will never be changed.'[43]

In the 1990s theologian Thomas Berry wrote that in times of great crisis the energy for change comes from two sources: 'terror and attraction.' He compared this to addiction, from which 'we seldom recover until we become somewhat terrified by what is happening. We become so frightened that we are willing to undertake a drastic restructuring of our lives, a reordering of our personal life, our environment, our associations—a kind of rebuilding of life from the ground up.' This is the *terror*. But terror alone is not enough. 'To do this effectively, there is also need of a dream. Jung frequently expressed the idea that "the dream drives the action." We need a creative dream, a vision.'[44] This is the attraction, the *vision*.

Terror and vision—could it be that these two things go together, *must go together*, for deep change to be possible? As anyone knows who has struggled with or supported those who have struggled with addiction, sometimes it is necessary to hit rock bottom, to be confronted with the devastating vision of what our lives have become—in order to achieve the capacity to even begin to look for change. So too it is often precisely the experience of the evils and injustices of the world, or the vision of a darkening future, that unsettle us, shock us out of our comfort zone, and call on us to 'change everything'.

This is the gift of Our Lady of Darkness.

Hope's Arrow

Now that we have reclaimed hopeful pessimism as a moral source, even a virtue for our times, it may be clear that 'hopeful' can be bracketed: the work it does is to emphasise that pessimism need not mean fatalism, but once that work is done, there is no reason why 'pessimism' should not suffice. Recall that *hopeful pessimism* is an invitation to reconsider how we think about pessimism but also how we think about hope. 'Hope' here can be seen as a ladder that we need to climb up to our destination: once we have climbed it successfully, we are welcome to let it go, and just be pessimists, committed to the cause.

Or, be optimists. As long as our vision is clear, what matters is to keep our eyes firmly on the cause, on what it is *right* to do— remembering always that those of us whose vision is darker or more desperate should not be blamed for this; that it does not mean they have given up. To despair of a better future does not mean one has forsaken it: as pessimists of the past have proven, and continue to prove each day, this may be the precise point at which resistance takes root.

The true test is not how hopeful or desperate, how optimistic or pessimistic we are. Either way, there is a risk that it becomes just about words and feelings; that it costs us nothing. The real test is in how our attitudes solidify; in how they come to ground. And so I turn, once more, to that hopeful pessimist Albert Camus:

> At this moment, when each of us must fit an arrow to his bow and enter the lists anew, to reconquer, within history and in spite of it, that which he owns already, the thin yield of his fields, the brief love of this earth, at this moment when at last a man is born, it is time to forsake our age and its adolescent rages. The bow bends; the wood complains. At the moment of supreme tension, there will leap into flight an unswerving arrow, a shaft that is inflexible and free.[45]

The test is not in the nature of the bow but in the trajectory of the arrow, the truth of the aim. Hope means nothing if it does not harden into action; pessimism means nothing if keeps us behind closed doors. The call is absolute, the test is in how we answer it. Without this, hope is just hope, pessimism is just pessimism, and this gets us nowhere. As the stone called out to Rilke: *'you must change your life.'*

And so it is time to turn the page on hopeful pessimism, and do the work. For duty, for justice, for truth, for those who are already suffering, and those who will come after us, for humans and for other species, for solidarity, for the frail lives beside us and the dark earth beneath us—in the knowledge that you, that I, have answered the call.

ACKNOWLEDGEMENTS

As readers of *Dark Matters* will know, *Hopeful Pessimism* grew out of its final pages as its necessary continuation; I thank Ben Tate and his colleagues at Princeton University Press for helping me bring it into life. But the book might not have been written if it were not for the invitation of *Aeon* magazine to write an essay on hope, pessimism, and climate change; I thank Sam Dresser and others at *Aeon* for this encouragement, and for allowing me to republish sections of that essay in this book. And my ongoing thanks go to the Leverhulme Trust and the University of St Andrews for supporting this work on hopeful pessimism.

In the preparation of this book, several wonderful scholars have shared their work with me: I thank Simon Hope, Quân Nguyen, Enrico Galvagni, Giuseppe Pezzini, Béatrice Han-Pile, and Robert Stern for their generosity in permitting me to read and cite unpublished or forthcoming work. For consulting on Václav Havel's Czech terms for hope and faith, I thank Matyáš Moravec. For their careful reading and commenting on the manuscript, I thank three anonymous reviewers. For conversations about hope and despair, optimism and pessimism, conceptual loss and climate change, I thank Quân Nguyen, Simon Hope, Bridget Bradley, Andreas Malm, Miguel de la Cal Moreno, Alex Douglas, and the warm community of philosophers at the University of St Andrews. For their friendship and support, I thank Colm Ó Siochrú, Roxani Krystalli, Jack Bonnamy, Margaret

Hampson, Jade Fletcher, King-Ho Leung, Joy Clarkson, and Adam Etinson. And I thank my friend Anna Thomas for allowing me to use her words on grief.

Above all, I thank my family, especially my mother, Mañec, without whom this book would not exist, and my three brothers, Manu, Remko, and Pablo, who have inspired many of its thoughts. I dedicate this book to them, and to activists past, present, and future—in gratitude and admiration.

NOTES

Epigraph

Toyohiko Kagawa, quoted in Peter W. Millar, *An Iona Prayer Book* (Norwich: Canterbury Press, 1998).

Introduction

1. Watts, cited in Bateman, 'Mr. G. F. Watts and His Art', 4.
2. Chomsky, *Optimism over Despair*, 196.
3. Goodall, *Book of Hope*, 78.
4. Solnit, *Hope in the Dark*, xii; Solnit, 'Why Climate Despair Is a Luxury'.
5. Dienstag, *Pessimism*, 40.
6. Peter Jackson, dir., *The Lord of the Rings: The Two Towers* (New Line Cinema, 2002).
7. I will return to Tolkien and the two hopes in chapter 6.
8. On the importance of 'seeing ourselves through dark moods' in general, see Alessandri, *Night Vision*.
9. For more on Lear, see chapter 5.
10. Leonard Cohen, 'Anthem', *The Future* (Columbia, 1992).

1: Optimism, Pessimism, Fatalism

Note to epigraph: Camus, in 1947/48, in journal *Caliban*; cited in Todd, *Camus*, 247 (slightly amended).

1. Chesterton, *G. F. Watts*, 98.
2. Chesterton, *G. F. Watts*, 98–103.
3. Alexander Pope wrote 'Whatever is, is right,' which in French became 'Tout est bien'; for more on this debate, see my *Dark Matters*, chap. 3.
4. Voltaire, *Candide*, 13.
5. See my *Dark Matters*, chap. 8.

6. For more on this, see my *Dark Matters*, especially chap. 2.

7. See Leibniz, *Theodicy*.

8. Citation from a letter from Voltaire to Élie Bertrand, 18 February 1756 (included in *Candide*, 134).

9. For these passages in Bayle and Hume, see my *Dark Matters*, chaps. 1 and 5.

10. Leibniz, *Theodicy*, 216, 248.

11. Note, however, that Popper explained his phrase as simply a rejection of fatalism: 'One must focus on the things that need to be done and for which one is responsible' (*All Life Is Problem Solving*, 125). In fact Popper insisted that he considered himself an optimist *only* about the present, not the future (see below, and chapter 6).

12. Van Lede and Luyendijk, *Pessimisme is voor losers*. There are some exceptions to this pattern: sometimes optimism is (negatively) associated with naivete, and pessimism (positively) with realism. But in the vast majority of cases, optimism tends to be positively, pessimism negatively charged. See Dienstag, preface to *Pessimism*.

13. See https://richardlangworth.com/optimist-pessimists.

14. Or 'everything happens for a reason' (see Kate Bowler's book of this title); see also Alessandri, *Night Vision*, and my *Dark Matters*, chap. 9.

15. *Volkskrant*, 'Een nieuwe kijk op crisis'; *Trouw*, 'Zo maken we de toekomst weer leuk' and 'Zin in morgen'. The illustration by Jip van den Toorn is featured in Sitalsing, 'Achter elke crisis'.

16. As suggested by Takken, 'Hoopvolle klimaat-tv, omdat de kijkers anders wegzappen'.

17. Dienstag, *Pessimism*, 40.

18. Popper, *All Life Is Problem Solving*, 143.

19. Popper, *All Life Is Problem Solving*, 109.

20. Popper, *All Life Is Problem Solving*, 109.

21. See, e.g., Ord, *The Precipice*, 9: 'this is not a pessimistic book. It does not present an inevitable arc of history culminating in our destruction' (thus equating pessimism with fatalism).

22. And in fact, by rejecting *both* kinds of fatalism, Popper shows that he recognised this.

23. In fact, this isn't quite what Leibniz meant, but it was what Voltaire *thought* he meant. See my *Dark Matters*, chap. 3.

24. Robinson, *Givenness of Things*, 29.

25. Wallace-Wells, *Uninhabitable Earth*, 35 (my emphasis). Approvingly cited in Malm, *How to Blow Up a Pipeline*, 146.

26. See, for instance, Stephen Gardiner's insistence that climate policies should not be founded on optimistic hopes about a 'green revolution' bringing economic growth

but on a sense of duty: 'such hope is and should not be our primary ground for acting. After all, morally speaking, *we must act in any case*. . . . The key point is that we should act on climate change even if doing so does not make us better off; indeed, even if it may make us significantly worse off' (*Perfect Moral Storm*, 68; original emphasis).

27. Scranton, *Learning to Die*, 22, 92. The term 'climate stoicism' is applied to Scranton by Stolze, 'Against Climate Stoicism'. See also Malm's criticism of Scranton and others in *How to Blow Up a Pipeline*, 133ff.

28. Miéville, 'The Limits of Utopia' (my emphasis).

29. Jessica Schmidt, cited in Malm, *Progress*, 108–9.

2: Pessimism and Activism

Note to epigraph: 'La seule lâcheté est de se mettre à genoux. . . . Le devoir c'est de faire ce qu'on sait être juste et bonne.' Camus (February or March 1943), cited in Todd, *Camus*, 164, or p. 326 of the French version.

1. For instance: 'We need utopias. That's almost a given in activism. If an alternative to this world were inconceivable, how could we change it?' (Miéville, 'The Limits of Utopia').

2. Chomsky, *Optimism over Despair*, 196.

3. The first two slogans appear on XR banners in the Dutch documentary *2Doc: Klimaatrebellen: Tussen hoop en wanhoop* [Climate rebels: Between hope and despair], directed by Ingeborg Jansen (2022), https://www.2doc.nl/documentaires/2022/06/klimaatrebellen.html; for the third, see figure 2.

4. See Malm, *How to Blow Up a Pipeline*, 151, dissecting here some baffling statements by Roy Scranton and Timothy Morton on learning to 'smile' by 'fully inhabiting catastrophe space' (Scranton, *We're Doomed*, 46–47).

5. In Dienstag's book 'pessimism' is used mainly in the future-oriented sense, but the argument made by Dienstag on the political efficacy of pessimism also holds for the value-oriented sense, especially in the case of Camus.

6. Dienstag, *Pessimism*, 123.

7. As Jacqueline Rose wrote in the *London Review of Books* in May 2020: 'By the end of March, monthly sales of the UK Penguin Classics edition had grown from the low hundreds to the mid-thousands and were rising (they are now up 1000 per cent)' ('Pointing the Finger').

8. Both in the future-oriented and value-oriented sense.

9. Camus, *Myth of Sisyphus*, 26.

10. Camus, *Myth of Sisyphus*, 7.

11. Camus, *Myth of Sisyphus*, 119.

12. Dienstag, *Pessimism*, 148.

13. Dienstag, *Pessimism*, 144.

14. Camus, *The Rebel*, 245.

15. Camus, *Resistance, Rebellion, and Death*, 57–58. Camus said he was pessimistic about the world and human destiny, though 'optimistic as to man' (*Resistance, Rebellion, and Death*, 73), adding: 'This means that the words "pessimism" and "optimism" need to be clearly defined and that, until we can do so, we must pay attention to what unites us rather than to what separates us.'

16. Dienstag, *Pessimism*, 155.

17. Camus, *Resistance, Rebellion, and Death*, 39–40.

18. Dienstag, *Pessimism*, 156.

19. Thus Jeffrey Isaac identifies a 'unique mixture of pessimism and courage' in the writings of Camus and Arendt (*Arendt, Camus, and Modern Rebellion*, 18) and emphasises that they both drew from the example of the French Resistance, drawing in turn from Norman Jacobson, who read in Camus, Arendt, and George Orwell a 'political theory without solace in the twentieth century' (*Pride and Solace*, 139).

20. Dienstag, *Pessimism*, 149n. See Isaac, *Arendt, Camus, and Modern Rebellion*, esp. chaps. 4 and 5.

21. Camus, letter to Roland Barthes on *The Plague*, Paris, 11 January 1955, in *Lyrical and Critical Essays*, 339.

22. Dienstag, *Pessimism*, 156, 145.

23. On this term, see chapter 8.

24. Mordecai Anielewicz to Yitzhak Cukierman, 23 April 1943, Jewish Virtual Library, https://www.jewishvirtuallibrary.org/the-last-letter-from-morde (emphasis in this online version).

25. See Dienstag, *Pessimism*, 41n.

26. Brossat and Klingberg, *Revolutionary Yiddishland*, 162; quoted by Malm in *How to Blow Up a Pipeline*, 198 (Malm's emphasis).

27. Malm, *How to Blow Up a Pipeline*, 150–51.

28. Camus, *The Rebel*, 3.

29. Camus, 'Are We Pessimists?', in *Speaking Out*, 37.

30. Camus, 'Crisis of Man', in *Speaking Out*, 32.

31. Camus, *The Plague*, 101.

32. Camus, *The Plague*, 96.

33. Camus, *The Plague*, 195.

34. Camus, *The Plague*, 120.

35. Consider the recent Shell windfall and the complicity of fossil-fuel companies BP and ExxonMobil in fuelling the denialism campaign as well as popularising the idea of a *personal* carbon footprint. For an excellent visual overview of the campaign history of fossil-fuel denialism, see Supran and Oreskes, 'The Forgotten Oil Ads'. For

more on the 'twin specters of moral corruption and shadow solutions' which haunt global climate negotiations, see Gardiner, *Perfect Moral Storm* (e.g., at 140).

36. Camus, *The Plague*, 140 (my emphasis).

37. Poe, 'The Masque of the Red Death', 485.

38. Robinson, *The Ministry for the Future*, 297.

39. Blumenfeld, 'Climate Barbarism', 163.

40. Butler, 'A Coal Mine for Every Wildfire'.

41. Klein, *On Fire*, 50.

42. Note, however, the recent surge of denialism in the far right; see Malm and the Zetkin Collective, *White Skin, Black Fuel*.

43. Blumenfeld, 'Climate Barbarism', 170.

44. Blumenfeld, 'Climate Barbarism', 172.

45. See the section 'Hope's Arrow' in chapter 9.

46. Klein, *On Fire*, 50 (my emphasis).

47. This is not to say Camus was himself always true to these principles, as his policy of silence in response to the question of Algeria's liberation continues to divide opinions. See below, note 73.

48. Camus, *The Plague*, 98–99.

49. Tooze, 'Ecological Leninism'.

50. Nguyen, 'Pessimism', 110, 112.

51. Nguyen, 'Pessimism', 121.

52. Nairn, 'Learning from Young People Engaged in Climate Activism', 442 (my emphasis); also quoted by Nguyen, 'Pessimism', 121–22.

53. Note that Nguyen's argument applies to both 'future-oriented climate optimism,' which is committed to future progress, and 'purpose-oriented climate optimism,' which appeals to 'a greater purpose behind hardships and suffering' ('Pessimism', 121). I am here focusing only on the former; it is possible that my argument for 'hopeful pessimism' shares some affinities with the latter.

54. Nguyen, 'Pessimism' (his emphasis), 126.

55. Nguyen, 'Pessimism' (my emphasis), 126; Harvey, 'Greta Thunberg Says School Strikes Have Achieved Nothing'. Note, however, that Thunberg did acknowledge the movement's efficacy in shifting awareness (see chapter 9) but not in achieving *concrete* results.

56. Nguyen, 'Pessimism', 127.

57. As in the words of the chief sustainability officer at Xbox: 'In a world that is full of despair and danger, play is the perfect remedy. It fosters imagination, hope, and cooperation. Play helps us feel like we can save the world, and that's what's most missing for the general public right now' (Trista Patterson, quoted in *Time*, 4 December 2023).

58. See also Alessandri, *Night Vision*.

59. Kleres and Wettergren, 'Fear, Hope, Anger', 514 (their emphasis).

60. Cited in Kleres and Wettergren, 'Fear, Hope, Anger', 512.

61. Sierra Club US, COY Lima, December 2014, cited in Kleres and Wettergren, 'Fear, Hope, Anger', 514 (my emphasis).

62. Kleres and Wettergren, 'Fear, Hope, Anger', 508; see again Nguyen, 'Pessimism', 116.

63. Activista/Action Aid 1, COY Paris, November 2015, cited in Kleres and Wettergren, 'Fear, Hope, Anger', 516.

64. Thunberg, 'Our House Is on Fire'.

65. Kleres and Wettergren, 'Fear, Hope, Anger', 516 (my emphasis).

66. Activista/Action Aid 2, COY Paris, November 2015, cited in Kleres and Wettergren, 'Fear, Hope, Anger', 516.

67. Swedish youth activist, COY Lima, December 2014, cited in Kleres and Wettergren, 'Fear, Hope, Anger', 513 (my emphasis).

68. Kleres and Wettergren, 'Fear, Hope, Anger', 516.

69. Kleres and Wettergren, 'Fear, Hope, Anger', 508.

70. Miéville, 'The Limits of Utopia'.

71. Salvage Editorial Collective, 'Pessimism after Corbyn' (their emphasis).

72. Camus, 'Are We Pessimists?', in *Speaking Out*, 36.

73. Camus, *Resistance, Rebellion, and Death*, 246. There is avowedly an irony in this passage, as Camus himself (while 'impeccably anti-colonial' [Gopnik]) at the very time of speaking these words had fallen silent over the Algerian question, showing, perhaps, just how persistent this temptation is. But the matter is complicated, and Camus himself was torn: see Hammer, 'Why Is Albert Camus Still a Stranger in His Native Algeria?' and Gopnik, 'Facing History'.

3: Losing the Future

Note to epigraph: Koethe, 'In Italy', section 2: 'Expulsion from the Garden', 140 (emphasis in original).

1. For instance, Byron's poem 'Darkness' of 1816 had been preceded by François Xavier Cousin de Grainville's *Le Dernier Homme* of 1805 and was followed by Thomas Campbell's poem 'The Last Man' in 1823–25. See Redford, 'The "Last Man on Earth" in Romantic Literature'.

2. Shelley, *The Last Man*, 273–74.

3. Shelley, *The Last Man*, 308.

4. Shelley, *The Last Man*, 448–49.

5. Shelley, *The Last Man*, 467. The story ends with Verney setting sail in the desperate hope of finding another human being on another continent.

6. Though focusing on 2100 is deceiving, as it suggests an end point to the crisis, when in fact things will likely just get worse once that date has passed: see Malm, *Progress*, 6–7.

7. The novel is very different from the 2006 film version directed by Alfonso Cuarón (which is set in 2027); for various reasons the film is better; but the novel gives some interesting background to the existential situation.

8. James, *The Children of Men*, 12.

9. James, *The Children of Men*, 13.

10. The lectures were originally held at UC Berkeley in 2012 as part of the Tanner Lectures on Human Values but later expanded into a book, with replies by critics.

11. Scheffler, *Death and the Afterlife*, 26.

12. Scheffler, *Death and the Afterlife*, 18.

13. Scheffler, *Death and the Afterlife*, 38.

14. Scheffler, *Death and the Afterlife*, 18.

15. Scheffler, *Death and the Afterlife*, 21.

16. Scheffler, *Death and the Afterlife*, 26.

17. Scheffler, *Death and the Afterlife*, 40.

18. Scheffler, *Death and the Afterlife*, 43.

19. Note that Scheffler is bracketing questions of personal immortality or the religious afterlife.

20. Scheffler, *Death and the Afterlife*, 29.

21. Scheffler, *Death and the Afterlife*, 30.

22. Scheffler, *Death and the Afterlife*, 34.

23. Scheffler, *Death and the Afterlife*, 30.

24. Scheffler, *Death and the Afterlife*, 45.

25. See, for instance, the replies by Susan Wolf and others in Scheffler, *Death and the Afterlife*.

26. Sebastiaan (twenty-one at the time of speaking), quoted in the Dutch documentary *Klimaatrebellen* at 10:26 (my translation, my emphasis).

27. Thunberg, speech at the Houses of Parliament.

28. Jessica Agar, quoted in Gayle, 'Just Stop Oil Campaigners Glue Themselves to Da Vinci Copy in Royal Academy'.

29. Sherrell, *Warmth*, 98.

30. I borrow the concept of 'a gap that is intensely active' from William James, who used this phrase to describe the tip-of-the-tongue-experience (*Principles of Psychology*, 1:251).

31. Yotam Marom, in Lakey and Marom, 'Can Now Really Be the Best Time to Be Alive?'

32. Magnason, *On Time and Water*, 61.

33. Thunberg, speech at the 'Declaration of Rebellion'.

34. There is a risk, however, in generalising the climate concerns of the young, as there are also many in this generation who are not aware of or do not care about the crisis: climate barbarism also rages among the young. Equally there is a risk in over-emphasising the old/young dichotomy, as there are many older people active in the climate movement.

35. Quoted in Hilton, 'Greenland Is Now a Country Fit for Broccoli Growers'.

36. Thus Sherrell in his memoir *Warmth* speaks of climate crisis only as 'the Problem'. See, however, Heglar, 'Climate Change Isn't the First Existential Threat', for an important critique of the perceived exceptionality of climate change as an existential threat (see also chapter 9).

37. Albrecht, *Earth Emotions*, 200.

38. Scheffler, *Death and the Afterlife*, 43.

39. This is a question also for parents. 'I have four children who are starting to make their own life choices,' says Andri Snær Magnason. 'What should I tell them, how should I explain what's happening? I feel bad taking away *their sense of purpose, their faith in the future*' (*On Time and Water*, 115; my emphasis).

40. McKinnon, 'Climate Change', 40; this passage is also cited by Malm, *How to Blow Up a Pipeline*, 147, who adds Solnit, *Hope in the Dark*, 4: 'Anything could happen, and whether we act or not has everything to do with it.' On hope/despair, see also chapter 8.

41. On intergenerational justice, see, e.g., Gardiner, *Perfect Moral Storm*.

42. Nakate, cited in Klein and Stefoff, *How to Change Everything*, 267 (my emphasis).

43. Thunberg, guest editorial (my emphasis).

44. Thunberg, *Climate Book*, 154–55.

45. 'Transcript: Greta Thunberg's Speech at the UN Climate Action Summit', NPR, 23 September 2019, https://www.npr.org/2019/09/23/763452863/transcript-greta-thunbergs-speech-at-the-u-n-climate-action-summit.

46. Camus, *The Rebel*, 246–47.

47. 'Wo aber Gefahr ist, wächst / Das Rettende auch' (Hölderlin, 'Patmos', in *Poems and Fragments*, 462–63).

48. Klein, *This Changes Everything*, 48.

4: The Ambiguity of Hope

Note to epigraph: Eliot, 'East Coker', in *Four Quartets*, 28.

1. Cited in Tromans, *Hope*, 17.

2. At least at first sight: recall that Chesterton thought that anyone standing in front of *Hope* for a while would end up with something more like faith, vitality, or the will to live (see chapter 1).

3. Cited in Tromans, *Hope*, 9.

4. Tromans, *Hope*, 15; for Keats's use of the lyre image, see Franklin, 'Once More the Poet'. On the portrayal of Christian hope as anchor (*anchora spei*), see also Potkay, *Hope*, 340n.

5. I thank an anonymous reviewer for pointing this out to me.

6. Potkay, *Hope*, 8.

7. Tromans, *Hope*, 11–12.

8. Tromans, *Hope*, 16.

9. Cited in Tromans, *Hope*, 70n.

10. Published in *Academy*, 29 May 1886; cited in Tromans, *Hope*, 21. Tromans calls this 'the first of what were to be many Christian responses to the image.'

11. Forsyth, *Religion in Recent Art*, 133; also cited in Tromans, *Hope*, 34.

12. See Tromans, *Hope*, 34, who points out that Forsyth saw *Hope* as a companion piece to Watts's painting *Mammom*, which shows 'the god of greed crushing humanity'; at the time the two images were often displayed together.

13. James Burns, cited in Tromans, *Hope*, 72n.

14. J. E. Pythian in 1906, cited in Tromans, *Hope*, 72n.

15. Tromans, *Hope*, 22. Tromans notes that the second version fits better in sequence with *Mammon* and *The Dweller in the Innermost* of 1884–86, which Watts also gave to the nation. Two other versions survive: see https://en.wikipedia.org/wiki/Hope_(Watts).

16. See Tromans, *Hope*, 21: Watts had offered to donate his most important pictures to the nation, but as there were offers from private collectors by the end of 1886, Watts had made a second version (probably with studio assistant Cecil Schott) to be gifted instead of the first. On the other hand, Mary Watts claimed her husband painted the new version to improve on the original (Tromans, *Hope*, 71n).

17. Tromans, *Hope*, 49, citing the *Western Mail*, Perth WA, 1 September 1888.

18. Chesterton, *G. F. Watts*, 102–3.

19. Wright, 'The Audacity to Hope', 102. Barack Obama famously writes about being moved by Wright's sermon in *Dreams from My Father* (291–95), later borrowing Wright's title for his book *The Audacity of Hope*, though he never mentions Watts by name (see Tromans, *Hope*, 74n).

20. Kazantzidis and Spatharas, introduction to their edited volume *Hope in Ancient Literature, History, and Art*, 2. See also Potkay, *Hope*, 61–62, on the influence of Eastern traditions on Hellenistic philosophy such as Stoicism. See both volumes for more on hope's hesitant history.

21. Lateiner, '*Elpis* as Emotion and Reason', 131–32 (his emphasis).

22. *Elpis* is usually translated as 'hope', but this is not straightforward: see again Kazantzidis and Spatharas, *Hope in Ancient Literature, History, and Art*.

23. Hesiod, cited in Lateiner, 'Elpis as Emotion and Reason', 133; see also Potkay, Hope, 31ff.

24. Potkay, Hope, 8, 32. See Bloch, The Principle of Hope, 1:333–36.

25. Kazantzidis and Spatharas, introduction, 2. See Lateiner, 'Elpis as Emotion and Reason', 132: 'The futility and fatuity of hope is a Hellenic commonplace'; he also notes that the Greek elpis, which comes closest to our 'hope', is often combined with negative epithets such as empty hope or blind hope.

26. Dated to 477 BC: see Kazantzidis and Spatharas, introduction, 24–27.

27. Kazantzidis and Spatharas, introduction, 24.

28. Lateiner, 'Elpis as Emotion and Reason', 132; Potkay, Hope, 29.

29. Potkay, Hope, 29: 'The first author to treat elpis as an unqualified good, given a very specific object of desire (eternal life in Christ), is St. Paul, the earliest writer in the New Testament.'

30. Potkay, Hope, 29. Strictly speaking, hope must be oriented on two objects, eternal life and God's assistance; see Aquinas, 'On Hope', art. 1, in Disputed Questions on the Virtues, 221.

31. Pieper, Faith, Hope, Love, 99 (drawing on Aquinas).

32. Aquinas, 'On Hope', art. 1, in Disputed Questions on the Virtues, 217.

33. Pieper, Faith, Hope, Love, 100.

34. Aquinas, 'On the Virtues in General', art. 2, in Disputed Questions on the Virtues, 14; cf. Pieper, Faith, Hope, Love, 100.

35. Aquinas, 'On Hope', art. 1, in Disputed Questions on the Virtues, 222. Note that Aquinas distinguishes hope as a (religious) virtue from hope as a (secular) emotion: see Miner, 'Hope and Despair', in Thomas Aquinas on the Passions, 215–30.

36. Aquinas, 'On Hope', art. 1, in Disputed Questions on the Virtues, 222; Pieper, Faith, Hope, Love, 98, 113 (on praesumptio).

37. Pieper, Faith, Hope, Love, 101–3.

38. Aquinas, 'On Hope', art. 1, in Disputed Questions on the Virtues, 222–23.

39. 1 Corinthians 13:13 (New International Version).

40. Pieper, Faith, Hope, Love, 103.

41. Dante, Purgatorio, canto 29, vv. 127–29 (trans. Mandelbaum).

42. I borrow the term 'countervailing' from Potkay, Hope, 170.

43. Voltaire, Letters on England (also known as the Philosophical Letters), 132.

44. Samuel Johnson, Rambler, no. 67, Tuesday, 6 November 1750, in Works, 3:353.

45. Johnson, Rambler, no. 67, Tuesday, 6 November 1750, in Works, 3:356. See Johnson's letter to an unidentified female correspondent (8 June 1762, in Letters, 1:203): 'Hope is itself a species of happiness, and perhaps the chief happiness which this world affords, but like all other pleasures immoderately enjoyed, the excesses of hope must be expiated by pain, and expectations improperly indulged must end in disappointment.'

46. Johnson, Rambler, no. 203, Tuesday, 25 February 1752, in Works, 5:295.

47. Rousseau, 'Letter to Voltaire', 246 (my emphasis).

48. Schopenhauer, *Parerga and Paralipomena*, 2:525. He adds in a footnote: 'Hope is a state to which our whole being, namely will and intellect, concurs; the former in that it desires the object of hope, the latter in that it calculates it to be probable. The bigger the share of the latter factor and the smaller the former, the better things will be for hope; in the opposite case, the worse.'

49. Schopenhauer, *Parerga and Paralipomena*, 2:265.

50. Schopenhauer, *Parerga and Paralipomena*, 2:525. For some ambiguities of hope in Schopenhauer, see my *Dark Matters*, 356–58.

51. Nietzsche, *Human, All Too Human*, § 71 (my emphasis). Note that Nietzsche is more positive about hope elsewhere, but not unambiguously so.

52. Camus 'Nuptials', in *Lyrical and Critical Essays* (written c. 1936–37), 91–92.

53. Camus, *Myth of Sisyphus*, 7, 133, 58.

54. Cited in Todd, *Camus*, 291.

55. Camus, 'Create Dangerously' (lecture, Uppsala, December 1957), in *Resistance, Rebellion, and Death*, 272.

56. Eagleton, *Hope without Optimism*, 103.

57. Cited at the beginning of this chapter.

58. Gay, 'The Case against Hope'.

59. Note that she writes: 'Realism is more my ministry than is unbridled optimism', thus seeming to equate optimism with hope.

60. Solnit, *Hope in the Dark*, 4.

61. Goodall, *Book of Hope*, xv (my emphasis); see also p. 8: 'Hope . . . is what enables us to keep going in the face of adversity. It is what we desire to happen, but we must be prepared to work hard to make it so.'

62. Solnit, *Hope in the Dark*, xvi.

63. Thunberg, *Climate Book*, 421 (my emphasis).

64. Aquinas gives two examples of false hope: 'the hope of drunkards' and the hope of fools (actually Aquinas speaks of the 'young', but as Miner suggests, this doesn't necessarily mean chronologically *young*—rather a kind of psychological immaturity: that is, foolishness). See Miner, 'Hope and Despair', 224.

65. Miner, 'Hope and Despair', 223–24, who cites Aquinas: 'all fools, without using deliberation, attempt everything and are of good hope.'

66. Matt Santos, a (fictional) presidential candidate in *The West Wing*, season 6, episode 10, 'Faith Based Initiative', https://www.quotes.net/show-quote/91191; see also the examples mentioned by Miner, 'Hope and Despair', 223.

67. Miner, 'Hope and Despair', 224 (my emphasis).

68. Miner, 'Hope and Despair', 224 (my emphasis).

69. Though note that there may be a case for resistance even in the absence of all hope: that is, a *just cause* may be enough. See chapters 2 and 8.

70. And so, ironically, it turns out that to ground the case for hope on probability makes it *less* robust, not more so.

71. Scranton, *We're Doomed*.

72. As rightly emphasised by Figueres and Rivett-Carnac, *The Future We Choose*, 51: 'When your mind tells you that it is too late to make a difference, remember that every fraction of a degree of extra warming makes a big difference, and therefore any reduction in emissions lessens the burden on the future.'

73. Franzen, 'What If We Stopped Pretending?' Note that Franzen does mention that we should still do what we can, but the point is drowned out by the insistence that it's too late.

74. Goodall, *Book of Hope*, 10–11.

75. 'Hope is hard to characterize because of the exceptional diversity of its applications,' as Béatrice Han-Pile notes, adding that we can express hope for ourselves but also for people we love and for complete strangers; we can hope for the future but also for things past or present (such as 'I hope that he made it home safely'), and so forth (Han-Pile, 'Hope, Powerlessness, and Agency', 175). She also points out differences in 'intensity and meaningfulness', in degrees of likelihood and so forth. 'Thus, hope can attach itself to objects that are close or remote to the self; its temporal modality spans all three dimensions of time; it can be mild, almost irrelevant to the self, or identity-defining.'

76. Han-Pile, 'Hope, Powerlessness, and Agency', 176. See also chapter 8 below.

77. See Han-Pile, 'Hope, Powerlessness, and Agency', 179: 'if we understood the outcome as theoretically certain, or for all practical purposes as within our control, we could still *desire* it, *expect* it or *look forward* to it, but we could not *hope* for it' (my emphasis).

78. Goodall, cited in Saner, 'Jane Goodall on Fires, Floods, Frugality and the Good Fight'.

79. Goodall, *Book of Hope*, 10. Similarly Solnit, *Hope in the Dark*, 11: 'Hope and action feed each other.' And Thunberg: 'It feels like people are obsessed today with asking "Is there hope?"—because they feel that without it, they cannot act. In fact, it's the exact opposite: when they act, they create hope' (cited in Mossman, '"I haven't met a politician ready to do what it takes"').

80. See chapter 8 (on despair).

81. Han-Pile and Stern, 'Is Hope a Secular Virtue?', 77, 105n40. Note also that hope is not straightforwardly a matter of control: Han-Pile and Stern argue that hoping 'is neither active, nor passive: it is what might be called medio-passive' (98); see Han-Pile, 'Hope, Powerlessness, and Agency', 197, and Eagleton, *Hope without Optimism*, 70.

82. Eagleton, *Hope without Optimism*, 58.

83. See also Lear, *Radical Hope*, 105, where he stresses that hopefulness is not necessarily a positive trait: it can also be 'a strategy for averting [one's] gaze.'

84. Han-Pile and Stern, 'Is Hope a Secular Virtue?', 87–89.

85. Or 'expectation': see Han-Pile and Stern, 'Is Hope a Secular Virtue?', 88, 93–95.

86. See chapters 5 and 6 below.

87. Miéville, 'The Limits of Utopia'.

5: Radical Hope Revisited

1. von Preussen, 'Don't Tread on Me'.

2. Attributed to Kafka by Max Brod in a slightly different version: 'Oh, hope enough, infinite hope,—just not for us.' See https://quoteinvestigator.com/2021/10/05/hope/.

3. von Preussen, 'Don't Tread on Me'.

4. Thunberg, *Climate Book*, 3.

5. Lear, *Radical Hope*, 1.

6. Cited in Lear, *Radical Hope*, 2, 56 (my emphases).

7. Lear, *Radical Hope*, 8, 24, 34 (my emphasis).

8. Lear, *Radical Hope*, 50, 24 (his emphasis).

9. Lear, *Radical Hope*, 64.

10. Lear, *Radical Hope*, 59, 64–65 (his emphasis).

11. Lear, *Radical Hope*, 68, 115.

12. Lear, *Radical Hope*, 83.

13. For more on these dreams, see Lear, *Radical Hope*, chap. 2.

14. Lear, *Radical Hope*, 95, 97.

15. Lear, *Radical Hope*, 103.

16. Or so Lear claims: 'unlike other tribes, the Crow were not displaced from their lands, they were not put on a forced march, they did not have to walk a "trail of tears"—and they could correctly say of themselves that they were never defeated' (*Radical Hope*, 136).

17. Lear, *Radical Hope*, 95.

18. Lear, *Radical Hope*, 104.

19. Lear, *Radical Hope*, 113, 123.

20. Lear, *Radical Hope*, 123.

21. Lear, *Radical Hope*, 132–34.

22. Lear, *Radical Hope*, 123 (my emphasis).

23. Lear, *Radical Hope*, 107.

24. Recall that while scientists voiced concern about climate change since at least the 1980s, and Bill McKibben published his book *The End of Nature* in 1989, the denialist campaign was successful enough to suspend widespread public awareness for several decades.

25. Lear, *Radical Hope*, 115, 83.
26. Lear, *Radical Hope*, 104.
27. Lear, *Radical Hope*, 115.
28. Williston, 'Climate Change and Radical Hope', 165.
29. Thompson, 'Radical Hope for Living Well in a Warmer World', 51, 52.
30. Williston, 'Climate Change and Radical Hope', 167.
31. Hope, 'Climate Change ', n. 49.
32. Hope, 'Climate Change', § 2.
33. Thompson defines radical hope as a kind of courage; Williston hardly discusses courage.
34. Lear, *Radical Hope*, 109.
35. Hope, 'Climate Change'.
36. Hope, 'Climate Change' (his emphases).
37. Note that Lear does not do this himself (at least, not *quite*—more on this below).
38. Oppenheimer, 'Out of Unbearable Loss' (my emphasis).
39. Lear, *Radical Hope*, 108.
40. Recounted in Lear, *Radical Hope*, 26–29; Wraps His Tail quoted on 28–29.
41. Lear, *Radical Hope*, 97, 32, 97.
42. Cited in Utley, *Sitting Bull*, 123.
43. Lear, *Radical Hope*, 148–49.
44. Lear, *Radical Hope*, 150–51.
45. Lear, *Radical Hope*, 108.
46. Hoxie, quoted in Lear, *Radical Hope*, 106.
47. Žižek, *Living in the End Times*, xiv.
48. See chapter 2.
49. Brossat and Klingberg, *Revolutionary Yiddishland*, 150–51 (my emphases).
50. Quoted in Brossat and Klingberg, *Revolutionary Yiddishland*, 151 (my emphasis).
51. Lear, *Imagining the End*, 39.
52. Brossat and Klingberg, *Revolutionary Yiddishland*, 162–63 (my emphasis). Part of this passage was also quoted in chapter 2 (and by Malm).
53. Brossat and Klingberg, *Revolutionary Yiddishland*, 166 (my emphasis).
54. This is the hope expressed by the late Hilary Mantel, who quoted Petrarch on the last page of her renowned Cromwell trilogy, which was also the last book of her life: see the quote at the opening of this chapter.
55. Frankl, *Man's Search for Meaning*, 90.
56. Eagleton, *Hope without Optimism*, 32–33, here discussing Walter Benjamin.
57. See Blumberg, 'Sitting Bull's Legacy'.

58. For one thing, both believed to be obeying divine guidance, but Plenty Coups's dreams were not about the climate crisis, nor were Sitting Bull's.

59. Taylor, 'A Different Kind of Courage'.

60. See chapter 7 below.

61. Oppenheimer ('Out of Unbearable Loss') reads Lear in the second way; Taylor ('A Different Kind of Courage') in the first.

62. Lear, *Imagining the End*, 24.

63. Lear, *Imagining the End*, 39–40 (his emphasis).

64. Lear, *Imagining the End*, 103–4 (my emphasis in final line).

65. Eagleton, *Hope without Optimism*, 65; on 'absolute hope' (which Eagleton calls 'fundamental hope'), see Marcel, *Homo Viator*, 26, 39–40. For more on Bloch and Marcel, see chap. 2 of Eagleton's book.

66. Franzen, 'What If We Stopped Pretending?'; Scranton, *Learning to Die* and *We're Doomed*.

67. This is a charitable interpretation that I think fails for Scranton, though perhaps not for Franzen, and, for example, Paul Kingsnorth (consider his 'Finnegas': 'Perhaps, if we're lucky, we could lay some ground for what is to come').

68. Wallace-Wells, *Uninhabitable Earth*, 35 (my emphasis).

69. Not to mention the suffering of other species.

70. Thunberg, *Climate Book*, 422.

71. Lear, *Radical Hope*, 123

72. Lear, *Radical Hope*, 75.

73. Han-Pile, 'Hope, Powerlessness, and Agency', 187, also notes the *spiritual* nature of radical hope.

74. Taylor, 'A Different Kind of Courage'. Note that this means that even those belonging to religious communities cannot draw from their spiritual sources any consensus for moral or political action: modern societies don't at all adhere to such sources in a collective mode as the Crow did.

75. Lear, *Radical Hope*, 94.

76. Lear, *Radical Hope*, 94; on the return to life, see *Imagining the End*, and chapter 7 below; on despair, see chapter 8 below.

6: Blue Hope

Note to epigraph: Camus, 'Summer' (1953), in *Lyrical and Critical Essays*, 169.

1. Eagleton, *Hope without Optimism*, 13.

2. And now, *Hopeful Pessimism*! But see the final pages of chapter 9. Note also the subtitles of Figueres and Rivett-Carnac, *The Future We Choose: The Stubborn Optimist's Guide to the Climate Crisis*, and Rutger Bregman, *Humankind: A Hopeful*

History (which in many languages is instead rendered 'an optimistic history'). In September 2023 the special climate issue of *Newsweek* bore the title 'Don't Lose Hope'.

3. Goodall, *Book of Hope*, 232; see also Kelsey, *Hope Matters*, chap. 2: 'The Collateral Damage of Doom and Gloom'.

4. The quote is from Eagleton, *Hope without Optimism*, 11; on the Roman *spes*, see chap. 4.

5. Potkay, *Hope*, 27; see below on Cornel West's hesitation with regard to the Obama campaign's use of hope.

6. Potkay, *Hope*, chap. 1.

7. Ronald Reagan, 'Acceptance Speech at the Republican National Convention,' 17 July 1980, https://www.youtube.com/watch?v=SBP2gvZTnwM, at 29:06.

8. Eagleton, *Hope without Optimism*, 4, 10–11 (the historian remains unnamed). Eagleton also quotes Henry James, 'although a conservative is not necessarily an optimist, I think an optimist is pretty likely to be a conservative' (James, *Literary Criticism*, quoted in Eagleton, *Hope without Optimism*, 4), and points out that optimism is 'almost a state ideology' in the United States (and North Korea) while 'pessimism is thought to be vaguely subversive' (Eagleton, *Hope without Optimism*, 10).

9. 'Boris Johnson's First Speech as Prime Minister', 24 July 2019, https://www.gov.uk/government/speeches/boris-johnsons-first-speech-as-prime-minister-24-july-2019

10. Clark, 'Carlota Perez and the Economics of Hope'.

11. 'Liz Truss's Final Speech as Prime Minister', 25 October 2022, https://www.gov.uk/government/speeches/liz-trusss-final-speech-as-prime-minister-25-october-2022.

12. 'Rishi Sunak's First Speech as Prime Minister', 25 October 2022, https://www.gov.uk/government/speeches/prime-minister-rishi-sunaks-statement-25-october-2022.

13. Jeremy Hunt, interview by Chris Mason, BBC News, 17 November 2022, https://www.bbc.co.uk/news/uk-politics-63665271.

14. West, *Hope on a Tightrope*, 15.

15. West, *Hope on a Tightrope*, 6.

16. West, *Hope on a Tightrope*, 216.

17. West, *Hope on a Tightrope*, 217.

18. Hanman, 'We Are Seeing the Beginnings'.

19. Mossman, '"I haven't met a politician ready to do what it takes"'.

20. In Mossman, '"I haven't met a politician ready to do what it takes"'.

21. Marvel, 'We Need Courage, Not Hope, to Face Climate Change'. See also Kimmerer, 'Mending Our Relationship with the Earth', 420: 'I'm often asked: where

do you find hope in these dark times? I'm not sure I really know what we mean by hope. A source of optimism? Wishful thinking? Evidence of a turning towards life and away from destruction? I don't know about hope, but I do know about love. I think we are in this perilous moment because we have not loved the Earth enough, and it is love that will lead us to safety.'

22. Thunberg, *Climate Book*, 436 (my emphasis).

23. Thunberg, *Climate Book*, 421, 3.

24. This is the vision of hope espoused by Thunberg and others when they emphasise that hope must be rooted in action (see above, chapter 4).

25. Eagleton, *Hope without Optimism*, 110.

26. Goodall, *Book of Hope*, 169–70.

27. 'hopepunk' entered the *Collins English Dictionary* in 2019: see https://www.collinsdictionary.com/dictionary/english/hopepunk.

28. Though Rowland later adjusted this: 'Whether the glass is half full or half empty, what matters is that there's water in that glass. And that's something worth defending' ('One Atom of Justice').

29. Rowland, Tumblr post: https://ariaste.tumblr.com/post/163500138919/ariaste-the-opposite-of-grimdark-is-hopepunk; see also 'One Atom of Justice'.

30. See https://www.youtube.com/watch?v=k6C8SX0mWP0.

31. E.g., Robson, 'The Sci-fi Genre Offering Radical Hope for Living Better'.

32. Goodall, *Book of Hope*, 169.

33. Pezzini, *Tolkien and the Mystery of Literary Creation*, chap. 5.

34. Tolkien, '*Ahtrabeth Finrod ah Andreth*': a dialogue written by J.R.R. Tolkien and published posthumously by Christopher Tolkien in *Morgoth's Ring* (320).

35. Pezzini, *Tolkien and the Mystery of Literary Creation*, chap. 5.

36. Tolkien, *The Lord of the Rings* (hereafter LotR), 1:331 (my emphasis).

37. Tolkien, LotR, 1:333.

38. Tolkien, LotR, 2:441. Note that just after Gandalf's fall Aragorn also mentions revenge, perhaps in the passion of the moment: 'At least we may yet be avenged. Let us gird ourselves and weep no more! Come! We have a long road and much to do' (LotR, 1:333).

39. Tolkien, LotR, 3:918, 924 (my emphases).

40. Tolkien, LotR, 1:357.

41. Tolkien, *Morgoth's Ring*, 320.

42. Tolkien, *Morgoth's Ring*, 332.

43. Tolkien, *Morgoth's Ring*, 320.

44. Tolkien, LotR, 1:404.

45. Tolkien, LotR, 2:495.

46. Pezzini, *Tolkien and the Mystery of Literary Creation*, chap. 5. Note the phrase Tolkien used when describing the occurrences of the War of the Ring in the

Appendix: 'how *hope beyond hope* was fulfilled' (Appendix A, LotR, 3:1062, my emphasis).

47. Both spoken by Éomer, in Tolkien, LotR, 3:848, 3:847.

48. Tolkien, LotR, 3:950.

49. Tolkien, LotR, 3:1029.

50. Note that in his *Letters* Tolkien repeatedly resisted the idea that the plot of LotR represented a straightforward victory of good over evil with all the good people going home happy and rewarded; note also that Sauron was 'defeated' but not destroyed.

51. Tolkien, *Letters*, 181.

52. Tolkien, *Letters*, 246, 327.

53. Tolkien, *Sauron Defeated*, 62 (final emphasis mine).

54. Tolkien, *Sauron Defeated*, 62.

55. See LotR, 3:933: 'Never for long had hope died in his staunch heart'; and 3:950: 'after coming all that way I don't want to give up yet. It's not like me, somehow, if you understand.'

56. Tolkien, LotR, 3:922. The 'song' referred to is 'Sam's Song in the Orc Tower'.

57. Tolkien, Appendix A, LotR, 3:1062 (my emphasis).

58. Tolkien, *Letters*, 181; see again Pezzini, *Tolkien and the Mystery of Literary Creation*, chap. 5.

59. Tromans, *Hope*, 20.

60. Dante, *Purgatorio*, canto I, v. 135 (trans. Hollander and Hollander); in contrast there is no hope in *Inferno*, whose gates are adorned with the damning phrase: 'Abandon all hope ye who enter here.'

61. See Pastoureau, *Blue: History of a Colour*.

62. See, e.g., Kelsey, *Hope Matters*, chap. 2; Figueres and Rivett-Carnac, *The Future We Choose*, chap. 5. I want to stress that there is much of value in these books, and the authors are absolutely correct in their opposition to fatalism (in the former: pp. 8, 24, 39; in the latter: pp. 3, 13, 60); I believe they go too far, however, in their emphasis on positive thinking and conflation of hope and optimism.

63. E.g., Figueres and Rivett-Carnac, *The Future We Choose*; Wong, 'How to Stay Optimistic When Everything Seems Wrong'.

64. Frankl, *Man's Search for Meaning*, 47.

65. Frankl, *Man's Search for Meaning*, 82.

66. Frankl, *Man's Search for Meaning*, 83–84.

67. Frankl, *Man's Search for Meaning*, 86, 46.

68. Recall that this was exactly the concern expressed by Cornel West in response to the high hopes for Obama's presidency in 2008 and by the Salvage Collective in response to the Corbyn candidacy: that too high hopes will end in disappointment and deflation. See chapter 2 on activists' disillusionment after failed COP events.

69. Amanda Ripley ('This Element Is Critical to Human Flourishing'): 'For journalists, hope is a defiant way of being in the world: ever on the lookout for what is but always alert to what might be.'

70. See Paul Wilson's preface to Havel, *Disturbing the Peace*.

71. Havel, *Disturbing the Peace*, 181 (my emphasis).

72. Havel, *Disturbing the Peace*, 182. See Dienstag, *Pessimism*, 156n, who connects Havel to Camus and suggests that 'a very strong case exists that it was on the basis of just such a pessimistic solidarity that, for example, the rebellious dissident movements of Eastern Europe in the 1970s and 1980s coalesced. The writings of Václav Havel—and the veneration of iconoclasts like Frank Zappa by the Czech underground—echo Camus' injunction to combat oppression with individuality.'

73. Havel, Letter 64, 17 January 1981, *Letters to Olga*, 150. This is missed by Figueres and Rivett-Carnac, who misquote Haval as describing 'optimism' in this passage (*The Future We Choose*, 52).

74. Havel seems to be using 'hope' (*naděje*) and 'faith' (*víra*) interchangeably in this text; both are presented as standing in sharp contrast to optimism. Many thanks to Matyáš Moravec for consulting on the Czech terms.

75. Havel, Letter 64, 17 January 1981, *Letters to Olga*, 150–51.

76. Havel, *Disturbing the Peace*, 181.

77. Frankl, *Man's Search for Meaning*, 85 (first emphasis his; second emphasis mine).

78. West, *Hope on a Tightrope*, 209, 78 (my emphasis).

79. Popper, *All Life Is Problem Solving*, 111, 109 (my emphases); see chap. 1 for the full quote.

80. George Perkins Marsh, quoted in Wulf, *The Invention of Nature*, 297.

81. Solnit, *Hope in the Dark*, xxi (in this book Solnit repeatedly, and interestingly, alternates between blue hope and green).

82. Virginia Woolf, quoted in Solnit, *Hope in the Dark*, 1.

83. Solnit, *Hope in the Dark*, 23.

84. Eagleton, *Hope without Optimism*, 120 (here discussing Quentin Meillassoux).

85. La Mettrie (my translation), fully quoted in my *Dark Matters*, 183.

86. Schopenhauer, *World as Will*, 1:184.

87. Eagleton, *Hope without Optimism*, 21.

88. Popper, *All Life Is Problem Solving*, 143 (my emphasis). See Bloch, *The Principle of Hope*, 1:246: 'The Authentic in man and in the world is outstanding, waiting, lives in fear of being frustrated, lives in hope of succeeding. Because what is possible can equally well turn into Nothing as into Being: the Possible, as that which is not fully conditional, is that which is not settled.'

89. McKinnon, 'Climate Change', 40 (see chapter 8).

90. West, *Hope on a Tightrope*, 217.

91. Marcel, *Being and Having*, 91n.; see also 93: 'It seems to me that the conditions that make it possible to hope are strictly the same as those which make it possible to despair.' Note, however, that for Marcel hope must ultimately be rooted in the transcendent: 'it is in the invisible world that Hope flows out to sea' (*Being and Having*, 78; see *Homo Viator*, 40–41).

92. Eagleton, *Hope without Optimism*, 65.

93. Epicurus, quoted in Eagleton, *Hope without Optimism*, 69.

94. See again Popper, *All Life Is Problem Solving*, 112: 'As far as the future is concerned, we should not seek to prophesy but simply try to act in a way that is morally right and responsible.'

95. Havel, *Disturbing the Peace*, 181.

96. Frankl, *Man's Search for Meaning*, 90.

97. West, *Hope on a Tightrope*, 99.

98. Brossat and Klingberg, *Revolutionary Yiddishland*, 132, 139, 143 (my emphases); the eastern European Jewish man remains unnamed.

99. Goodall, *Book of Hope*, 194, 197 (my emphases).

100. Nakate, *A Bigger Picture*, 10–17 (her emphasis). See chapter 9 for the full quote.

101. Thunberg, *Climate Book*, 389.

102. Ghosh, 'Climate Change Is Becoming an All-out War' (my emphasis).

103. Jordan to Solnit, August 2003, cited in Solnit, *Hope in the Dark*, 93.

104. 'Activism' is an avowedly vague term, which can be narrowly or broadly defined: I deliberately leave the door open to competing definitions, as my aim is not to defend a specific mode of activism but the potential of pessimism as a motivational source.

105. West, *Hope on a Tightrope*, 209.

106. Rowan Williams and Peter Fenwick, comments during online discussion, 12 December 2022, https://www.youtube.com/watch?v=taC3YPuV7mM, at 1:07:47.

107. E.g., Goodall (*Book of Hope*, 234) writes of spurring a crowd to declare with her, 'Together we CAN! Together we WILL!'

108. Recall also that it can be focused on the past; see chapter 5.

109. For instance, climate justice.

110. Miéville, 'The Limits of Utopia'.

111. Goodall, *Book of Hope*, 144.

112. Rowland, 'One Atom of Justice'.

113. Solnit, *Hope in the Dark*, 109, 21–22, 139. There is a tension here which Solnit does not see. In fact there are two kinds of hope at work in Solnit's book: on the one hand, hope based on positive information (reasons/grounds for hope), such as past successes or 'hopeful' signs that things are moving in the right direction; on the other, hope based on radical uncertainty.

114. Solnit, *Hope in the Dark*, 4.

115. Tolkien, LotR, 3:933. Sam also realises that, somehow, Gandalf's fall is crucial: 'Things all went wrong when we went down in Moria.'

116. Watts, cited in Bateman, 'Mr. G. F. Watts and His Art', 4.

7: Our Lady of Tears: On Grief

Note to epigraph: De Quincey, *Suspiria*, 156.

1. De Quincey, *Suspiria*, 146 (I am mainly quoting from the essay 'Levana and Our Ladies of Sorrow').

2. De Quincey, *Suspiria*, 148–49.

3. De Quincey, *Suspiria*, 149: '*Theirs* were the symbols,—*mine* are the words' (his emphasis).

4. Helen Macdonald, interview by Michael Berkeley, *Private Passions*, 28 June 2020, https://www.bbc.co.uk/sounds/play/m000kh8f.

5. I draw the term 'companion on the road' from Kingsnorth, *Confessions*, 147 (fully quoted in the next chapter).

6. De Quincey, *Suspiria*, 149–50.

7. Lemon, 'Dress in Relation to Animal Life', 172; see Boase, *Etta Lemon*, chap. 16.

8. G. F. Watts, *A Dedication (To all those who love the beautiful and mourn over the senseless and cruel destruction of bird life and beauty)*, 1898–99 (Lemon mentions in her 1899 pamphlet that 'while he was painting it Mr. Watts called it his "Shuddering Angel"' ['Dress in Relation to Animal Life', 175]).

9. Leopold, *A Sand County Almanac*, 103.

10. Cunsolo and Ellis, 'Ecological Grief', 275.

11. Leopold, 'The Round River—A Parable' (c. 1941), in *The Essential Aldo Leopold*, 265.

12. Hamilton, *Requiem*, 212. See also chapter 3 above.

13. Hamilton, *Requiem*, 214.

14. Appears in the Dutch documentary *Klimaatrebellen* at 51:22.

15. Klein, cited in Hanman, 'We Are Seeing the Beginnings'. See also Sherrell, *Warmth*, 95: 'In organizing daily against the Problem, we've become so adept at compartmentalization that these actions are often our only chance to really grieve. The sit-in creates a context for it, a moment of heightened drama into which we can finally pour our anger and our disbelief and—scariest of all, because we guard it so closely—our flickering but still unextinguished sense of hope.'

16. Cited in the documentary *Lament for the Land*, by Ashlee Cunsolo Willox and the communities of Nunatsiavut, http://www.lamentfortheland.ca/, at approximately 29:40.

17. Albrecht, *Earth Emotions*, 200, 40. See chapter 3 above.

18. Lewis, *A Grief Observed*, 5.

19. See, e.g., https://therevelator.org/species-extinct-2022/.

20. Tolkien, LotR, 1:351. Tolkien refers to this specific passage in his *Letters*, noting that 'The heart remains' in this description: it still moves him (*Letters*, 221).

21. Cited in Lear, *Radical Hope*, 130.

22. Jetñil-Kijiner, 'Dear Matafele Peinem' (emphasis added). The Carteret and Taro islanders are mentioned because both are early examples of communities having to relocate because of rising sea levels.

23. Hamilton, *Requiem*, 211.

24. Lear, *Imagining the End*, 41. Note that, of these three categories of crisis, the last seems to occupy Lear the most: it is in context of the *pandemic* that he says, 'We are anxious and uncertain about the future, and the past no longer provides clear guidance' (22–23).

25. Lear, *Imagining the End*, 41.

26. Lear, *Imagining the End*, 41–42 (his emphasis).

27. Lear, *Imagining the End*, 62 (emphases removed).

28. Lear, *Imagining the End*, 8 (his emphasis).

29. Lear, *Imagining the End*, 10, 15.

30. Lear, *Imagining the End*, 15.

31. Lear *Imagining the End*, 17.

32. Lear *Imagining the End*, 18–19.

33. Lear *Imagining the End*, 24. Lear thus suggests a similarity between the anxiety surrounding World War I and that surrounding the Covid-19 pandemic (at least at the time of writing).

34. Lear *Imagining the End*, 38–40 (his emphasis): note that, while this sounds a little like 'radical hope', Lear does not use this term in the new book (wisely, perhaps: see chap. 5).

35. Lear *Imagining the End*, 63.

36. Lear *Imagining the End*, 64.

37. Freud, 'Mourning', 245. (The word Freud uses is *Vollendung*, 'completion'; in German: *nach der Vollendung der Trauerarbeit*).

38. Butler, *Precarious Life*, 20, who also mentions that Freud changed his mind about some aspects of mourning.

39. I am here citing Cholbi's distinction in *Grief*, 21–22: note, however, that the terms are fluid. As Cholbi notes, many who mourn are also grieving but it's possible to mourn without grieving (*Grief*, 22).

40. I am here paraphrasing a friend of mine who, after the sudden death of a beloved friend, spoke of the grief having become a part of her life: 'a quiet grief I don't want or need to go away.'

41. Cunsolo and Ellis, 'Ecological Grief', 279.

42. Freud, 'Mourning', 243.

43. Hamilton, *Requiem*, 211. See Boehm and Cronk, 'Dark Extinction'.

44. See Cunsolo and Ellis, 'Ecological Grief', 279, who note that it may not be possible to return to 'a new point of relative stability after experiencing a significant loss'—in 'the context of unending or ongoing environmental losses.'

45. Freud, 'Mourning', 257

46. Sherrell, *Warmth*, 245 (his emphasis).

47. See Freud, 'Mourning', 243–44: 'although mourning involves grave departures from the normal attitude to life, it never occurs to us to regard it as a pathological condition and to refer it to medical treatment.'

48. *The Simpsons*, 'The Good, the Sad and the Drugly', season 20, episode 17.

49. Which is not to say that melancholia or depression cannot be a response to real loss (as Freud also noted)—but that our ordinary language suggests otherwise.

50. Butler, *Precarious Life*, 30, 21.

51. Lear, *Radical Hope*, 132.

8: Our Lady of Sighs: On Despair

Note to epigraph: Shelley, *The Last Man*, 470.

1. De Quincey, *Suspiria*, 150–51.

2. De Quincey, *Suspiria*, 150.

3. Goodall, *Book of Hope*, 78.

4. Solnit, 'Why Climate Despair Is a Luxury'; Solnit, *Hope in the Dark*, ix.

5. See, e.g., McKinnon, 'Climate Change'; Malm, *How to Blow Up a Pipeline*, chap. 3, 'Fighting Despair'; Monbiot and Wrigley, 'Rewilding', 351: 'Rewilding enables us to begin to heal some of the great damage we have inflicted on the living world and, with it, the wounds we have inflicted on ourselves. And this could be our best defence against despair. We can replace our silent spring with a raucous summer.'

6. Thunberg, guest editorial; Thunberg, *Climate Book*, 42.

7. Frankl, *Man's Search for Meaning*, 32: the half-remembered quote comes from Lessing's play *Emilia Galotti*, act IV, scene 7, where Countess Orsina says: 'Wer über gewisse Dinge den Verstand nicht verlieret, der hat keinen zu verlieren.' (I thank an anonymous reviewer for the reference.)

8. Han-Pile, 'Hope, Powerlessness and Agency', 176; Meirav, 'The Nature of Hope', 219. See chapter 4.

9. Meirav, 'The Nature of Hope', 222–23 (his emphasis). Meirav also gives another example, where one person is hopeful of winning the lottery and another sceptical, though their assessments of the probability and desirability of winning are exactly the same (223–24).

10. E.g., by Meirav, Han-Pile, and recently Whyman (*Infinitely Full of Hope*, 31–32).

11. Note that here certainty includes the certainty of impossibility. Paul Tillich is often attributed the quote that 'the opposite of faith is not doubt, but certainty,' which is roughly but not literally what he claims in *Dynamics of Faith*.

12. See Eagleton, *Hope without Optimism*, 44: 'There are accordingly times when [hope] does not sound all that different from despair.'

13. Mann, 'Resisting the New Denialism', 373.

14. Solnit, 'Why Climate Despair Is a Luxury' (my emphasis).

15. McKinnon, 'Climate Change', 33 (my emphasis).

16. The conclusion is often implied. See especially Scranton, *We're Doomed*; also Franzen, 'What If We Stopped Pretending?' (though Franzen says there is still reason for action on a local level); for critics, see Malm, *How to Blow Up a Pipeline*, chap. 3, and Stolze, 'Against Climate Stoicism'.

17. Sherrell, *Warmth*, 153; though he adds that in his heart he wasn't really sure about this argument.

18. Sonia Seneviratne at ETH Zurich, cited in Abnett, 'Explainer'; see the 2023 IPCC report: https://www.ipcc.ch/report/sixth-assessment-report-cycle/.

19. On differences between degrees of warming, see Lyon et al., 'Climate Change Research and Action Must Look beyond 2100'; McCarthy, 'Climate Crisis'; and Carbon Brief, 'The Impacts of Climate Change'.

20. Broome, 'Against Denialism', discussing here the 'joyguzzling' scenario (going for a high-emission fun ride in an SUV on a Sunday afternoon). For other arguments for the efficacy of individual action, see Nefsky, 'How You Can Help'; McKinnon, 'Climate Change'.

21. I've already cited Malm, Thunberg, Wallace-Wells, and Sherrell, who have all made this point. See also Solnit, *Hope in the Dark*, 131: 'the difference between the best and worst case scenarios is vast, and the future is not yet written.'

22. See chapter 1.

23. Scranton, *We're Doomed*, 67, 68, 73 (my emphasis).

24. Malm, *How to Blow Up a Pipeline*, 147 (his emphasis); McKinnon, 'Climate Change', 40.

25. Solnit, *Hope in the Dark*, 12.

26. Solnit, *Hope in the Dark*, 23; Solnit, 'Why Climate Despair Is a Luxury'; see also Ripley, 'This Element Is Critical to Human Flourishing', and Goodall, *Book of Hope*, 97: 'If only the media would give more space to the uplifting, hopeful news that we find everywhere.'

27. Thunberg, *Climate Book*, 91.

28. Thunberg, *Climate Book*, 355.

29. Solnit, 'Why Climate Despair Is a Luxury' (my emphasis); she also contrasts despair as feeling/forecast.

30. Solnit, *Hope in the Dark*, e.g., 21, 7.

31. See chapter 9.

32. See Han-Pile and Stern, 'Is Hope a Secular Virtue?', 89.

33. Solnit, 'Why Climate Despair Is a Luxury'.

34. Spinoza, *Ethics*, 3p50schol (p. 132), and 'Definitions of the Emotions' 13ex (pp. 146–57). See Han-Pile, 'Hope, Powerlessness, and Agency', 183, who also cites Hume, La Rochefoucauld, and Seneca for similar views. Contrast Solnit, *Hope in the Dark*, 4: 'To hope is dangerous, and yet it is the opposite of fear, for to live is to risk.'

35. Austen, *Persuasion*, 284.

36. See Han-Pile and Stern, 'Is Hope a Secular Virtue?', 88–92.

37. See chapters 2 and 5.

38. On Provo, see especially Roel van Duijn (the founding member and activist who went on to have a career in local politics), *Provo*, and his autobiography *Diepvriesfiguur* (both in Dutch).

39. Provo Manifesto, in Van Duijn, *Provo*, 28 (my translation; my emphasis).

40. Provo Manifesto 1967, in Van Duijn, *Provo*, 71 (my emphasis).

41. 'Inleiding tot het Provocerend Denken,' in Van Duijn, *Provo*, 29 (Johnson and Kosygin were then, respectively, president of the United States and premier of the Soviet Union).

42. Thunberg, 'Our House Is on Fire'.

43. This is a loose citation from Bayle, 'Xenophanes.F' (quoted in full in my *Dark Matters*, 50).

44. Kierkegaard, *The Sickness unto Death*, 142; see Eagleton, *Hope without Optimism*, 128. (Note, however, that Kierkegaard was analysing despair in a firmly religious context.)

45. See Alessandri, *Night Vision*.

46. West, *Hope on a Tightrope*, 217 (my emphasis); see chapter 6 (of this book) for the full quote.

47. Miéville, 'The Limits of Utopia' and 'From Choice to Polarity', respectively (my emphasis).

48. Klein, in Hanman, 'We Are Seeing the Beginnings'; see also Sherrell, *Warmth*, 122: 'The rhythmic oscillation between buildup and breakdown, between hope and hopelessness.'

49. Kingsnorth, *Confessions*, 147.

50. Solnit, *Hope in the Dark*, 138 ('the teddy bear of despair'), 142 ('the ease of despair'), 7.

51. Eagleton, *Hope without Optimism*, 12.

52. Alessandri, *Night Vision*, 11.

53. Solnit, *Hope in the Dark*, 4: 'hope should shove you out the door.'

9: Our Lady of Darkness

Note to epigraph: Rilke, 'Archaic Torso of Apollo' (translation slightly adjusted), in *Selected Poems*, 82.

1. De Quincey, *Suspiria*, 151–52.

2. De Quincey, *Suspiria*, 152–53 (his emphasis): in De Quincey's text it is the first sister (the Madonna) addressing the third, as they stand by De Quincey's bed and decide the shape *his* life will take.

3. See Galvagni, 'Climate Change' for a helpful overview of the debate; Chappell, 'Virtue Ethics and Climate Change'.

4. The first description comes from Galvagni, 'Climate Change', 590, who discusses these two benefits for virtue ethics. On the now standard distinction between luxury and subsistence emissions, see Shue, 'Subsistence Emissions'.

5. Galvagni, 'Climate Change', 591–93.

6. See Broome, 'Against Denialism'; Nefsky, 'How You Can Help'.

7. Note that I say 'virtue-oriented approach' because this works for a variety of theories, not just standard virtue ethics: see Galvagni, 'Climate Change', 592–93; and Chappell, 'Virtue Ethics', 185, who argues that 'a conception of the virtues is *a necessary part* of any humanly adequate ethical outlook.'

8. Lenzi, 'How Should We Respond to Climate Change?', 424; see again Galvagni, 'Climate Change', 593.

9. On 'tangible results', see chapter 5. Note that this is not to endorse mere 'purity activism' (where individual abstention is the end and limit of action) but to suggest that the cultivation of virtues can unfold into active commitment on a varied scale.

10. Chappell, 'Virtue Ethics', 188–89 (her emphasis).

11. Chappell, 'Virtue Ethics', 190.

12. Chappell, 'Virtue Ethics', 191.

13. Chappell, *Epiphanies*, 8: 'An epiphany is an overwhelming existentially significant manifestation of value in experience, often sudden and surprising, which feeds the psyche, which feels like it "comes from outside" . . . which teaches us something new, which "takes us out of ourselves", and to which there is a natural and correct response.' She calls it a 'peak experience' while noting this does not mean epiphanies are necessarily positive; they can also be epiphanic by reaching a peak of horror, terror, or anger (9).

14. Chappell, *Epiphanies*, 50.

15. Chappell, *Epiphanies*, 50–51.

16. Owen Jones, cited in Chappell, *Epiphanies*, 52.

17. Chappell, *Epiphanies*, 52.

18. Goodall, *Book of Hope*, 197.

19. Nakate, *A Bigger Picture*, 10–17 (her emphasis).

20. Sherrell, *Warmth*, 25.

21. Chappell, *Epiphanies*, 280.

22. Chappell, *Epiphanies*, 121.

23. Chappell, *Epiphanies*, 53.

24. Chappell, *Epiphanies*, 51.

25. Chappell, *Epiphanies*, 132.

26. When the campaign for denialism became unsustainable, fossil-fuel companies were quick to popularise the idea of the personal carbon footprint, thus exploiting awareness for business as usual: see, e.g., Crist, 'Is It OK to Have a Child?'

27. Blumenfeld, 'Climate Barbarism': see chapter 2.

28. Chappell, Q&A after her presentation on *Epiphanies* at the 'Epistemic Breakthroughs' conference, held in St Andrews in June 2022.

29. On the dangers of 'neo-optimism', see also Malm and Zetkin Collective, *White Skin, Black Fuel*, 486–92, 537. Note that overt optimism and the mocking of climate concerns ('Doomsday is cancelled', 'Apocalypse no') was an explicit strategy of fossil-fuel greenwashing from the 1980s onwards: see, e.g., Supran and Oreskes, 'The Forgotten Oil Ads'.

30. See my *Dark Matters*; and Alessandri, *Night Vision*, 2: 'What we need going forward is to stop trying to shed light on darkness and instead learn to see in the dark.'

31. Hume, *An Enquiry Concerning the Principles of Morals* (1751), section 9.1.

32. Robinson, *The Givenness of Things*, 29.

33. E.g., Colby and Damon, *Some Do Care*, chap. 10, 'Positivity and Hopefulness'. The authors stress, however, that these exemplars weren't aiming for positivity: 'The moral values were primary, and if the pursuit of these values leads to misery and dejection rather than exhilaration, so be it' (271).

34. Malm, *How to Blow Up a Pipeline*, 19.

35. Thunberg, *Climate Book*, 354.

36. Tarrou, in Camus, *The Plague*, 195.

37. Heglar, 'Climate Change Isn't the First Existential Threat'.

38. That is, the *active* tenses: see chapter 8.

39. Sometimes explicitly so: see, e.g., Malm, *Progress*, 195: 'As long as there are only few signs of [capitalism] being toppled on a global scale, there is reason to be pessimistic—and correspondingly intransigent in militancy and negativity.' In a footnote he refers to Eagleton, *Hope without Optimism* (hope!) and *Salvage* (pessimism!).

40. See again my *Dark Matters*, especially chap. 9; and Alessandri, *Night Vision*.

41. Kingsnorth, *Confessions*, 143.

42. Alessandri, *Night Vision*, 5.

43. West, *Hope on a Tightrope*, 85–86.

44. Berry, *Befriending the Earth*, 90.

45. Camus, *The Rebel*, 248.

BIBLIOGRAPHY

All online sources last consulted December 2023, unless otherwise stated.

Abnett, Kate. 'Explainer: What's the Difference between 1.5°C and 2°C of Global Warming?' Reuters, 9 November 2021. https://www.reuters.com/business/cop /whats-difference-between-15c-2c-global-warming-2021-11-07/.

Albrecht, Glenn A. *Earth Emotions: New Words for a New World*. Ithaca: Cornell University Press, 2019.

Alessandri, Mariana. *Night Vision: Seeing Ourselves through Dark Moods*. Princeton: Princeton University Press, 2023.

Aquinas, Thomas. *Disputed Questions on the Virtues*. Ed. E. Atkins and T. Williams. Cambridge: Cambridge University Press, 2005.

Austen, Jane. *Persuasion*. London: Macmillan Collector's Library, 2016.

Bateman, Charles T. 'Mr. G. F. Watts and His Art'. *Windsor Magazine* 14 (1901): 3–16.

Berry, Thomas, with Thomas Clarke. *Befriending the Earth: A Theology of Reconciliation between Humans and the Earth*. Mystic, CT: Twenty-Third Publications, 1991.

Bloch, Ernst. *The Principle of Hope*. 1954–59. 3 vols. Trans. Neville Plaice, Stephen Plaice, and Paul Knight. Oxford: Blackwell, 1985.

Blumberg, Jess. 'Sitting Bull's Legacy: The Lakota Sioux Leader's Relics Return to His Only Living Descendants'. *Smithsonian Magazine*, 30 October 2007. https:// www.smithsonianmag.com/history/sitting-bulls-legacy-175332903/.

Blumenfeld, Jacob. 'Climate Barbarism: Adapting to a Wrong World'. *Constellations* 30 (2023): 162–78.

Boase, Tessa. *Etta Lemon: The Woman Who Saved the Birds*. London: Aurum, 2021.

Boehm, Mannfred M. A., and Quentin C. B. Cronk. 'Dark Extinction: The Problem of Unknown Historical Extinctions'. *Biology Letters* 17, no. 3 (March 2021).

Bowler, Kate. *Everything Happens for a Reason. And Other Lies I've Loved*. London: SPCK, 2018.

Broome, John. 'Against Denialism'. *The Monist* 102, no. 1 (2019): 110–29.

Brossat, Alain, and Sylvie Klingberg. *Revolutionary Yiddishland: A History of Jewish Radicalism*. London: Verso, 2016.

Butler, James. 'A Coal Mine for Every Wildfire: James Butler Writes about Andreas Malm's Climate Manifestos'. *London Review of Books* 43, no. 22 (18 November 2021). https://www.lrb.co.uk/the-paper/v43/n22/james-butler/a-coal-mine-for-every-wildfire.

Butler, Judith. *Precarious Life: The Powers of Mourning and Violence*. London: Verso, 2020.

Camus, Albert. *Lyrical and Critical Essays*. Ed. Philip Thody. Trans. Ellen Conroy Kennedy. New York: Vintage Books, 1970.

———. *The Myth of Sisyphus*. Trans. Justin O'Brien. 1942. London: Penguin, 2005.

———. *The Plague*. Trans. Robin Buss. 1947. London: Penguin, 2013.

———. *The Rebel*. Trans. Anthony Bower. 1951. London: Penguin, 2013.

———. *Resistance, Rebellion, and Death: Essays*. Trans. Justin O'Brien. New York: Vintage, 1995.

———. *Speaking Out: Lectures and Speeches, 1937–1958*. Trans. Quintin Hoare. New York: Vintage Books, 2021.

Carbon Brief. 'The Impacts of Climate Change at 1.5C, 2C and Beyond'. https://interactive.carbonbrief.org/impacts-climate-change-one-point-five-degrees-two-degrees/.

Chappell, Sophie Grace. *Epiphanies: An Ethics of Experience*. Oxford: Oxford University Press, 2022.

———. 'Epiphanies'. Presentation at the *Epistemic Breakthroughs* workshop at St Andrews, June 2022.

———. 'Virtue Ethics and Climate Change'. In *Moral Theory and Climate Change*, ed. D. E. Miller and B. Eggleston, 177–92. New York: Routledge, 2020.

Chesterton, G. K. *G. F. Watts*. 1904. New York: Cosimo, 2007.

Cholbi, Michael. *Grief: A Philosophical Guide*. Princeton: Princeton University Press, 2022.

Chomsky, Noam. Interviewed by C. J. Polychroniou. *Optimism over Despair: On Capitalism, Empire and Social Change*. London: Penguin, 2017.

Clark, Tom. 'Carlota Perez and the Economics of Hope'. *Prospect*, 29 October 2021. https://www.prospectmagazine.co.uk/ideas/economics/38086/carlota-perez-and-the-economics-of-hope.

Colby, Anne, and William Damon. *Some Do Care: Contemporary Lives of Moral Commitment*. New York: Free Press, 1992.

Crist, Meehan. 'Is It OK to Have a Child?' *London Review of Books* 42, no. 5 (5 March 2020). https://www.lrb.co.uk/the-paper/v42/n05/meehan-crist/is-it-ok-to-have-a-child.

Cunsolo, A., and N. R. Ellis. 'Ecological Grief as a Mental Health Response to Climate Change–Related Loss'. *Nature Climate Change* 8 (2018): 275–81.

Dante Alighieri. *Purgatorio*. Trans. Jean Hollander and Robert Hollander. New York: Anchor Books, 2003.

————. *Purgatorio*. Trans. Allen Mandelbaum. London: Random House, 2016.

De Quincey, Thomas. *Suspiria de Profundis* [1845–91]. In *Confessions of an English Opium-Eater and Other Writings*, ed. Grevel Lindop, 87–181. Oxford: Oxford University Press, 1989.

Dienstag, Joshua Foa. *Pessimism: Philosophy, Ethic, Spirit*. Princeton: Princeton University Press, 2006.

Eagleton, Terry. *Hope without Optimism*. New Haven: Yale University Press, 2017.

Eliot, T. S. *Four Quartets*. 1943. Boston: Mariner Books, 1971.

Figueres, Christiana, and Tom Rivett-Carnac. *The Future We Choose: The Stubborn Optimist's Guide to the Climate Crisis*. London: Manilla Press, 2020.

Foer, Jonathan Safran. *We Are the Weather*. London: Hamish Hamilton, 2019.

Forsyth, Peter Taylor. *Religion in Recent Art: Expository Lectures on Rossetti, Burne-Jones, Watts, Holman Hunt and Wagner*. Manchester: Abel Heywood & Son, 1889.

Frankl, Viktor. *Man's Search for Meaning*. Partly translated from the German by Ilse Lasch. 1946. London: Rider, 2004.

Franklin, John Curtis. 'Once More the Poet: Keats, Severn, and the Grecian Lyre'. *Memoirs of the American Academy in Rome* 48 (2003): 227–40.

Franzen, Jonathan. 'What If We Stopped Pretending?' *New Yorker*, 8 September 2019. https://www.newyorker.com/culture/cultural-comment/what-if-we-stopped -pretending.

Freud, Sigmund. 'Mourning and Melancholia'. In *The Standard Edition of the Complete Psychological Works of Sigmund Freud*, trans. James Strachey et al., 14:243–58. London: Hogarth Press, 1953–66.

Galvagni, Enrico. 'Climate Change and Virtue Ethics'. In *Handbook of Philosophy of Climate Change*, ed. G. Pellegrino, and M. Di Paola, 587–600. Cham: Springer, 2023.

Gardiner, Stephen M. *A Perfect Moral Storm: The Ethical Tragedy of Climate Change*. Oxford: Oxford University Press, 2013.

Gay, Roxane. 'The Case against Hope'. *New York Times*, 6 June 2019. https://www .nytimes.com/2019/06/06/opinion/hope-politics-2019.html.

Gayle, Damien. 'Just Stop Oil Campaigners Glue Themselves to Da Vinci Copy in Royal Academy'. *Guardian*, 5 July 2022. https://www.theguardian.com /artanddesign/2022/jul/05/just-stop-oil-campaigners-glue-themselves-to-da -vinci-copy-in-royal-academy.

Ghosh, Amitav. 'Climate Change Is Becoming an All-out War'. *New Statesman*, 19 October 2022. https://www.newstatesman.com/environment/2022/10/amitav -ghosh-climate-change-war.

Goodall, Jane, and Douglas Abrams, with Gail Hudson. *The Book of Hope: A Survival Guide for Trying Times*. London: Penguin, 2022.

Gopnik, Adam. 'Facing History'. *New Yorker*, 2 April 2012. https://www.newyorker .com/magazine/2012/04/09/facing-history.

Gravlee, G. Scott. 'Aristotle on Hope'. *Journal of the History of Philosophy* 38, no. 4 (2000): 461–77.

Hamilton, Clive. *Requiem for a Species: Why We Resist the Truth about Climate Change.* London: Routledge, 2015.

Hammer, Joshua. 'Why Is Albert Camus Still a Stranger in His Native Algeria?' *Smithsonian Magazine,* October 2013. https://www.smithsonianmag.com /innovation/why-is-albert-camus-still-a-stranger-in-his-native-algeria-13063/.

Hanman, Natalie, interviewing Naomi Klein. 'We Are Seeing the Beginnings of the Era of Climate Barbarism'. *Guardian*, 14 September 2019. https://www .theguardian.com/books/2019/sep/14/naomi-klein-we-are-seeing-the -beginnings-of-the-era-of-climate-barbarism.

Han-Pile, Béatrice. 'Hope, Powerlessness, and Agency'. *Midwest Studies in Philosophy* 41, no. 1 (2017): 175–201.

Han-Pile, Béatrice, and Robert Stern. 'Is Hope a Secular Virtue? Hope as the Virtue of the Possible'. In *The Virtue of Hope*, ed. Nancy E. Snow, 73–108. Oxford: Oxford University Press, 2024.

Harvey, Fiona. 'Greta Thunberg Says School Strikes Have Achieved Nothing'. *Guardian*, 6 December 2019. https://www.theguardian.com/environment/2019/dec /06/greta-thunberg-says-school-strikes-have-achieved-nothing.

Havel, Václav. *Disturbing the Peace: A Conversation with Karel Hvížďala.* Trans. Paul Wilson. New York: Vintage Books, 1991.

———. *Letters to Olga, June 1979–September 1982.* Trans. Paul Wilson. 1983. London: Faber and Faber, 1990.

Heglar, Mary Annaïse. 'Climate Change Isn't the First Existential Threat'. *Zora*, 18 February 2019. https://zora.medium.com/sorry-yall-but-climate-change-ain-t -the-first-existential-threat-b3c999267aa0.

Hilton, Isabel. 'Greenland Is Now a Country Fit for Broccoli Growers'. *Guardian*, 14 September 2007. https://www.theguardian.com/commentisfree/2007/sep/14 /comment.climatechange.

Hölderlin, Friedrich. *Poems and Fragments.* Bilingual ed. Trans. Michael Hamburger. London: Routledge and Kegan Paul, 1966.

Hope, Simon. 'Climate Change as a Philosophical Problem'. Unpublished manuscript.

Hume, David. *An Enquiry Concerning the Principles of Morals.* 1751. Ed. Tom L. Beauchamp. Oxford: Oxford University Press, 2010.

Isaac, Jeffrey C. *Arendt, Camus, and Modern Rebellion.* New Haven: Yale University Press, 1992.

Jacobson, Norman. *Pride and Solace: The Functions and Limits of Political Theory.* Berkeley: University of California Press, 1978.

James, William. *The Principles of Psychology*. 2 vols. New York: Henry Holt, 1890.

James, P. D. *The Children of Men*. London: Faber & Faber, 2018.

Jetñil-Kijiner, Kathy. 'Dear Matafele Peinem'. https://www.kathyjetnilkijiner.com /united-nations-climate-summit-opening-ceremony-my-poem-to-my-daughter/.

Johnson, Samuel. *The Letters of Samuel Johnson*. Ed. Bruce Redford. 5 vols. Princeton: Princeton University Press, 1992–94.

———. *The Yale Edition of the Works of Samuel Johnson*. 23 vols. General editor, Allen T. Hazen. New Haven: Yale University Press, 1955–.

Johnston, Alexandre. '"Poet of Hope": Elpis in Pindar'. *Hope in Ancient Literature, History, and Art: Ancient Emotions I*, ed. Kazantzidis and Spatharas, 35–52.

Kazantzidis, George, and Dimos Spatharas, eds. *Hope in Ancient Literature, History, and Art: Ancient Emotions I*. Berlin: De Gruyter, 2018.

Kelsey, Elin. *Hope Matters: Why Changing the Way We Think Is Critical to Solving the Environmental Crisis*. Vancouver: Greystone Books, 2020.

Kierkegaard, Søren. *The Sickness unto Death*. 1849. Trans. Bruce H. Kirmmse. New York: W. W. Norton, 2023.

Kimmerer, Robin Wall. 'Mending Our Relationship with the Earth'. In Thunberg et al., *Climate Book*, 415–20.

Kingsnorth, Paul. *Confessions of a Recovering Environmentalist*. London: Faber & Faber, 2017.

———. 'Finnegas'. *Emergence Magazine*, 20 March 2020. https://emergencemagazine .org/op_ed/finnegas/.

Klein, Naomi. *On Fire: The Burning Case for a Green New Deal*. London: Allen Lane, 2019.

———. *This Changes Everything: Capitalism vs. the Climate*. London: Penguin, 2014.

Klein, Naomi, with Rebecca Stefoff. *How to Change Everything: The Young Human's Guide to Protecting the Planet and Each Other*. London: Penguin, 2022.

Kleres, Jochen, and Åsa Wettergren. 'Fear, Hope, Anger, and Guilt in Climate Activism'. *Social Movement Studies* 16, no. 5 (2017): 507–19.

Koethe, John. 'In Italy'. *Southwest Review* 86, no. 1 (2001): 139–42. http://www.jstor .org/stable/43472144.

Lakey, George, and Yotam Marom. 'Can Now Really Be the Best Time to Be Alive? A Dialogue across Generations'. *Waging Nonviolence*, 26 December 2019. https:// wagingnonviolence.org/2019/12/can-now-really-be-the-best-time-to-be-alive.

Lateiner, Donald. '*Elpis* as Emotion and Reason (Hope and Expectation) in Fifth-century Greek Historians'. In *Hope in Ancient Literature, History, and Art: Ancient Emotions I*, ed. Kazantzidis and Spatharas, 131–50.

Lear, Jonathan. *Imagining the End: Mourning and Ethical Life*. Cambridge, MA: Belknap Press of Harvard University Press, 2022.

———. *Radical Hope: Ethics in the Face of Cultural Devastation*. Cambridge, MA: Harvard University Press, 2006.

Leibniz. *Theodicy: Essays on the Goodness of God, the Freedom of Man, and the Origin of Evil*. Trans. E. M. Huggard. Chicago: Open Court, 1998.

Lemon, Etta. 'Dress in Relation to Animal Life' (1899). In *In Nature's Name: An Anthology of Women's Writing and Illustration, 1780–1930*, ed. Barbara Gates, 170–75. Chicago: University of Chicago Press, 2002.

Lenzi, Dominic. 'How Should We Respond to Climate Change? Virtue Ethics and Aggregation Problems'. *Journal of Social Philosophy* 54, no. 3 (2023): 421–36.

Leopold, Aldo. *The Essential Aldo Leopold: Quotations and Commentaries*. Ed. Curt Meine and Richard L. Knight. Madison: University of Wisconsin Press, 1999.

———. *A Sand County Almanac: And Sketches Here and There*. 1949. Oxford: Oxford University Press, 2020.

Lewis, C. S. *A Grief Observed*. London: Faber and Faber, 1966.

Lyon, C., et al. 'Climate Change Research and Action Must Look beyond 2100'. *Global Change Biology* 28 (2022): 349–61.

Magnason, Andri Snær. *On Time and Water: A History of Our Future*. Trans. Lytton Smith. London: Serpents Tail, 2021.

Malm, Andreas. *How to Blow Up a Pipeline: Learning to Fight in a World on Fire*. London: Verso, 2021.

———. *The Progress of This Storm: Nature and Society in a Warming World*. London: Verso, 2020.

Malm, Andreas, and the Zetkin Collective. *White Skin, Black Fuel: On the Danger of Fossil Fascism*. London: Verso, 2021.

Mann, Michael E. 'Resisting the New Denialism'. In Thunberg, *Climate Book*, 372–74.

Mantel, Hilary. *The Mirror and the Light*. London: 4th Estate, 2020.

Marcel, Gabriel. *Being and Having*. Trans. Katharine Farrer. Westminster: Dacre Press, 1949.

———. *Homo Viator: Introduction to the Metaphysic of Hope*. 1952. Trans. Emma Craufurd and Paul Seaton. South Bend, IN: St Augustine's Press, 2010.

Marvel, Kate. 'We Need Courage, Not Hope, to Face Climate Change'. *On Being*, 1 March 2018. https://onbeing.org/blog/kate-marvel-we-need-courage-not-hope-to-face-climate-change/.

McCarthy, Joe. 'Climate Crisis: What's the Difference between a Rise of 1.5, 2, and 3 Degrees Celsius?' *Global Citizen*, 30 July 2021. https://www.globalcitizen.org/en/content/the-difference-in-global-warming-levels-explained/.

McKinnon, Catriona. 'Climate Change: Against Despair'. *Ethics & the Environment* 19, no. 1 (2014): 31–48.

Meirav, Ariel. 'The Nature of Hope'. *Ratio* 22 (2009): 216–33.

Miéville, China. 'From Choice to Polarity: Politics of, and, and in Art'. *Salvage*, 20 June 2016. https://salvage.zone/from-choice-to-polarity-politics-of-in-and-and-art/.

———. 'The Limits of Utopia'. *Salvage*, 1 August 2015. https://salvage.zone/the-limits-of-utopia/.

Miner, Robert. *Thomas Aquinas on the Passions: A Study of Summa Theologiae, 1a2ae 22–48*. Cambridge: Cambridge University Press, 2009.

Monbiot, George, and Rebecca Wrigley. 'Rewilding'. In Thunberg, *Climate Book*, 348–51.

Mossman, Kate. '"I haven't met a politician ready to do what it takes": Greta Thunberg and Björk in Conversation'. *New Statesman*, 17 October 2022. https://www.newstatesman.com/environment/2022/10/greta-thunberg-bjork-guomunds dottir-interview-climate-change.

Nairn, Karen. 'Learning from Young People Engaged in Climate Activism: The Potential of Collectivizing Despair and Hope'. *YOUNG* 27, no. 5 (2019): 435–50. https://doi.org/10.1177/1103308818817603.

Nakate, Vanessa. *A Bigger Picture: My Fight to Bring a New African Voice to the Climate Crisis*. London: One Boat, 2022.

Nefsky, Julia. 'How You Can Help, without Making a Difference'. *Philosophical Studies: An International Journal for Philosophy in the Analytic Tradition* 174, no. 11 (2017): 2743–67.

Neruda, Pablo. *The Captain's Verses*. Trans. Brian Cole. London: Anvil Press Poetry, 2004.

Nguyen, Anh-Quân. 'Pessimism for Climate Activists'. *Ethics and the Environment* 29, no. 1 (2024): 109–37.

Nietzsche, Friedrich. *Human, All Too Human*. Trans. R. J. Hollingdale. Cambridge: Cambridge University Press, 2002.

Obama, Barack. *Dreams from My Father: A Story of Race and Inheritance*. Edinburgh: Canongate, 2016.

Oppenheimer, Daniel. 'Out of Unbearable Loss, a Vision of Radical Hope'. *Washington Post*, 9 November 2022. https://www.washingtonpost.com/books/2022/11/09/imagining-end-mourning-ethics-lear-review/.

Ord, Toby. *The Precipice: Existential Risk and the Future of Humanity*. London: Bloomsbury, 2021.

Pastoureau, Michel. *Blue: History of a Colour*. Princeton: Princeton University Press, 2018.

Pezzini, Giuseppe. *Tolkien and the Mystery of Literary Creation*. Cambridge: Cambridge University Press, 2024.

Pieper, Josef. *Faith, Hope, Love*. 1935. Trans. Richard Winston, Clara Winston, and Sister Mary Frances McCarthy. San Francisco: Ignatius Press, 1997.

Poe, Edgar Allen. 'The Masque of the Red Death'. In *Poetry and Tales*, 485–90. New York: Library of America, 1984.

Popper, Karl. *All Life Is Problem Solving*. Trans. Patrick Camiller. London: Routledge, 2009.

Potkay, Adam. *Hope: A Literary History*. Cambridge: Cambridge University Press, 2022.

Redford, Catherine. 'The "Last Man on Earth" in Romantic Literature'. https://wordsworth.org.uk/blog/2014/11/06/the-last-man-on-earth-in-romantic-literature/.

Rilke, Rainer Maria. *Selected Poems*. Trans. Susan Ranson and Marielle Sutherland. Ed. Robert Villain. Oxford: Oxford University Press, 2011.

Ripley, Amanda. 'This Element Is Critical to Human Flourishing—yet Missing from the News'. *Washington Post*, 30 March 2023. https://www.washingtonpost.com/opinions/2023/03/30/amanda-ripley-hope-news.

Robinson, Kim Stanley. *The Ministry for the Future*. London: Orbit, 2020.

Robinson, Marilynne. *The Givenness of Things*. London: Virago, 2015.

Robson, David. 'The Sci-fi Genre Offering Radical Hope for Living Better'. *BBC Culture*, 14 January 2022. https://www.bbc.com/culture/article/20220113-the-sci-fi-genre-offering-radical-hope-for-living-better.

Rose, Jacqueline. 'Pointing the Finger: Jacqueline Rose on "The Plague"'. *London Review of Books* 42, no. 9 (7 May 2020). https://www.lrb.co.uk/the-paper/v42/n09/jacqueline-rose/pointing-the-finger.

Rousseau, Jean-Jacques. 'Letter to Voltaire'. In *The Discourses and Other Early Political Writings*, ed. Victor Gourevitch, 232–46. Cambridge: Cambridge University Press, 2016.

Rowland, Alexandra. 'One Atom of Justice, One Molecule of Mercy, and the Empire of Unsheathed Knives'. *Stellar Beacon* (Winter 2019). https://festive.ninja/one-atom-of-justice-one-molecule-of-mercy-and-the-empire-of-unsheathed-knives-alexandra-rowland/.

Salvage Editorial Collective. 'Pessimism after Corbyn'. *Salvage*, 14 September 2015. https://salvage.zone/pessimism-after-corbyn/.

Saner, Emine. 'Jane Goodall on Fires, Floods, Frugality and the Good Fight: "People have to change from within"'. *Guardian*, 20 October 2021. https://www.theguardian.com/science/2021/oct/20/jane-goodall-on-fires-floods-frugality-and-the-good-fight-people-have-to-change-from-within.

Scheffler, Samuel. *Death and the Afterlife*. Ed. Niko Kolodny. Oxford: Oxford University Press, 2013.

Schopenhauer, Arthur. *Parerga and Paralipomena: Short Philosophical Essays*. 2 vols. Trans. and ed. Sabine Roehr, Christopher Janaway, and Adrian Del Caro. Cambridge: Cambridge University Press, 2014–17.

———. *The World as Will and Representation*. 2 vols. Trans. E.F.J. Payne. New York: Dover Publications, 1966–69.

Scranton, Roy. *Learning to Die in the Anthropocene: Reflections on the End of a Civilization*. San Francisco: City Lights Books, 2015.

———. *We're Doomed. Now What?: Essays on War and Climate Change*. New York: Soho Press, 2018.

Shelley, Mary. *The Last Man*. Ed. Morton D. Paley. Oxford: Oxford University Press, 2008.

Sherrell, Daniel. *Warmth: Coming of Age at the End of Our World*. New York: Penguin, 2021.

Shue, Henry. 'Subsistence Emissions and Luxury Emissions'. *Law & Policy*, no. 15 (1993): 39–60.

Sitalsing, Sheila. 'Achter elke crisis schuilt een bestuurlijke clusterfuck'. *Volkskrant*, 23 December 2022. https://www.volkskrant.nl/nieuws-achtergrond/achter-elke -crisis-schuilt-een-bestuurlijke-clusterfuck~bc21fda4/#&gid=1&pid=2.

Solnit, Rebecca. *Hope in the Dark: Untold Histories, Wild Possibilities*. Edinburgh: Canongate, 2016.

———. 'Why Climate Despair Is a Luxury'. *New Statesman*, 19 October 2022. https://www.newstatesman.com/environment/2022/10/rebecca-solnit-climate -despair-luxury.

Spinoza, Benedict de. *Ethics*. Trans. Michael Silverthorne and Matthew J. Kisner. Cambridge: Cambridge University Press, 2018.

Stangl, Rebecca. *Neither Heroes nor Saints: Ordinary Virtue, Extraordinary Virtue, and Self-cultivation*. Oxford: Oxford University Press, 2020.

Stolze, Ted. 'Against Climate Stoicism: Learning to Fight in the Anthropocene'. In *Interrogating the Anthropocene: Ecology, Aesthetics, Pedagogy, and the Future in Question*, ed. jan jagodzinski, 317–37. New York: Palgrave Macmillan, 2018.

Supran, Geoffrey, and Naomi Oreskes. 'The Forgotten Oil Ads That Told Us Climate Change Was Nothing'. *Guardian*, 18 November 2021. https://www.theguardian .com/environment/2021/nov/18/the-forgotten-oil-ads-that-told-us-climate -change-was-nothing.

Takken, Wilfred. 'Hoopvolle klimaat-tv, omdat de kijkers anders wegzappen' [Hopeful Climate TV, as otherwise viewers change the channel]. NRC, 2 November 2022, https://www.nrc.nl/nieuws/2022/11/02/hoopvolle-klimaat-tv-omdat -de-kijkers-anders-wegzappen-2-a4146985.

Taylor, Charles. 'A Different Kind of Courage'. *New York Review*, 26 April 2007. https://www.nybooks.com/articles/2007/04/26/a-different-kind-of-courage/.

Thompson, Allen. 'Radical Hope for Living Well in a Warmer World'. *Journal of Agricultural and Environmental Ethics* 23, nos. 1–2 (2009): 43–55.

Thunberg, Greta. *The Climate Book*. London: Allen Lane, 2022.

———. Guest editorial. *New Statesman*, 19 October 2022. https://www.newstatesman .com/environment/2022/10/greta-thunberg-guest-edit-politicians-rescue -planet.

———. 'Our House Is on Fire'. *Guardian*, 25 January 2019. https://www.theguardian .com/environment/2019/jan/25/our-house-is-on-fire-greta-thunberg16 -urges-leaders-to-act-on-climate.

———. Speech at the 'Declaration of Rebellion'. Parliament Square, London, 31 October 2018. https://medium.com/wedonthavetime/the-rebellion-has-begun -d1bffe31d3b5.

———. Speech at the Houses of Parliament. 23 April 2019. https://www.theguardian .com/environment/2019/apr/23/greta-thunberg-full-speech-to-mps-you -did-not-act-in-time.

Tillich, Paul. *Dynamics of Faith*. New York: HarperOne, 2009.

Todd, Olivier. *Albert Camus: A Life*. Trans. Benjamin Ivry. London: Vintage, 1998.

———. *Albert Camus: Une vie*. Paris: Gallimard, 1996.

Tolkien, J.R.R. *The Letters of J.R.R. Tolkien: A Selection*. Ed. Humphrey Carpenter and Christopher Tolkien. London: Harper Collins, 2006.

———. *The Lord of the Rings*. 3 vols. London: Harper Collins, 2011.

———. *Morgoth's Ring*. Ed. Christopher Tolkien. London: Harper Collins, 2015.

———. *Sauron Defeated*. Ed. Christopher Tolkien. London: Harper Collins, 2015.

Tooze, Adam. 'Ecological Leninism: Adam Tooze on Andreas Malm's Post-pandemic Climate Politics'. *London Review of Books* 43, no. 22 (18 November 2021). https:// www.lrb.co.uk/the-paper/v43/n22/adam-tooze/ecological-leninism.

Tromans, Nicholas. *Hope: The Life and Times of a Victorian Icon*. Compton: Watts Gallery, 2011.

Trouw. 'Zo maken we de toekomst weer leuk' [This is how we'll make the future fun again] and 'Zin in morgen' [Excited about tomorrow]. 31 December 2022.

Utley, Robert. *Sitting Bull: The Life and Times of an American Patriot*. New York: Holt Paperbacks, 2008.

Van der Lugt, Mara. *Dark Matters: Pessimism and the Problem of Suffering*. Princeton: Princeton University Press, 2021.

———. 'Look on the Dark Side'. *Aeon*, 26 April 2022. https://aeon.co/essays/in -these-dark-times-the-virtue-we-need-is-hopeful-pessimism.

Van Duijn, Roel. *Diepvriesfiguur: Autobiografie van PD106043 in samenwerking met de AIVD*. Amsterdam: Van Praag, 2012.

———. *Provo: De Geschiedenis van de Provotarische Beweging 1965–1967*. Amsterdam: Meulenhoff, 1985.

Van Lede, Kees, and Joris Luyendijk. *Pessimisme is voor losers*. Amsterdam: Balans, 2020.

Volkskrant. 'Een nieuwe kijk op crisis' [A new perspective on crisis]. 24 December 2022.

Voltaire. *Candide and Related Texts*. Trans. David Wootton. Indianapolis: Hackett, 2000.

———. *Letters on England* [*Lettres philosophiques*]. Trans. Leonard Tancock. London: Penguin, 2005.

von Preussen, Brigid. 'Don't Tread on Me'. *London Review of Books* 44, no. 24 (15 December 2022). https://www.lrb.co.uk/the-paper/v44/n24/brigid-von-preussen/don-t-tread-on-me.

Wallace-Wells, David. *The Uninhabitable Earth: Life after Warming*. New York: Tim Duggan Books, 2019.

West, Cornel. *Democracy Matters: Winning the Fight against Imperialism*. New York: Penguin, 2005.

———. *Hope on a Tightrope*. London: SmileyBooks, 2015.

Whyman, Tom. *Infinitely Full of Hope: Fatherhood and the Future in an Age of Crisis and Disaster*. London: Repeater, 2021.

Williston, Byron. 'Climate Change and Radical Hope'. *Ethics and the Environment* 17, no. 2 (2012): 165–86.

Wong, Kristin. 'How to Stay Optimistic When Everything Seems Wrong'. *New York Times*, 29 April 2020. https://www.nytimes.com/2020/04/29/smarter-living/coronavirus-how-to-stay-optimistic-.html.

Wright, Jeremiah A., Jr. 'The Audacity to Hope'. In *What Makes You So Strong? Sermons of Joy and Strength from Jeremiah A. Wright Jr.*, 91–110. Valley Forge, PA: Judson Press, 1993.

Wulf, Andrea. *The Invention of Nature: The Adventures of Alexander von Humboldt, the Lost Hero of Science*. London: John Murray, 2015.

Žižek, Slavoj. *Living in the End Times*. London: Verso, 2018.

ILLUSTRATIONS

Figures

Color Plates (following p. 74)

INDEX

Page numbers in *italics* indicate figures and tables.

Leibniz, G. W., 5; *Essais de Theodicée*,
7; on God creating worlds, 7–8; on
goods of life, 9; optimism as cruel
philosophy, 5; on system as a whole
is good, 17
Lemon, Etta, Royal Society for the
Protection of Birds, 154
Leopold, Aldo, on grief expression,
154, 155
Letters to Olga (Havel), 136
Lewis, C. S., on grief, 157
Lisbon earthquake (1756), 8
logotherapy, psychological theory of,
132–33
Lord of the Rings, The (Tolkien), 146–47,
165; film, xviii; hopes *Amdir* and
Estel, 124–30; trilogy, 124–30

magnanimity, 75–76
Magnason, Andri Snær, response to
climate change, 56, 310n39
Malm, Andreas: case for committed
climate action, 106; *How to Blow Up
a Pipeline*, 30, 205n4; on resistance,
31; rise of climate movement, 193–94;
Tooze on, 37
Mann, Michael E., despair-mongering,
173
Manson, James, Tate Gallery, 68
Man's Search for Meaning (Frankl),
132–34
Mantel, Hilary, hope of, 216n54
Marcel, Gabriel, on absolute hope, 112,
140–41, 222n91
Marom, Yotam, on living with dread, 56
Marsh, George Perkins, on uncer-
tainty of future, 138
Martin, George R. R.: *Game of Thrones*,
124; *Song of Ice and Fire*, 124

Marvel, Kate, climate scientist on
hope, 121–22
Mason, Chris, interviewing Jeremy
Hunt, 120
'Masque of the Red Death, The' (Poe),
33–34, 163
McKibben, Bill, *The End of Nature*,
215n24
McKinnon, Catriona: on climate
change, 173; on principle of action, 60
Meirav, Ariel, on hope in *The
Shawshank Redemption*, 172
melancholia: mourning and, 158–65;
open wound of, 164
Melbourne International Exhibition
(1888), 70
mental health, 38
Miéville, China: bad pessimism and
bad optimism, 20; on bad rap of
pessimism, 44; on despair and
hope, 145, 181; price of hope, 90
Miner, Robert, on false hope, 83
Ministry of the Future, The (Robinson),
33–34
moral education, 187
mourning, 71; climate grief and, 166–68;
grief and, 153–58; melancholia and,
158–65
'Mourning and Melancholia' (Freud),
160–62
Myth of Sisyphus, The (Camus), 26–27,
79

Nairn, Karen, on burnout, 38, 45
Nakate, Vanessa: becoming a climate
activist, 143; on climate change, 62;
on extreme events, 189
Nazi occupation, 142
Nazism, 106